ANXIETY

Current Trends in Theory and Research

VOLUME I

CONTRIBUTORS

ERNEST S. BARRATT
RAYMOND B. CATTELL
SEYMOUR EPSTEIN
CARROLL E. IZARD
EUGENE E. LEVITT
BEEMAN N. PHILLIPS
CHARLES D. SPIELBERGER
SILVAN S. TOMPKINS

ANXIETY

Current Trends in Theory and Research

Edited by CHARLES D. SPIELBERGER
Department of Psychology
Florida State University
Tallahassee, Florida

VOLUME I

ACADEMIC PRESS New York and London 1972

ACADEMIC PRESS, INC.
111 Fifth Avenue, New York, New York 10003

United Kingdom Edition published by
ACADEMIC PRESS, INC. (LONDON) LTD.
24/28 Oval Road, London NW1

LIBRARY OF CONGRESS CATALOG CARD NUMBER: 70-182630

PRINTED IN THE UNITED STATES OF AMERICA

CONTENTS

List of Contributors ix
Preface xi
Acknowledgements xiii
Contents of Volume II xv

Part I **INTRODUCTION**

Chapter 1. **Current Trends in Theory and Research on Anxiety**

Charles D. Spielberger

Historical Perspective 3
Anxiety: Current Trends in Theory and Research 9
References 18

Part II **THE NATURE AND MEASUREMENT OF ANXIETY**

Chapter 2. **Anxiety as an Emotional State**

Charles D. Spielberger

The Concept of Emotion 24
Anxiety as an Emotional State 28
The Measurement of Anxiety States 31

Toward a Trait-State Theory of Anxiety 38
Summary 45
References 46

Chapter 3. **Anxiety: A Variable Combination of Interacting Fundamental Emotions**
Carroll E. Izard

A Conceptual Analysis of Anxiety 55
Some Differences among Theories of Emotion and Anxiety 65
Empirical Analysis of "Anxiety" 76
Summary and Conclusions 102
References 104

Comments on Dr. Izard's paper 107
Silvan S. Tomkins

Comments on Dr. Izard's paper 113
Eugene E. Levitt

Chapter 4. **The Nature and Genesis of Mood States: A Theoretical Model with Experimental Measurements Concerning Anxiety, Depression, Arousal, and Other Mood States**
Raymond B. Cattell

Introduction 115
The Basis for Differentiating the Concepts of States, Traits, and Trait Change Factors 120
The Expansion of the Traditional R-technique Specification Equation to Incorporate States and Trait-Change Factors 122
The Use of Coordinated R-, dR-, and P-technique Experiments to Effect Separation and Identification of Trait, Trait Change, and State Structures 127
Further Characteristics Needing Definition in the State Model: Measurement Origins, Frequency, and Speed of Oscillation 138
The Integration of State Research with the Concepts of State Liability and Modulation 141
The State and Trait Variances to be Expected under R-, dR-, and P-Designs 145

Conditions Required for Defining Anxiety, in Relation to Effort Stress, Arousal, Depression, and Fear 153
The Nature and Theoretical Distinction of Anxiety, Effort Stress, Arousal, Depression, and Fear 159
Anxiety and Other States Defined in a Theory of Dynamic Process 165
References 178

Comments on Dr. Cattell's paper 185

Seymour Epstein

References 192

Part III **NEUROPHYSIOLOGICAL AND BIOCHEMICAL ASPECTS OF ANXIETY**

Chapter 5. **Anxiety and Impulsiveness: Toward a Neuropsychological Model**

Ernest S. Barratt

Overview of Research Project and Rationale 195
Psychometric Research (Human) 198
Laboratory Behavioral Research (Human) 204
Psychophysiological Research (Human) 212
Everyday Life Experiences (Human) 213
Infrahuman Research 215
Toward a Neuropsychological Model of Impulsiveness and Anxiety 218
References 220

Comments on Dr. Barratt's paper 223

Beeman N. Phillips

Chapter 6. **A Brief Commentary on the "Psychiatric Breakthrough" with Emphasis on the Hematology of Anxiety**

Eugene E. Levitt

The Hematology of Anxiety 228
A Critical Commentary on Breakthrough Research 232
References 234

Comments on Dr. Levitt's paper 235
Ernest S. Barratt

Author Index I-1
Subject Index I-7

LIST OF CONTRIBUTORS

Numbers in parentheses indicate the pages on which the authors' contributions begin.

ERNEST S. BARRATT, Behavioral Science Laboratories, The University of Texas Medical Branch, Galveston, Texas (195, 235)

RAYMOND B. CATTELL, Laboratory of Psychology and Group Analysis, University of Illinois, Urbana, Illinois (115)

SEYMOUR EPSTEIN, Department of Psychology, University of Massachusetts, Amherst, Massachusetts (185)

CARROLL E. IZARD, Department of Psychology, Vanderbilt University, Nashville, Tennessee (55)

EUGENE E. LEVITT, Psychology Section, Indiana University School of Medicine, Indianapolis, Indiana (113, 227)

BEEMAN N. PHILLIPS, Doctoral Training Program in School Psychology, University of Texas, Austin, Texas (223)

CHARLES D. SPIELBERGER, Department of Psychology, Florida State University, Tallahassee, Florida (3, 24)

SILVAN S. TOMPKINS, Department of Psychology, Rutgers University, New Brunswick, New Jersey (107)

PREFACE

The importance of anxiety as a fundamental human emotion is widely recognized by behavioral and medical scientists, and many regard anxiety as a basic condition of human existence. In keeping with the increasing concern with the stress of life in contemporary society, theories of anxiety have proliferated in recent years, and publication rates for investigations of anxiety and related phenomena such as stress and fear have continued to accelerate. While consensus is still lacking with regard to the conceptual meaning of anxiety, and there is as yet little agreement as to how it should be measured, nevertheless, considerable progress may be noted in these areas during the past decade.

In order to facilitate a more comprehensive understanding of anxiety phenomena, the views on this subject of a group of distinguished behavioral and medical scientists were brought together in 1966 in a book entitled *Anxiety and Behavior.* While this volume accurately reflected the then current opinions and convictions of a number of persons whose work and thought on anxiety had significantly contributed to existing knowledge, each of the contributors seemed to approach the problem of anxiety with his own unique theoretical orientation and research methods. It was also apparent that there was relatively little interaction among leading contributors to this field and a definite need for confrontation among different viewpoints.

The present work may be regarded as a sequel to *Anxiety and Behavior* in that many of the same scientists have contributed revisions and modifications of their earlier views, along with descriptions of their current work. This work grows out of a symposium on *Anxiety: Current Trends in Theory and Research* held at Florida State University in the spring of 1970. The format of the symposium brought together persons who have made important contributions to the understanding of anxiety phenomena and provided them with an opportunity to react to each other's ideas. One of the main goals of the symposium was to stimulate confrontation among opposing views with the expectation that this would, at least, provide clarification of terminology and elimination of the semantic confusion that now plagues the field. Hopefully, it might also lead to conceptual advances that would help to integrate the burgeoning empirical literature on anxiety and related phenomena.

This work is intended primarily for psychologists and students of psychology, but it should be of interest to any behavioral or medical scientist who is concerned with a more comprehensive understanding of personality and psychopathology. For the sake of greater convenience to the reader, the contents are divided into two volumes. The introductory chapter in Volume I provides background information and historical perspective with regard to theory and research on anxiety and a brief overview of the unique theoretical perspective and research objectives with which each contributor has approached this topic. The chapters in Volume I by Izard, Cattell, and Spielberger are concerned with the nature and measurement of anxiety, and those by Levitt and Barratt discuss neurophysiological and biochemical aspects of anxiety.

Two major categories of anxiety research are singled out for special attention in Volume II. Lazarus and Averill, Epstein, and Mandler consider the effects of stress on anxiety, with special emphasis on the role of cognition and uncertainty, and Beck discusses the interaction of stress, cognition, and anxiety in the development of psychosomatic symptoms. The second category of research considered in Volume II is concerned with anxiety in college students and school children. I. G. Sarason reviews and evaluates the literature on test anxiety; Phillips, Martin, and Meyers are concerned with the effects of anxiety on school-related behavior and methods of intervention designed to reduce anxiety; and S. B. Sarason considers the problem of intervening in the schools to relieve anxiety in the context of the school culture. In the final chapter of Volume II, Spielberger examines salient conceptual and methodological issues encountered in anxiety research that seem to cut across different theoretical orientations.

ACKNOWLEDGMENTS

The symposium on which these volumes are based was made possible by a grant from the Florida State University Graduate Committee for the Social Sciences. I would like to express my appreciation to Paul G. Craig, Vice-President for Academic Affairs, and Robert O. Lawton, Dean of the College of Arts and Sciences, for their encouragement in the development of the symposium, and for taking time from their busy schedules to present opening remarks at the beginning of each of the symposium sessions. I am also indebted to Joseph H. Grosslight, Edward E. McClure, and Ronald M. Pavalko, Chairmen, respectively, of Psychology, Urban and Regional Planning, and Sociology, for contributing departmental funds to help defray the costs of the symposium, and to D. N. Hansen, Director of the School Psychology Training Program, and Kent S. Miller, Director of the Community Mental Health Research Program in Sociology, for their contributions to the planning and development of the symposium.

Special thanks are due to my administrative assistant, Pam Harrison, for her invaluable contribution in arranging and coordinating the symposium. I would also like to express my gratitude to Helen Thomas, Jan Stewart, and Susan Atwater for their expert technical and clerical assistance in the processing and preparation of the manuscript for publication, and to Academic Press, whose enthusiasm for this endeavor never waivered and was clearly evidenced by their representation at the symposium and their willing assistance whenever called upon.

Finally, for their special role in stimulating the development of the symposium and their enthusiasm and willing assistance in helping to make it a rich learning experience for all those who participated, these volumes are dedicated to the graduate students and colleagues who have worked with me on anxiety research at Florida State University: Dana C. Ackley, Stephen M. Auerbach, C. Drew Edwards, Fernando Gonzalez-Reigosa, J. Kenneth Kling, Douglas H. Lamb, Robert E. Lushene, W. George McAdoo, Angel C. Martinez-Urrutia, Joseph J. Montuori, Stephen E. J. O'Hagan, Harold F. O'Neil, Jr., Denna J. Platzek, Edward Rappaport, David P. Rice, and Herbert A. Speir.

CONTENTS OF VOLUME II

Part IV. **STRESS, COGNITION, AND ANXIETY**

Chapter 7. **Emotion and Cognition with Special Reference to Anxiety**
Richard S. Lazarus and James R. Averill

Comments on Dr. Lazarus' and Dr. Averill's paper
Raymond B. Cattell

Chapter 8. **The Nature of Anxiety with Emphasis upon Its Relationship to Expectancy**
Seymour Epstein

Comments on Dr. Epstein's paper
Aaron T. Beck

Chapter 9. **Cognition, Anxiety, and Psychophysiological Disorders**
Aaron T. Beck

Chapter 10. **Helplessness: Theory and Research in Anxiety**

George Mandler

Comments on Dr. Mandler's paper

Richard S. Lazarus

Part V. **TEST ANXIETY AND ANXIOUS SCHOOL CHILDREN**

Chapter 11. **Experimental Approaches to Test Anxiety: Attention and the Uses of Information**

Irwin G. Sarason

Comments on Dr. Sarason's paper

George Mandler

Chapter 12. **School-Related Interventions with Anxious Children**

B. N. Phillips, R. P. Martin, and J. Meyers

Comments on Dr. Phillip's paper

Carroll E. Izard

Chapter 13. **Anxiety, Intervention, and the Culture of the School**

Seymour B. Sarason

Part VI. **SUMMARY**

Chapter 14. **Conceptual and Methodological Issues in Research on Anxiety**

Charles D. Spielberger

Author Index–Subject Index.

PART I

Introduction

Chapter 1

CURRENT TRENDS IN THEORY AND RESEARCH ON ANXIETY

Charles D. Spielberger

These volumes seek to facilitate a more comprehensive understanding of anxiety phenomena by bringing together the current views of behavioral scientists who have made significant contributions to our present knowledge. The principal goal in this introductory chapter is to present an overview of the unique theoretical perspective and research objectives with which each contributor has approached the topic of anxiety. A second goal is to provide background information and historical perspective for the reader with limited familiarity with this area.

Historical Perspective

Fear and anxiety have long been regarded as fundamental human emotions. The concept of fear, according to Cohen (1969), is clearly reflected in ancient

Egyptian hieroglyphics. James Kritzeck, of the Department of Oriental Studies at Princeton, noted a central concern with anxiety in the work of the medieval Arab philosopher, Ala ibn Hazm, of Cordova. In a treatise entitled *A Philosophy of Character and Conduct,* written in the eleventh century, Ibn Hazm unequivocally asserts the universality of anxiety as a basic condition of human existence.

> In his investigations, Ibn Hazm writes, he had constantly tried to single out "one end in human actions which all men unanimously hold as good, and which they all seek. I have found only this: the aim of escaping anxiety . . . . Not only have I discovered that all humanity considers this good and desirable, but also that . . . no one is moved to act or moved to speak a single word who does not hope by means of this action or word to release anxiety from his spirit [Kritzeck, 1956, p. 573]."

In his classic book, *The Meaning of Anxiety,* May (1950) surveys the evidence of the centrality of the problem of anxiety in contemporary literature, music, art, and religion, as well as in psychiatry, psychoanalysis, and psychology. He also documents the concern with anxiety in current political and philosophical thought and examines in some detail the views of those philosophers who have most significantly influenced modern anxiety theory. For Spinoza, fear was essentially a state of mind or attitude, a subjective condition of uncertainty in which there was the expectation that something painful or unpleasant might happen. Spinoza held that to entertain fear was a sign of "weakness of the mind," and that fear could be overcome by a "courageous dedication to reason [May, 1950, p. 24]."

While Spinoza's views were shared by most of the intellectual leaders of the seventeenth century, his faith in reason was questioned by Pascal who observed much irrationality and "perpetual restlessness" in himself and his fellow man. Pascal clearly recognized the power of the emotions to influence human behavior, and the obvious insufficiency of reason in overcoming passion. Belief in the rational control of emotions was further challenged by nineteenth century philosphers such as Schelling, Nietzsche, Schopenhauer, and, especially, by Kierkegaard. All these existential thinkers ". . . insisted that reality can be approached and experienced only by the whole individual as a feeling and acting as well as a thinking organism [May, 1950, p. 30]."

The nineteenth century also witnessed the increasing concern of biologists with fear and anxiety. Darwin believed that the potential for experiencing fear was an inherent characteristic of men and animals which had evolved as an adaptive mechanism over countless generations. The specific nature of fear reactions was presumably shaped through a process of natural selection of those who were successful in coping with or escaping the many dangers that imperiled their lives. In *The Expression of Emotion in Man and Animals,* first published in

1872, Darwin provides a vivid description of the typical manifestations of fear–rapid palpitation of the heart, trembling, increased perspiration, erection of the hair, dryness of the mouth, change in voice quality, dilation of the pupils, and the like. An important characteristic of the expression of fear was that it varied in its level of intensity, "... in its gradations from mere attention to a start of surprise, into extreme terror and horror [Darwin, 1965, p. 306]."

In the twentieth century, anxiety has emerged as a central problem and a predominant theme of modern life. This era is referred to as "the century of fear" by the French author, Albert Camus, and as the *Age of Anxiety* in the title of a sensitive poetic work by W. H. Auden (May, 1950). The *Age of Anxiety* is also the title of Leonard Bernstein's Second Symphony, as well as a modern ballet choreographed by Jerome Robbins that was inspired by Bernstein's music and Auden's poem (Mason, 1954).

Sigmund Freud is undoubtedly the most important contributor to our present understanding of anxiety phenomena. In 1894, he conceptualized anxiety neurosis as a discrete clinical syndrome to be differentiated from neurasthenia (Freud, 1953), and subsequently came to regard anxiety as the fundamental problem in all neurotic symptom formation (Freud, 1936). Freud defined anxiety as "something felt," an unpleasant emotional (affective) state that is universally experienced:

> Anxiety (or dread) itself needs no description; everyone has personally experienced this sensation, or to speak more correctly this affective condition, at some time or other. But in my opinion not enough serious consideration has been given to the question why nervous persons in particular suffer from anxiety so much more intensely, and so much more altogether, than others ... one thing is certain, that the problem of anxiety is a nodal point, linking up all kinds of most important questions: a riddle of which the solution must cast a flood of light upon our whole mental life [Freud, 1969, p. 341].

Thus, for Freud, anxiety was not only a central problem in neurosis, but understanding anxiety was also essential to the development of a comprehensive theory of human behavior. Freud's theoretical views on fear and anxiety were continually modified over a period of nearly 50 years as he searched for the "right abstract ideas" with which to clarify the essential nature of these concepts.

Since the turn of the century, clinical studies of anxiety have appeared in the psychiatric literature with increasing regularity. Pavlov's (1927) discovery of experimental neurosis also served to stimulate numerous investigations of fear and anxiety in animals. Prior to 1950, however, there were relatively few experimental investigations of anxiety in humans. The complexity of anxiety phenomena, the lack of appropriate instruments for assessing anxiety, and ethical problems associated with inducing anxiety in the laboratory have all contributed to the paucity of research.

Theory and research on anxiety were greatly stimulated in 1950 by the publication of three important books—May's *The Meaning of Anxiety*, Mowrer's *Learning Theory and Personality Dynamics*, and Dollard and Miller's *Personality and Psychotherapy*. A collection of papers presented in a symposium sponsored by the American Psychopathological Association was also published that same year in a volume entitled *Anxiety* (Hoch & Zubin, 1950).

Interest in anxiety research at mid-century was further stimulated by the development of Taylor's (1951, 1953) Manifest Anxiety Scale and Mandler and Sarason's (1952: Sarason & Mandler, 1952) Test Anxiety Questionnaire, the first of a number of psychometric instruments designed to assess fear and anxiety in adults (e.g., Cattell, 1957; Endler, Hunt, & Rosenstein, 1962; Freeman, 1953; McReynolds, 1968; Spielberger, Gorsuch, & Lushene, 1970; Zuckerman & Lubin, 1965). More recently, self-report scales have been developed for measuring general and test anxiety in children (e.g., Castaneda, McCandless, & Palermo, 1956; Sarason, Davidson, Lighthall, Waite, & Ruebush, 1960; Spielberger, Edwards, Montouri, & Lushene, 1971).

Since 1950, more than 2500 articles and books have been indexed in *Psychological Abstracts* under the heading, "Anxiety" (Spielberger, 1966a),[1] and the percentage of anxiety studies relative to the total number of annual entries in the Abstracts has increased almost eightfold, from approximately 0.2 percent in the 1930s to almost 1.6 percent at the present time. During this same period, more than 4000 studies on anxiety and closely related topics have appeared in medical journals. Since there is surprisingly little overlap between the psychological and medical literature, it seems safe to estimate that over 5000 articles or books on anxiety have been published during the past two decades. Thus, the behavioral scientist who wishes to study anxiety phenomena is confronted not only with a burgeoning empirical literature, but also with a diversity of theoretical orientations that reflect important differences in the professional training, experience, and research goals of those who work in this area.

Anxiety and Behavior

In 1964, the topic of anxiety was selected as the subject of a series of colloquia jointly sponsored by the Psychology Departments of Vanderbilt University and George Peabody College. This topic was to be covered in depth

[1] These estimates of publication rates in the psychological and medical literature on anxiety are probably conservative. Research on stress and fear are generally not included unless the term "anxiety" appeared in the title of an article or book. The present estimates are based on extrapolations from the data reported by Spielberger (1966a) and assume that annual publication rates for studies of anxiety have remained essentially unchanged since the early 1960s.

by psychologists and psychiatrists who represented a number of different points of view. We invited as speakers distinguished scientists whose work on anxiety was already well known, and requested that each spend two days with us. In addition to a formal colloquium presentation, we asked each speaker to meet with a graduate seminar on "Experimental Approaches to Personality" and to be available for informal discussions with interested graduate students and faculty.

The papers presented in the Vanderbilt-Peabody colloquium series were subsequently revised and published in a volume entitled *Anxiety and Behavior* (Spielberger, 1966b), along with several additional papers by scientists who could not participate in person. The contributors to this book included: Raymond B. Cattell, Charles W. Eriksen, Roy R. Grinker, Sr., Carroll E. Izard, Richard S. Lazarus, Robert B. Malmo, George Mandler, O. Hobart Mowrer, Edward M. Opton, Jr., Seymour B. Sarason, Stanley Schachter, Janet Taylor Spence, Kenneth W. Spence, Charles D. Spielberger, Silvan S. Tomkins, David L. Watson, and Joseph Wolpe. In his introductory chapter, the editor noted that each of the contributors had approached the problem of anxiety with his own theoretical orientation and research methods, and concluded that a meaningful integration or synthesis of their diverse views was not yet possible (Spielberger, 1966a).

Since the publication of *Anxiety and Behavior,* the literature on anxiety and related topics, such as stress and fear, has continued to grow, and the publication rate for research reports and clinical case studies has accelerated. Important book-length contributions in the past five years that were specifically concerned with these subjects include: *Psychological Stress and the Coping Process* (Lazarus, 1966), *Psychological Stress* (Appley & Trumbull, 1967), *The Psychology of Anxiety* (Levitt, 1967), *Aspects of Anxiety* (Branch, 1968), *Fear of Failure* (Birney, Burdick, & Teevan, 1969), *Explorations in the Psychology of Stress and Anxiety* (Rourke, 1969), *Fears and Phobias* (Marks, 1969), and *Theories of Anxiety* (Fischer, 1970). The past 5 years have also witnessed increased interest in stress and anxiety in children (Brody & Axelrad, 1970; Wolff, 1969) and in the effects of anxiety on education (Kurzweil, 1968), academic achievement (Gaudry & Spielberger, 1971), and executive effectiveness (Schoonmaker, 1969). Two recent books on anxiety and neurosis should also be noted (Martin, 1971; Rycroft, 1968).

Confrontation among Differing Views of Anxiety

A basic shortcoming in current theory and research on anxiety, as was previously suggested, is that scientists who research this area represent many different theoretical orientations and employ a wide variety of research methods. In his review of *Anxiety and Behavior* which appeared in *Contemporary Psychology,* Sarason (1967) criticized the format of the

Vanderbilt-Peabody colloquium series because it did not provide for interaction among the participants and needed confrontation among different points of view. With respect to the communication gap in anxiety research, Sarason (1967) writes:

> . . . most of the writers usually display little interest in what their colleagues between the hard covers have to say. Therefore, they do not comment on ideas and experiments other than those rather directly related to their specific preoccupations. . . . How might Mowrer and Grinker cope with each other's analyses of anxiety and its meaning? Which nonfactor analytic psychologist would risk incursions into the land of Cattell? Would Kenneth Spence have ventured into what he surely would have regarded as the Izard-Tomkins conceptual quicksand [p. 601]?

To gauge, at least superficially, the extent to which the contributors to *Anxiety and Behavior* had influenced one another, the references at the end of each of the twelve chapters were examined, excluding the two chapters contributed by the editor. Consistent with Sarason's observation, in seven of the twelve chapters, there were no citations of any other contributor. But, in four chapters, the authors cited the work of at least three other contributors, and Spence and Spence listed a total of eleven references to the research publications of other contributors. Nevertheless, it is difficult to escape the conclusion that, circa 1966, there was relatively little effort to integrate theory and research on anxiety among leading authorities in this area.

Challenged by Sarason's criticism, and prodded by my own graduate students, the writer set about to determine the feasibility of holding a symposium on stress and anxiety that would stimulate confrontation among opposing views. The goals of this symposium were to bring together persons who have made important contributions to the understanding of anxiety phenomena, and to provide them with an opportunity of reacting to each other's ideas on this subject. At the very least, it was felt that this type of confrontation might result in clarification of terminology and elimination of some of the semantic confusion that now plagues the field. Hopefully, it might also lead to conceptual advances that would help to integrate the burgeoning empirical literature on anxiety.

As a first step in the organization of a symposium on current trends in theory and research on anxiety, the principal contributors to *Anxiety and Behavior* were invited to participate. Specifically, each of them was asked to present a paper describing his current work on anxiety, stress, and related phenomena, and to exchange views with other leading scholars who have contributed to these areas. Raymond B. Cattell, Carroll E. Izard, Richard S. Lazarus, George Mandler, Seymour B. Sarason, and Silvan S. Tomkins accepted our invitation. Other behavioral scientists who had published extensively on stress and anxiety, and who were currently working in these areas, were also invited to attend the symposium. Those who agreed to participate included Ernest S. Barratt, Aaron T. Beck, Seymour Epstein, Eugene E. Levitt, Beeman N. Phillips, and Irwin G. Sarason.

The symposium was held in Tallahassee, Florida, in March and April of 1970, under the sponsorship of Florida State University. To maximize interaction among the participants, there were two sessions, with six participants in each session. Each participant was asked to develop his presentation with the expectation that it would be revised and published in a sequel to *Anxiety and Behavior.* In addition to presenting a paper based on his own current work, each participant was assigned as the primary discussant for one other paper. The format of the symposium also provided for the spontaneous exchange of ideas among participants, as well as interaction with the audience which consisted primarily of psychology graduate students and faculty.

The present volumes are based on the papers presented at the Tallahassee symposium and comments on each of these papers by the primary discussants. While spontaneous interactions among the participants were also duly recorded, transforming the spoken word into the printed page for this aspect of the symposium proved to be an impossible task. In many cases, the remarks of the participants were stimulated by between-session interactions that made little sense without extensive clarification of context. Another difficulty was that some of the questions from the audience required the introduction of a great deal of background information that would be of limited interest to the sophisticated reader. While the impact of each symposium participant on his colleagues must ultimately be evaluated in future research contributions, there is substantial evidence nevertheless that the "colleagues between the hard covers" in these volumes have given considerable attention to each other's work.

Anxiety: Current Trends in Theory and Research

This work is organized into two volumes, consisting of six main parts. Following this introductory overview (Part I), the chapters in Volume 1 focus upon the nature and measurement of anxiety (Part II), and its neurophysiological and biochemical aspects (Part III). While the chapters in Volume 2 are also concerned with these topics, two major subcategories of anxiety research are singled out for special attention. Part IV is concerned with stress and anxiety, with special emphasis on the role of cognition and uncertainty. Test anxiety, the antecedents, concomitants, and consequences of anxiety in school settings, and methods of reducing anxiety in school children are the subject matter of the chapters in Part V. A number of important conceptual and methodological issues encountered in anxiety research are discussed in Part VI.

The Nature and Measurement of Anxiety

Spielberger discusses the nature and measurement of anxiety as a transitory emotional state (A-State) which consists of feelings of apprehension and tension, and heightened activity of the autonomic nervous system. It is assumed that A-States vary in intensity and fluctuate over time as a function of the stresses that impinge upon the individual. State anxiety is distinguished from anxiety proneness or trait anxiety (A-Trait), which is defined in terms of individual differences in the frequency that anxiety states are manifested over time. After considering several general approaches to the measurement of feelings and emotions, four self-report measures of anxiety as an emotional state are briefly described, and the development of the State-Trait Anxiety Inventory is discussed in some detail. A trait-state theory of anxiety is proposed which specifies the effects of different classes of stressful stimuli on level of A-State for persons who differ in A-Trait.

Izard takes as his point of departure the theoretical position developed by Izard and Tomkins in their chapter in *Anxiety and Behavior*. In the earlier work, Izard and Tomkins equated anxiety with fear, which they regarded as a primary or fundamental emotion. The main thesis in the present chapter is that anxiety is a "pattern of emotions," a complex emotional reaction that includes fear as well as other fundamental emotions. To support this interpretation, Izard describes the results of several recent studies which employed the Differential Emotion Scale, an instrument developed through factor-analytic procedures to measure the fundamental emotions posited by Izard's theory. Of particular interest is a study of patterns of emotion in a highly threatening, real-life situation experienced by Black students at Jackson (Mississippi) State College shortly after a police–student confrontation resulted in the death of two students and injuries to many more.

It should come as no surprise that Cattell is critical of traditional bivariate research on anxiety. He feels that only through the use of appropriate multivariate approaches guided by an adequate conceptual model will a scientific understanding of anxiety be possible. Cattell distinguishes between anxiety as a mood state and as a personality trait and discusses the technical procedures he considers appropriate for measuring states and traits. The emphasis in the present chapter is on anxiety as a unitary source state that is defined by a distinctive pattern of "behavioral and physiological changes coordinated in time." On the basis of the results of numerous factor-analytic studies over the past 25 years, Cattell contends that state anxiety has been consistently differentiated from other similar mood states, such as depression, fear ("a reaction to a definite external stimulus"), effort stress, and arousal by the unique pattern of response that characterizes variations in each of these mood states over time. In Cattell's theory of emotion, there are a limited number of unitary source states, but these may be found in widely varying combinations which produce a great many apparent but superficial differences in surface states.

Neurophysiological and Biochemical Aspects of Anxiety

Barratt's main interest is in developing a neuropsychological model to account for anxiety and impulsiveness. He discusses the results of a number of recent studies in his programmatic research and reports data from observations of everyday life experiences, psychometric tests and rating scales, traditional laboratory behavioral tasks, and psychophysiological measures such as heart rate, galvanic skin response, and cortical evoked potentials. While recognizing that the facts are not yet sufficiently clear to warrant a definitive theory, on the basis of his findings to date Barratt speculates that "feelings" of anxiety may be determined by hypothalamic-hypophyseal control of endocrine functions which influence changes in the autonomic nervous system. He also suggests that a person's "awareness" of such feelings may result from nonspecific reticular control of cortical activity in which the orbitofrontal cortex is a key area relative to feelings of tenseness.

In 1969, an article by Ferris N. Pitts on "The biochemistry of anxiety" appeared in the *Scientific American.* The main conclusions were that anxiety symptoms result from a high concentration of lactate ion and that anxiety attacks can be induced in neurotic patients by lactate infusion. It was also suggested that the injection of calcium ion can reduce these symptoms. Pitts' findings were widely hailed as a scientific breakthrough, with potentially revolutionary implications for the psychiatric treatment of neurotic individuals.

In Chapter 6, Levitt discusses Pitts' work on the hematology of anxiety in the context of earlier "breakthrough" research on the biochemical determinants of mental illness. He compares the initial reactions to this research with the flurry of excitement produced by Heath's investigations of the role of taraxein in schizophrenia in the 1950s. After a detailed evaluation of the methodological limitations in Pitts's studies of anxiety and lactic acid, the findings of subsequent experiments are examined which tend to refute the hypothesis that lactate causes anxiety. Levitt then offers a critical general commentary on breakthrough research.

Stress, Cognition, and Anxiety

The importance of cognitive factors in anxiety phenomena is a common theme that is emphasized in the four chapters in Part IV (Volume 2). In

Chapter 7, Lazarus and Averill propose a theory of emotion which seems to reflect a significant departure from the views expressed by Lazarus and Opton in *Anxiety and Behavior.* In the earlier chapter, the authors were primarily concerned with the development of a theory of psychological stress that specified the conditions under which stress reactions were evoked, the processes that intervened between the "stress" stimulus and the "stress" response, and how individuals coped with stress. In the present chapter, the authors' concept of emotion encompasses the stress stimulus, the stress response, and the cognitive and physiological processes that intervene between them. Anxiety is defined as "an emotion based on the appraisal of threat, an appraisal that entails symbolic, anticipatory, and other uncertain elements." Lazarus and Averill differentiate between anxiety and fear-related emotions such as fright, separation distress, and instrumental fear in terms of the developmental origins of these emotional states, the conditions which elicit them, and the pattern of responses by which they are characterized. But the most unique and important criteria for distinguishing anxiety from other fear-related emotions are the cognitive mechanisms or appraisals that mediate between the emotional response and the stressful stimuli that evoke it.

Taking seriously Sarason's criticism that the contributors to *Anxiety and Behavior* displayed little interest in each other's work, Lazarus and Averill compare and contrast their own theoretical conceptions with those of other anxiety theorists on such topics as the relation between fear and anxiety, the motivational or drive aspects of anxiety states, and the role of cognitive mediators in evoking emotions. They also report the results of several recent investigations in which anticipation of the occurrence of a stressful stimulus and threat ambiguity were experimentally manipulated.

Epstein begins his paper with a lucid analysis of the nature of anxiety as this concept is employed by a number of major personality theorists. On the basis of this analysis, he concludes that anxiety is an acutely unpleasant "state of diffuse arousal following the perception of threat." According to Epstein, anxiety states are evoked by three basic conditions: primary overstimulation, cognitive incongruity, and response unavailability. Fear and anxiety are distinguished in terms of whether or not the arousal evoked by threatening circumstances is channeled into appropriate purposive action. Fear is viewed as an avoidance motive in which a high level of arousal is directed into flight. Anxiety is regarded as a state of "unresolved fear" in which the arousal that occurs following the perception of threat persists and becomes diffuse because the individual is unable to direct it into purposive behavior. Indecision, conflict, and external restraint contribute to the evocation of anxiety reactions by producing cognitive incongruity and response unavailability.

Expectancy is considered by Epstein to be a basic parameter in determining level of arousal, and he reports the results of several recent studies in his research program concerned with investigating the relationship between expectancy and anxiety. In Epstein's research, expectancy with regard to the onset and the intensity of noxious stimulation was experimentally manipulated, and the effects of these manipulations on changes in heart rate, skin conductance, and self-report ratings of fear and anxiety were observed during anticipation, impact, and recovery periods. Data are also reported on the effects on fear reactions of incubation and habituation to noxious stimulation, and on patterns of autonomic reactivity when there is uncertainty with regard to the occurrence of a threat.

The reader will find Epstein's analysis of a number of viewpoints regarding the nature of anxiety especially helpful. Indeed, the first half of this chapter could well serve as the introduction to these volumes. This chapter is included in Part IV because of the striking convergence which may be noted between Epstein's work and the research reported by Lazarus and Averill with respect to experimental methodology, the specific variables that are manipulated, and the response measures that are obtained as reactions to stress and indicants of anxiety.

In Chapter 9, Beck examines the interaction of cognition and anxiety in the development of psychophysiological (psychosomatic) symptoms. Brief descriptions are given of eight different models that have been proposed to account for the role of anxiety in the etiology of psychophysiological disorders. Anxiety is viewed as an unpleasant emotional reaction to real or imagined dangers that is accompanied by autonomic discharge and subjectively experienced as "tension," "fright," or "nervousness." If the cues associated with the anxiety reaction, either cognitive or physiological, are themselves interpreted as danger signals, then additional anxiety is evoked, and a spiral or cyclical effect may occur. Psychosomatic symptoms develop when an anxiety-prone individual who is disposed to excessive reactions in one or more physiological systems is continually exposed, over a long period of time, to situations he interprets as threatening. Examples are given of the operation of this threat–anxiety–physical symptom cycle in several different types of psychosomatic disorders such as peptic ulcer and angina pectoris.

The contents of Mandler's chapter may be divided into two major parts. In the first, Mandler offers a critical commentary on the lack of scientific progress in theory and research on anxiety over the past twenty years. Failure to develop determinate theory is attributed to unrealistic concerns with "megalotheories" of the "whole personality." The absence of cumulative research is seen as resulting from a preoccupation with the demonstration of "new" phenomena. Mandler is especially critical of research with anxiety scales that has produced hundreds of studies with little theoretical import. As an approach to the construction of determinate theory in the anxiety domain, Mandler recommends that subareas be delineated for the development of relevant mini-theories concerned with a limited number of potent variables which are subjected to intensive empirical investigation.

In the second half of his chapter, Mandler follows his own recommendation in providing a theoretical analysis of the relationship between helplessness and anxiety. He assumes that stressful circumstances initially produce distress and arousal, and that "helplessness," which is cognitively interpreted as anxiety, results when an organism has no behavior available to him that will relieve his distress. In Mandler's analysis of anxiety, the interruption of organized plans or sequences of behavior is a fundamental condition that leads to states of distress and arousal. When no appropriate behavior is available as an alternate for the original plan, helplessness and anxiety result. Thus, helplessness and anxiety are defined, not by the objective situation, but by the individual and his repertory of behavior.

Test Anxiety and Anxious School Children

The chapters in Part V are concerned with the effects of anxiety on test performance and with school-related aspects of anxiety in children. In Chapter 11, I. G. Sarason examines the research literature on test anxiety and describes the results of a series of his own studies conducted over the past fifteen years which demonstrate that the performance of high test-anxious persons may be both facilitated and impaired by experimental conditions. Personal evaluation or threat leads to decrements in the performance of high test-anxious students, whereas reassurance facilitates their performance. Achievement-oriented instructions impair the performance of high test-anxious subjects but seem to have a salutary effect on low test-anxious subjects. Observing a successful model facilitates the performance of high test-anxious subjects, while observing models who fail results in poorer performance.

On the basis of his evaluation of the literature and his own research findings, Sarason concludes that "persons who differ in assessed test anxiety differ with regard to their attentiveness to environmental stimuli and how they interpret and employ these cues in problem-solving." In essence, high test-anxious persons are characterized by acquired habits and attitudes that involve negative self-perceptions and expectations. These self-deprecating habits and attitudes dispose test-anxious persons to experience fear and heightened physiological activity in situations such as examinations in which they are being evaluated, and influence the manner in which they interpret and respond to events in the environment. In keeping with these conclusions, Sarason discusses implications of research on test anxiety for therapeutic interventions with anxious students, for curriculum development in the schools, and for the behavior of teachers in the classroom.

The general goal of the paper by Phillips and his colleagues was to review the literature in psychology and education that pertains to the relation between anxiety and school-related behavior in children. A major focus is on school-related interventions that are designed to facilitate the adjustment of anxious school children. The review begins with a discussion of the nature of anxiety on the basis of which the authors conclude that, despite a diversity of theoretical perspectives, there are nevertheless three important points of convergence: (1) the conceptual distinction between state and trait anxiety appears to be gaining general acceptance; (2) stress produced by environmental or internal factors precipitates anxiety reactions; (3) the consequences of elevations in anxiety are usually negative or debilitating, but this depends on the nature of the task and the situation.

Phillips *et al.* examine the research literature on the antecedents, the phenomenological, physiological, and behavioral concomitants, and the proximal and distal consequences of anxiety in school children. Two general strategies are defined for intervening in the schools to reduce anxiety. The first involves identifying sources of stress in the school environment; the second is concerned with discovering and developing learning situations which take into account the relationship between anxiety and task requirements. A number of specific intervention strategies for helping anxious school children are also discussed. These include: teacher training, the appropriate use of psychological consultants and teacher aides, special diagnostic classes, therapeutic tutoring, programmed instruction, behavior modification, and modeling approaches.

The paper by S. B. Sarason is an invited commentary on the Phillips *et al.* paper.[2] Sarason observes that changing the schools to reduce the detrimental effects of anxiety on the behavior of children will require knowledge of the school culture and a sophisticated conception of social system intervention as well as a theory of anxiety. As a case in point, Sarason reviews the impact of the Russian launching of Sputnik, which spotlighted the need to produce more scientists in the U.S. and led to the development of new curricula for teaching mathematics. He concludes that the new math was no more successful than the old because the persons responsible for bringing about desired changes in the teaching of math lacked understanding of the nature of the schools as a social system. Consequently, too much emphasis was placed on the curriculum and not enough on factors affecting how it was implemented. Thus, in addition to explicit ideas as to what needs changing, intervention in the schools requires knowledge of the complexities of the school culture. Sarason describes some of his own recent work that was designed to develop a systematic description of selected aspects of the ecology of the kindergarten child and of life in the

[2] Professor Sarason originally planned to participate in the symposium, but personal circumstances prevented him from attending. However, he agreed to review and comment on the Phillips *et al.* paper in the context of his own earlier work on anxiety in elementary school children and in the context of his more recent work on psychoeducational intervention in the schools and the analysis of the school culture.

classroom. He concludes that unquestioned assumptions and traditional modes of thinking often determine the practices that take place in kindergarten classes.

The principal goal in the preceding brief descriptions of the contents of the individual chapters was to provide an overview of the theoretical orientation and research objectives of each contributor. Particular attention was given to the authors' definition of anxiety as a theoretical concept, and points of theoretical and empirical convergence were noted. A more critical evaluation of each chapter is provided by the symposium participant who served as the primary discussant for that paper.[3] Within the constraints imposed by the fact that there were two symposium sessions, each attended by half of the participants, the discussants were assigned on the basis of the editor's judgment of complimentarity in general interest and some degree of difference in theoretical orientation and/or methodological approach.

It should be noted that Tomkins presented a paper at the symposium on "Affect Theory: The Role of a Vascular Facial Response and Its Inhibition," in which he clarified his current theoretical views on anxiety as an emotional state. He also served as the principal discussant on Izard's paper. Professor Tomkins was unable to revise his paper so that it might be included in these volumes, but his discussion of Izard's paper highlights important points of agreement and difference between Izard's views and his own. Levitt was assigned as principal discussant for Tomkins' paper, but opted to comment on Izard's paper as well since his critique seemed to be equally applicable to both.

One of the major goals of the symposium on anxiety was to stimulate confrontation and give those with opposing theoretical views an opportunity to react to each others ideas. Consequently, perhaps a word or two would be in order with regard to how the comments of the discussants that are reported here came into being. Each contributor was asked to provide his principal discussant with a copy of his paper in advance of the symposium, but this was not always possible. In general, the discussants had relatively little time prior to the symposium to prepare their comments. Hence, the critique of each paper by the principal discussant was based primarily on the paper as it was presented at the symposium.

Each discussant's comments were tape recorded, transcribed, and returned to him, along with a copy of the paper on which he had commented, as it was subsequently revised for publication, so that he might edit his words before they were set into print. In several cases, the contributors made substantial changes in their original papers that could be directly traced to the comments of the discussant. While this provided concrete evidence of the value of direct confrontation in bringing about clarification, if not change, in opposing points

[3] Spielberger's chapter, "Anxiety as an Emotional State," was distributed to the participants in advance of the symposium. Since this paper was not presented at the symposium, no discussant was assigned.

of view, it also placed an additional strain on the discussant whose task it was to edit his original comments so that they would reflect what he said at the symposium while, at the same time, making sense in terms of the revisions in the paper on which he had commented.

To illustrate the impact of one discussant on one contributor, the following is extracted from a letter received by the editor from the discussant approximately four months following the conclusion of the symposium:

> As you may have guessed I reacted strongly to reading ________'s second (revised) paper. He includes all the points I discussed with him and borrows freely from my paper in organization as well as the phrases used in my critique. . . . To put it mildly, I was furious when I read the paper and wanted to immediately check to see if my impression was correct that any resemblance to the original paper was purely coincidental. It now appears that it obviously is and I will have to decide if I shall handle it by writing to him and having him at least correctly acknowledge my position and similarity of his to it, or whether I should simply clobber him in my critique.

The editor was, of course, delighted with this evidence of the discussant's impact on his colleague since it seemed to provide convincing justification for the symposium format, and supported the conclusion that we had been effective, at least in this one case, of bringing about immediate confrontation between opposing points of view. This conviction was obviously shared by another contributor who wrote as follows to the symposium participant who served as the principal discussant of his paper:

> I have just received your comments on my paper; and I think they are excellent in that they produce interaction on all important issues and also reduce differences to "more or less" rather than "categorical" ones. When the latter rear their heads, I always expect the scientific method of misfiring somewhere. Your commentary fully achieves the interactions which (Spielberger) rightly emphasized, and it does so while maintaining an objectivity and closeness of reasoning which is the only way of fulfilling the real function of interaction. . . . While a man must naturally continue with the momentum of his own emphasis, I really feel that this interaction may produce some positive bridging in future research which could never have happened without it.

While these brief comments cannot adequately convey the flavor of the symposium, they should serve to alert the reader to the fact that several of the papers were rather dramatically revised as a function of the discussion which took place. In addition to the value of the spontaneous exchange of ideas, it appears that lines of communication have been established that could result in increased future efforts to integrate and establish bridges between different points of view with regard to anxiety phenomena. While a meaningful synthesis of the various points of view that are described in these volumes is still not possible, several of the more salient conceptual and methodological issues in anxiety research that seem to cut across various theoretical orientations are identified and discussed in the final chapter of this work.

References

Appley, M. H., & Trumbull, R. (Eds.). *Psychological stress.* New York: Appleton-Century-Crofts, 1967.

Birney, R. C., Burdick, H., & Teevan, R. C. *Fear of failure.* Princeton, New Jersey: Van Nostrand-Reinhold, 1969.

Branch, C. H. *Aspects of anxiety.* Philadelphia, Pennsylvania: Lippincott, 1968.

Brody, S., & Axelrad, S. *Anxiety and ego formation in infancy.* New York: International Universities Press, 1970.

Castaneda, A., McCandless, B. R., & Palermo, D. S. The Children's Form of the Manifest Anxiety Scale. *Child Development,* 1965, **27**, 317–326.

Cattell, R. B. *Handbook for the I.P.A.T. Anxiety Scale.* Champaign, Illinois: Institute for Personality and Ability Testing, 1957.

Cohen, J. *Personality dynamics.* Chicago, Illinois: Rand McNally, 1969.

Darwin, C. *The expression of emotions in man and animals.* Chicago, Illinois: The University of Chicago Press, 1965.

Dollard, J., & Miller, N. E. *Personality and psychotherapy.* New York: McGraw-Hill, 1950.

Endler, N. S., Hunt, J. M., & Rosenstein, A. J. An S-R inventory of anxiousness. *Psychological Monographs,* 1962, **76**, No. 17, whole No. 536.

Fischer, W. F. *Theories of anxiety.* New York: Harper & Row, 1970.

Freeman, M. J. The development of a test for the measurement of anxiety: a study of its reliability and validity. *Psychological Monographs,* 1953, **67**, No. 3, whole No. 353.

Freud, S. *The problem of anxiety.* New York: Norton, 1936.

Freud, S. The justification for detaching from neurasthenia a particular syndrome: The anxiety neurosis (1894). In S. Freud (Ed.) *Collected Papers.* London: Hogarth Press, 1953.

Freud, S. *A general introduction to psychoanalysis.* New York: Simon & Schuster, 1969.

Gaudry, E., & Spielberger, C. D. *Anxiety and academic achievement.* Sidney: Wiley–Australasia, 1971.

Hoch, P. H., & Zubin, J. (Eds.). *Anxiety.* New York: Grune & Stratton, 1950.

Kritzeck, J. Philosophers of anxiety. *Commonweal,* 1955/56, **63**, 572–574.

Kurzweil, Z. E. *Anxiety and education.* New York: Thomas Yoseloff, 1968.

Lazarus, R. S. *Psychological stress and the coping process.* New York: McGraw-Hill, 1966.

Levitt, E. E. *The psychology of anxiety.* Indianapolis, Indiana: Bobbs–Merrill, 1967.

Mandler, G., & Sarason, S. B. A study of anxiety and learning. *Journal of Abnormal and Social Psychology,* 1952, **47**, 166–173.

Marks, I. M. *Fears and phobias.* New York: Academic Press, 1969.

Martin, B. *Anxiety and neurotic disorders.* New York: Wiley, 1971.

Mason, F. (Ed.). *Balanchine's complete stories of the great ballets.* Garden City, New York: Doubleday, 1954.

May, R. *The meaning of anxiety.* New York: Ronald Press, 1950.

McReynolds, P. The assessment of anxiety: A survey of available techniques. In P. McReynolds (Ed.), *Advances in Psychological Assessment.* Palo Alto, California: Science and Behavior Books, 1968.

Mowrer, O. H. *Learning theory and personality dynamics.* New York: Ronald Press, 1950.

Pavlov, I. P. *Conditioned reflexes.* London & New York: Oxford University Press, 1927.

Pitts, F. N. The biochemistry of anxiety. *Scientific American,* 1969, **220,** 69–75.

Rourke, B. P. (Ed.). *Explorations in the psychology of stress and anxiety.* Don Mills, Ontario: Longmans Canada, 1969.

Rycroft, C. *Anxiety and neurosis.* Baltimore, Maryland: Penguin Books, 1968.

Sarason, I. G. Anxious words. *Contemporary Psychology,* 1967, **12,** 601–602.

Sarason, S. B., Davidson, K. S., Lighthall, F. F., Waite, R. R., & Ruebush, B. K. *Anxiety in elementary school children.* New York: Wiley, 1960.

Sarason, S. B., & Mandler, G. Some correlates of test anxiety. *Journal of Abnormal and Social Psychology,* 1952, **47,** 810–817.

Schoonmaker, A. N. *Anxiety and the executive.* Washington: American Management Association, 1969.

Spielberger, C. D. Theory and research on anxiety. In C. D. Spielberger (Ed.), *Anxiety and behavior.* New York: Academic Press, 1966. Pp. 3–20. (a)

Spielberger, C. D. (Ed.). *Anxiety and behavior.* New York: Academic Press, 1966. (b)

Spielberger, C. D., Edwards, C. D., Montouri, J., & Lushene, R. *The State-Trait Anxiety Inventory for Children (How-I-Feel Questionnaire).* Palo Alto, California: Consulting Psychologists Press, 1970.

Spielberger, C. D., Gorsuch, R. L., & Lushene, R. E. *Manual for the State-Trait Anxiety Inventory (Self-Evaluation Questionnaire).* Palo Alto, California: Consulting Psychologists Press, 1970.

Taylor, J. A. The relationship of anxiety to the conditioned eyelid response. *Journal of Experimental Psychology,* 1951, **41,** 81–92.

Taylor, J. A. A personality scale of manifest anxiety. *Journal of Abnormal and Social Psychology,* 1953, **48,** 285–290.

Wolff, S. *Children under stress.* London: Penguin Press, 1969.

Zuckerman, M., & Lubin, B. *Manual for the Multiple Affect Adjective Check List.* San Diego, California: Educational & Industrial Testing Service, 1965.

PART II

The Nature and Measurement of Anxiety

Chapter 2

ANXIETY AS AN EMOTIONAL STATE[1]

Charles D. Spielberger

Freud regarded anxiety as "something felt," an unpleasant affective state or condition of the human organism. This state, as he observed it in patients who suffered with anxiety neuroses, was characterized by "all that is covered by the word 'nervousness [Freud, 1924].' " More specifically, an anxiety state was defined by: "(1) a specific unpleasurable quality, (2) efferent or discharge phenomena, and (3) the perception of these [Freud, 1936, p. 70]."

Anxiety, according to Freud, could be distinguished from other unpleasant affective states, such as anger, grief, or sorrow, by its unique combination of experiential and physiological qualities. The experiential qualities associated with anxiety which gave it a special "character of unpleasure" consisted of

[1] I am greatly indebted to Dr. Robert E. Lushene and Dr. W. George McAdoo for their contributions to this chapter, and to Professor Raymond B. Cattell for his comments on an earlier version that was prepared by C. D. Spielberger, R. E.Lushene, and W. G. McAdoo for R. B. Cattell (Ed.), *Handbook of Modern Personality Theory*.

feelings of apprehension, tension, or dread. The physiological and behavioral discharge phenomena associated with anxiety, for example, heart palpitation, disturbances in respiration, sweating, restlessness, tremor, shuddering, and the like, were considered by Freud to be essential components of anxiety states (and important contributors to their unpleasantness) but were of little theoretical interest to him.

The term "anxiety" is perhaps most commonly used in contemporary psychology to denote a palpable but transitory emotional state or condition characterized by feelings of tension and apprehension and heightened autonomic nervous system activity. Research on transitory anxiety has focused upon delineating the general properties of anxiety states and identifying the specific conditions that evoke them. The major goals of this chapter are to present a conceptualization of anxiety as an emotional state and to discuss theoretical and methodological issues that arise in the measurement of anxiety states.

The chapter is arranged in four sections. In the first section, the concept of emotion is considered in historical perspective, and a set of general characteristics for defining emotional states is suggested. A conception of anxiety as a specific emotional state is proposed in the second section, and some important methodological and terminological issues and problems that arise in research on anxiety are discussed. In the third section, general approaches to the measurement of feelings and emotions are considered, and five different self-report measures of anxiety as an emotional state are described. In the final section, two distinct anxiety concepts, state anxiety and trait anxiety, are defined, and a trait-state theory of anxiety is outlined.

The Concept of Emotion

While it is generally conceded that specific emotions may profoundly influence the lives of men, research on emotion reveals a discouraging degree of conceptual ambiguity and empirical inconsistency (Plutchik, 1962; Young, 1943). The observations of William James before the turn of the century on the psychology of emotion are no less pertinent today:

> The merely descriptive literature of the emotions is one of the most tedious parts of psychology. And not only is it tedious, but you feel that its subdivisions are to a great extent either fictitious or unimportant, and that its pretenses to accuracy are a sham [1890, p. 449].

This state of affairs has led some psychologists to conclude that there is no justification for the study of "emotions" since emotional reactions cannot be meaningfully distinguished from nonemotional responses characterized by a high degree of physiological activatión (e.g., Duffy, 1941, 1962). Yet the English language abounds with terms that are descriptive of emotions, and such terms serve to communicate nuances of feeling with clarity and power. Common sense and personal experience tell us that "feeling angry" and "being afraid" reflect different states or conditions of the organism which, more often than not, lead to different courses of action.

Concepts relating to emotional phenomena are found in almost all general theories of behavior. While many different conceptions of emotion have been proposed, none has achieved any wide degree of acceptance as yet. Nor has there been much agreement among the explanations offered to account for specific classes of emotional phenomena such as anger, fear, joy, or grief. Nevertheless, most authorities seem to regard emotions as complex states or conditions–human reactions that are characterized by specific experiential or feeling qualities and by widespread bodily changes, particularly in the autonomic nervous system.

The confusion and inconsistency in the literature on emotion appears to stem, in part, from the very complexity of emotional phenomena (Lindsley, 1951). Because of this complexity, individual investigators have tended to select either the phenomenological-experiential or the physiological-behavioral aspects of emotion for special study.

Most early studies of emotion were based on highly restricted observations of "immediate experience." For example, Titchener (1897) regarded "a vivid feeling" as the core of an emotion. Although he recognized that alterations in physiological response systems (e.g., pulse rate, respiration, muscular tension) were associated with emotional reactions, such bodily changes were considered relevant only in terms of their influence on reportable sensory experiences. Wundt (1896) also emphasized the phenomenological aspects of emotional reactions. He regarded emotions as unitary, relatively intense feeling-states that could be classified on the basis of three general psychological principles: (1) the qualitative characteristics of the feelings entering into the emotion, (2) the intensity of these feelings, and (3) the form of their occurrence, i.e., whether the emotion was sudden or gradual in onset and/or persistent or intermittent in duration.

The goals of early research on emotion were to discover, from an analysis of the introspective reports of trained observers, the basic qualitative feeling-states or "mental elements" which comprised different emotions. But this approach generated findings that were obviously artificial and unrelated to other kinds of behavior. Consequently, early research on the phenomenology of emotion was rejected or ignored, and the method of introspection itself was discredited and all but abandoned. Moreover, subjective reports about emotional states came to be viewed with extreme suspicion because they were unverifiable and easily falsified. This distrust of verbal reports was further intensified by psychoanalytic formulations which emphasized the distortions in mood and thought that may be produced by unconscious mental processes.

With the advent of behaviorism shortly after the turn of the century, psychology accepted the physicalistic assumptions of logical positivism, and research on emotion shifted from the investigation of subjective feeling-states to the evaluation of behavioral and physiological variables. Interest in general theories of emotion has declined in recent years, but there has been a noticeable increase in theory and research on specific emotions such as aggression (Berkowitz, 1962; Buss, 1961) and anxiety (Cattell & Scheier, 1961; Eysenck, 1957; Levitt, 1967, Sarason, Davidson, Lighthall, Waite, & Ruebush, 1960; Spielberger, 1966). Given the complexity of emotional phenomena, the decision to study individual emotions rather than emotions in general seems justified.

Research on the circumstances and conditions that produce changes in specific emotions such as fear or anxiety has also increased. This is evident, for example, in the number of recent books on psychological stress (Appley & Trumbull, 1967; Janis, 1958; Lazarus, 1966; Langer & Michael, 1963). For many psychologists, the word "emotion" has "mentalistic" connotations whereas the concept of stress, taken from physics and engineering, is more objective and therefore more "scientific." As Lazarus (1966) has noted, much of what was previously studied under the rubric of emotion is now considered in terms of the concept of psychological stress.

Arnold (1960a) has attributed the changing emphasis in theory and research on emotional phenomena to the fact that phenomenological conceptions of emotional states do not readily fit with current scientific methods. The epistemology and methodology of S–R psychology, and especially the prevailing bias against subjective experience as a *desideratum* for the science of psychology, require investigators to evaluate the impact of carefully defined and manipulated antecedent (stimulus) conditions on specific physiological and behavioral responses. While such methods have resulted in the development of scientifically rigorous procedures to measure the physiological and behavioral aspects of emotions, the feelings that are consciously experienced in emotional states have been largely neglected until very recently.

The typical paradigm employed in current research on emotion involves the manipulation of experimental conditions designed to influence a particular emotional state, and observation of the effects of these manipulations on behavioral and/or physiological responses that presumably reflect (define) changes in the emotional state. For example, in order to induce high levels of fear or anxiety, subjects may be threatened with electric shock, required to participate in stressful psychiatric interviews, or told that they are failing or performing poorly on a specific task. The impact of these experimental manipulations on behavior or physiological indicants of fear or anxiety (e.g., blood pressure, heart rate, muscle tension, electrodermal response) is then determined.

While the objective methods of S–R psychology have certainly helped to clarify the complex physiological and behavioral reactions produced by stressful experimental conditions, emotional reactions cannot be defined by stimulus and response operations alone. Differences in personality and past experience must also be taken into account because these dispose people to respond to similar stimulus objects and circumstances in radically different ways (Lazarus, Deese, & Osler, 1952). The savage who is unexpectedly confronted by a lion in the jungle is likely to react with intense fear, but the same lion may evoke feelings of exhilaration in the big game hunter, and mere amusement in children at the zoo. Whether or not an emotional response occurs during a psychological experiment often depends more on the subject's perception or interpretation of the situation than on the experimenter's manipulations (Ax, 1964). There can be little doubt that an individual's appraisal of a particular situation will greatly influence his reactions to it (Arnold, 1960; Lazarus & Opton, 1966).

In this chapter, the term, "emotion," will be used much as it is used in common language to refer to complex, qualitatively different, feeling-states or conditions of the human organism that have both phenomenological and physiological properties. A major point to be emphasized is that the long-neglected phenomenological-experiential properties of emotions must be investigated in their own right, along with the patterns of physiological and behavioral response associated with emotional arousal.

While some progress has been made in identifying specific patterns of physiological response associated with different emotions (e.g., Ax, 1953; Funkenstein, 1955; Schachter, 1957), very little current psychological research is concerned with the phenomenological aspects of emotional reactions. Yet the quality and intensity of the feelings experienced in emotional states seem to be their most unique and distinctive features. A comprehensive theory of personality will require concepts that take into account both the phenomenological and the physiological aspects of emotional reactions.

In order to achieve a comprehensive understanding of emotional phenomena, appropriate methods must be developed to distinguish between qualitatively different feeling-states, and to evaluate the intensity of such states as they change over time. The phenomenological aspects of emotion can be investigated most directly by using structured introspective reports about personal experience as a research tool. Of course, there must be adequate safeguards to permit evaluation of the veridicality of subjective reports, and the pitfalls associated with early introspective research on emotions must certainly be avoided. However, once objective procedures have been established for defining and measuring specific emotional states, it should be possible to draw upon rigorous experimental procedures to establish the construct validity of these measures.

Anxiety as an Emotional State

Research on anxiety as an emotional state has focused upon delineating the general properties of transitory anxiety states and identifying the specific conditions that evoke them. On the basis of an extensive review of the literature in psychology and psychiatry, Krause (1961) concluded that transitory anxiety is typically inferred from: (1) introspective verbal reports, (2) physiological signs, (3) "molar" behavior (i.e., body posture, restlessness, distortions in speech), (4) task performance, (5) clinical intuition, and (6) the response to stress. Introspective verbal reports, according to Krause's interpretation of conventional usage, provide the most widely-accepted basis for defining transitory anxiety.

Basowitz, Persky, Korchin, and Grinker (1955, p. 3) define anxiety as "the conscious and reportable experience of intense dread and foreboding, conceptualized as internally derived and unrelated to external threat." This definition is consistent with Freud's conception of anxiety as an emotional state and the prevailing convention of inferring transitory anxiety from introspective reports. Basowitz *et al.* also posit, as did Freud, that the unpleasant phenomenological qualities associated with anxiety states are consciously experienced. Thus, an individual who is "anxious" can observe and describe his unpleasant feelings, and can report the intensity and duration of these feelings.

In contrast to Krause's emphasis on introspective reports in the definition of anxiety, Martin (1961) proposes that anxiety reactions be viewed as complex neurophysiological responses that must be distinguished, conceptually and operationally, from the external or internal stimuli that evoke these responses. Thus, Martin emphasizes the importance of identifying and measuring the observable physiological and behavioral response patterns associated with states of fear or anxiety, and of differentiating between anxiety states and other emotional reactions. Martin also makes clear the need to distinguish between anxiety reactions and "defenses" against anxiety, i.e., responses that have been learned in order to reduce the intensity of anxiety states.

Schachter (1964) presents impressive evidence that emotional states consist of two major components: physiological arousal and socially determined cognitions. On the basis of research in which arousal of the sympathetic nervous system was induced by injections of epinephrine, Schachter (1967, p. 124) concludes:

> . . . precisely the same physiological state . . . can be manifested as anger, euphoria, amusement, fear, or . . . no emotion at all. Such results are virtually

> incomprehensible if we persist in the assumption of identity between physiological and psychological stress, but they fall neatly into place if we specify the fashion in which cognitive and physiological factors interact.

According to Schachter, an individual labels the feeling states associated with physiological arousal in terms of the social interpretations he gives to the situations in which these states are experienced. With regard to the natural occurrence of fear as an emotional reaction, Schachter suggests that:

> . . . cognitive or situational factors trigger physiological processes, and the triggering stimulus usually imposes the label we attach to our feelings. We see the threatening object; this perception-cognition initiates a state of sympathetic arousal and the joint cognitive-physiological experience is labeled "fear" [1967, p. 124].

Cattell and Scheier (1961) have pioneered in the application of multivariate techniques to the definition and measurement of anxiety. In their research, both phenomenological and physiological variables presumed to be related to anxiety have been studied with factor analytic procedures, notably such methods as P-technique, dR (differential R) technique, and chain-P technique (Cattell, 1966). In this multivariate approach, which permits investigation of the covariation of a number of different measures over time, "state" and "trait" anxiety have consistently emerged as principal personality factors. Many of the variables that load Cattell and Scheier's state-anxiety factor also have high loadings on their trait anxiety factor. Since the pattern of these loadings is quite different, Cattell hypothesizes that it should be possible to assess both state and trait anxiety from a single personality questionnaire by applying different weights to each scale item according to its unique contribution to the state and trait factors.

In summary, the clinical and research literature on transitory anxiety suggests that the presence of anxiety states in humans can be most meaningfully and unambiguously defined in terms of some combination of introspective verbal reports and physiological-behavioral signs. It is also apparent that anxiety states must be conceptually distinguished from the stimulus conditions that arouse them, and from the cognitive and behavioral maneuvers that are learned because they lead to anxiety reduction.

Transitory or state anxiety (A-State) may be conceived of as a complex, relatively unique emotional condition or reaction that may vary in intensity and fluctuate over time. More specifically, A-States may be conceptualized as consisting of unpleasant, consciously-perceived feelings of tension and apprehension, with associated activation or arousal of the autonomic nervous system. This conception, it may be noted, is quite comparable in many respects to the conception of anxiety as an emotional state originally suggested by Freud (1936) and elaborated upon by Basowitz *et al.* (1955).

In essence, if an individual reports that he feels anxious (frightened or apprehensive), this introspective verbal report defines an anxiety state. The use of introspective reports in the measurement of anxiety states assumes, of course, that people are capable of distinguishing between different feeling-states, and that they are motivated to report accurately and honestly.

In establishing the construct validity of measures of A-State based on introspective verbal reports, experimental procedures must be employed to determine the relationship between these self-report measures and physiological and behavioral indicants of anxiety. The application of self-report procedures in the measurement of state anxiety will be considered further in the section on Measurement of Anxiety States. At this point, however, it will be helpful to introduce several important terminological distinctions that will facilitate our discussion of anxiety phenomena in the remainder of the chapter.

Stress, Threat, and Anxiety

The words stress, threat, and anxiety are often used interchangeably by those who research anxiety phenomena. It is proposed here that the terms stress and threat be used to denote different aspects of a temporal sequence of events that results in the evocation of an anxiety state.

Stress will be used to refer to the objective stimulus properties of a situation. These may include variations in environmental conditions or circumstances that occur naturally, or that are introduced or manipulated by an experimenter. In essence, stress will denote external stimulus conditions or situations that are characterized by some degree of objective danger as defined by an experimenter, or as consensually validated by two or more observers.

A situation that is objectively stressful will be perceived as dangerous or threatening by most people. But whether or not a stressful situation is perceived as threatening by a particular person will depend upon his own subjective appraisal of the situation. Moreover, objectively nonstressful situations may be appraised as threatening by individuals who, for some reason, perceive them as dangerous. Thus, where *stress* refers to the objective stimulus properties of a situation, *threat* refers to an individual's idiosyncratic perception of a particular situation as physically or psychologically dangerous. The appraisal of a situation as dangerous or threatening will be determined, in part, by an individual's personality dispositions and past experience with similar situations.

The term, *anxiety,* or more specifically, *state anxiety* (A-State), will be used to refer to the complex emotional reactions that are evoked in individuals who interpret specific situations as personally threatening. If a person perceives a situation as threatening, irrespective of the presence of real (objective) danger, it is assumed that he will respond to it with an elevation in A-State, i.e., he will experience an immediate increase in the intensity of an emotional state characterized by feelings of tension and apprehension, and by heightened autonomic nervous system activity. The intensity and duration of this A-State reaction will be determined by the amount of threat that is perceived, and by the persistence of the individual's interpretation of the situation as dangerous.

The Measurement of Anxiety States

Although there has been notable progress in the assessment of personality characteristics in the past two decades, most of the advances have occurred in the measurement of personality traits rather than in the evaluation of psychological states. Since personality traits and states reflect different types of psychological constructs, the conceptual differences between them must be clarified in order to make our discussion of the measurement of state anxiety more meaningful.

Personality States and Traits

Personality states may be regarded as temporal cross sections in the stream-of-life of a person (Thorne, 1966). A personality state exists at a given moment in time, and at a particular level of intensity. Although personality states are often transitory, they can recur when evoked by appropriate stimuli, and they may endure over time when the evoking conditions persist. Emotional reactions may be viewed as expressions of personality states.

In contrast to the transitory nature of personality states, personality traits may be conceptualized as relatively enduring individual differences among people in specifiable tendencies to perceive the world in a certain way and/or in dispositions to react or behave in a specified manner with predictable regularity. Personality traits have the characteristics of a class of constructs which Atkinson (1964) calls "motives" and which Campbell (1963) refers to as "acquired behavioral dispositions." Atkinson defines motives as dispositional tendencies acquired in childhood that are latent until the cues of a situation activate them. Acquired dispositional concepts, according to Campbell, involve residues of past experience that dispose an individual both to view the world in a particular way and to manifest "object-consistent" response tendencies.

Personality traits may also be regarded as reflecting individual differences in the frequency and the intensity with which certain emotional states have been manifested in the past, and differences in the probability that such states will be experienced in the future. The stronger a particular personality trait, the more probable it is that an individual will experience the emotional state that corresponds to this trait, and the greater the probability that behaviors associated with the trait will be manifested in a variety of situations.

Furthermore, the stronger the personality trait, the more likely that these emotional states and associated behaviors will be characterized by high levels of intensity.

In certain respects, personality states and traits may be conceived of as analogous to the concepts of kinetic and potential energy in physics. Personality states, like kinetic energy, refer to palpable empirical reactions or processes taking place here and now at a given level of intensity. Personality traits, like potential energy, represent latent dispositions to respond with certain types of reactions, if triggered by appropriate stimuli.

Whether or not a particular personality trait will be expressed in overt behavior at a given moment in time will depend upon the strength of the trait and the presence of appropriate evoking stimuli. Although some people are more prone than others to be angry or anxious, these traits will not be manifested in behavior unless they are stimulated by appropriate circumstances. For example, in persons who are strongly disposed to experience anger, angry feelings will be more readily evoked by frustrating situations or by internal processes such as the thought that one has been treated unfairly. But under happy or pleasant circumstances, in which anger-provoking stimuli are absent or minimal, even persons highly disposed to react with angry feelings are not likely to do so.

The Measurement of Personality States

Thorne (1966) has cogently argued that psychological states should be the basic units of measurement in the study of human behavior, and especially in the study of personality. But because of methodological difficulties, transitory states have been largely ignored in psychological research. Attempts to develop instruments for the quantitative assessment of personality states have been infrequent because objective research methods for effectively measuring these constantly changing, subjective inner experiences have not been available. Over the past decade, however, a number of investigators have developed structured self-report scales that show promise as measures of transitory moods and emotional states.

Responses to self-report scales are certainly subject to falsification through a variety of mechanisms, and response sets often operate to distort the scores obtained with verbal report measures. It must be recognized, therefore, that the use of self-report scales to measure personality states rests upon the acceptance of what Wilde (1972) has termed the "inventory premise"—the assumption that people are willing, and able, to correctly describe their own feelings and behavior. A discussion of the complex methodological factors that are encountered with self-report measures is beyond the scope of the present chapter, but an excellent critical analysis of the assumptions that underlie the use of these techniques is provided by Wilde. It will suffice here to note Wilde's two general conclusions: (1) self-report scales may be regarded as verbal surrogates for behavior samples, and (2) the construct validity of self-report measures must be determined empirically within a theoretical context in the same manner that the validity of any other personality scale or performance measure is evaluated.

The first comprehensive battery of self-report scales for the assessment of feelings was apparently developed by Hildreth (1946). From the verbal reports of military patients, he derived 175 phrases that typified moods and attidues, and classified these into six categories. Each category was then scaled on the basis of the judgmental responses of psychiatric patients and hospital staff, using a modified Thurstone technique. The result was the Hildreth Feeling and Attitude Battery, a set of scales that measured various moods and affect states.

Wessman and Ricks (Wessman, Ricks, & Tyl, 1960; Wessman & Ricks, 1966) used rational and clinical criteria to develop a number of "Personal Feeling Scales" which defined affect dimensions such as tranquility versus social contempt, personal freedom versus constraint, harmony versus anger, energy versus fatigue, and others. The Wessman–Ricks and Hildreth scales are cumulative scales (Stouffer, Guttman, Suchman, Lazarsfeld, Star, & Clausen, 1950) in that the items are ordered to reflect increasing intensities of a particular feeling state.

A rather different approach to the measurement of affective states was taken by Nowlis and Green (Green & Nowlis, 1957; Nowlis & Green, 1964; Green, 1964). They collected a large number of adjectives that could be used to complete the sentence, "I feel ________ ." Subjects were then instructed to respond to sentences containing these adjectives by rating themselves on a mood-intensity dimension. On the basis of factor analytic studies, scales were derived for measuring twelve different mood dimensions.[2] Unfortunately, the range and reliability of these scales is limited by the fact that many of the dimensions are defined by as few as three adjectives, and one dimension, nonchalance, is assessed by only two adjectives.

Zuckerman and his colleagues (Zuckerman, 1960; Zuckerman & Lubin, 1965; Zuckerman, Lubin, Vogel, & Valerius, 1964) developed the Multiple Affect Adjective Check List (MAACL) for the assessment of affective states. The MAACL differs from the adjective rating-scales developed by Nowlis and Green in at least two important respects. First, the subject is required to check only those items that describe how he feels, rather than to indicate the intensity of specific feelings. Second, the adjectives that define the three affective

[2] A paper by Nowlis (1961) provides one of the best general introductions to the methods and problems associated with the measurement of affective states. Nowlis' approach has been subsequently extended by others (McNair & Lorr, 1964; Lorr, Daston, & Smith, 1967; Borgatta, 1961; Clyde, 1963). An excellent summary of the research findings is reported by Nowlis (1965).

dimensions–anxiety, hostility, and depression–were selected rationally rather than by factor-analytic procedures, and the resulting scales were validated by contrasting high and low groups on the three personality dimensions. An additional feature of the MAACL is that the same set of adjectives can be used to measure both states and traits. In the assessment of personality states, the subject is instructed to respond on the basis of how he feels "today;" in the assessment of personality traits, the subject is asked to respond according to how he generally feels.

THE MEASUREMENT OF STATE ANXIETY

In the mood scales developed by Wessman and Ricks, state anxiety (tranquility versus anxiety) is measured by a single, ten-item cumulative scale. Subjects are required to indicate "how calm or troubled you feel" by checking one of the ten scale items. The item that defines the lowest point on the tranquility-anxiety scale is: "Perfect and complete tranquility. Unshakably secure." The item representing the highest point on this scale is: "Completely beside myself with dread, worry, fear. Overwhelmingly distraught and apprehensive. Obsessed or terrified by insoluble problems and fears [Wessman & Ricks, 1966, p. 271]." The other eight scale points reflect intermediate levels along an inferred dimension of increasing anxiety. Wessman and Ricks were primarily concerned with the elation–depression dimension, and they report only limited information with regard to the validity of their anxiety scale.

An anxiety factor emerged as one of the basic mood dimensions in the research of Nowlis and Green (1965). This factor was defined by the adjectives "clutched up," "fearful," and "jittery" (1965, pp. 45–46). Other adjectives that also had loadings on the anxiety factor were "apprehensive," "uncertain," "helpless," and "weak," but the findings for these adjectives were not entirely consistent. Consequently, the Nowlis–Green measure of state anxiety in subsequent research has consisted of only three adjectives–clutched up, fearful, and jittery–each of which is rated on a four-point scale.

The IPAT 8-Parallel Form Anxiety Battery (8-PF) was developed by Scheier and Cattell (1960) for the "repeated measurement of changes in anxiety level over time." Each of the eight forms of this battery consists of subtests for which high loadings on a state-anxiety factor were demonstrated in differential-R and P-technique factor analysis. Only limited validity data have been reported for this test as a measure of state anxiety (Barrett & Dimascio, 1966; Dimascio, Meyer, & Stifler, 1968).

It should be noted that several of the subtests in the 8-PF Anxiety Battery were taken from the Objective–Analytic (O–A) Anxiety Battery (Cattell & Scheier, 1960) which measures trait anxiety as defined by Factor *U.I. 24* (Cattell & Scheier, 1961). Four of these subtests ("Susceptibility to Common

Annoyances," "Lack of Confidence in Untried Skills," "Honesty in Admitting Common Frailties," and "Susceptibility to Embarrassment") appear to reflect behavioral dispositions associated with trait anxiety, rather than anxiety states. Another subtest ("Questions") requires subjects to report the frequency a given symptom has been experienced in the past ("often," "sometimes," "never"), rather than the intensity of the experience in the present. Thus, it would appear that the 8-PF Anxiety Battery is more closely related to trait anxiety than to state anxiety.

Zuckerman and his associates (Zuckerman, 1960; Zuckerman & Biase, 1962) developed the Affect Adjective Check List (AACL) to measure both state and trait anxiety. The AACL was subsequently extended to include measures of hostility and depression, and renamed the Multiple Affect Adjective Check List (MAACL), which was described in the previous section. State anxiety is measured with the "Today" version of the AACL. This form requires the subject to check those adjectives that describe how he feels on the particular day the test is administered. The instructions may be modified, however, to require the subject to indicate how he feels at a certain time.

Zuckerman and Lubin (1968) have recently published an extensive bibliography of studies in which the AACL and the MAACL were used to evaluate changes in anxiety states as a function of a variety of stress-producing and stress-reducing conditions. In these studies the usefulness of the AACL as a measure of day-to-day fluctuations in state anxiety has been clearly demonstrated. While evidence for the validity of the Today Form of the AACL as a measure of state anxiety is impressive, the General Form of the AACL typically shows lower correlations with other standard measures of trait anxiety (e.g., The Taylor Manifest Anxiety Scale and the IPAT Anxiety Scale) than these measures correlate with one another (Spielberger, Gorsuch, & Lushene, 1970).

The State-Trait Anxiety Inventory

The State–Trait Anxiety Inventory (STAI) was developed to provide reliable, relatively brief self-report measures of both state (A-State) and trait (A-Trait) anxiety. Item selection and validation procedures for the STAI are described in detail by Spielberger and Gorsuch (1966) and by Spielberger *et al.* (1970).

In developing the STAI, it was assumed that items with a demonstrated relationship to other measures of anxiety would be most useful in an inventory designed to measure both A-State and A-Trait. Since most anxiety scales measure trait anxiety (Spielberger, 1966a), a large number of items embodying content of proven relationship to the most widely used A-Trait scales were rewritten so that each item could be administered with different instructions to measure either A-State or A-Trait. It was discovered, however, that the psycholinguistic properties of some of the items or, more precisely, the connotations of key words in these items, conveyed meanings that interfered with their use as measures of both A-State and A-Trait. For example, "I feel upset" turned out to be a good A-State item, but a relatively poor measure of A-Trait.

The test construction strategy for the STAI was subsequently modified to develop separate scales for the measurement of A-State and A-Trait. The STAI A-Trait scale consists of twenty statements that ask people to describe how they generally feel. Subjects respond to each scale item (e.g., "I lack self confidence") by checking one of the following: "Almost never," "Sometimes," "Often," "Almost always." Individual items were selected for the STAI A-Trait scale on the basis of significant correlations with other anxiety scales that were widely accepted as measures of individual differences in A-Trait, e.g., the Taylor (1953) Manifest Anxiety Scale, and the IPAT Anxiety Scale. Individual A-Trait items were also expected to be impervious to situational stress and relatively stable over time.

Three important characteristics determined the test construction strategy for the development of the STAI A-State scale:

1. When the scale was given with instructions that required the subject to report his present feelings ("Indicate how you feel *right now*"), each item was expected to reflect the subject's level of anxiety (A-State) at that particular moment in time. Only those items were retained for the final scale that showed higher means in a priori stressful situations than in nonstressful or nonthreatening situations.

2. A second characteristic that was sought in the development of the STAI A-State scale was high reliability. In evaluating the effects of various stressor conditions on level of A-State, the major interest is in the differences obtained on two or more occasions of measurement. Since difference scores between any two occasions contain the error components of both the initial and final scores, if the components of the difference score are only moderately reliable, the resulting difference score will itself be low in reliability.

3. To maximize its usefulness in psychological research, a third characteristic that was desired in the STAI A-State scale was ease and brevity of administration. In the investigation of the effects of emotional states on performance, a long involved test would be unsuitable for experimental tasks in which taking the test might interfere with performance on the task. Furthermore, since rapid fluctuations in A-State may occur in a changing environment, a long test would be less sensitive to such variations.

The STAI A-State scale consists of twenty statements that ask people to describe how they feel at a particular moment in time; subjects respond to each A-State item by rating themselves on the following four point scale: (1) Not at all, (2) Somewhat, (3) Moderately so, (4) Very much so. The item selection and item validation procedures for the STAI are described in detail by Spielberger *et al.* (1970). Sample items from the STAI A-State scale are given in Table 2.1.

TABLE 2.1
Selected Items from the A-State Scale of the State-Trait Anxiety Inventory

I feel calm	1	2	3	4
I am tense	1	2	3	4
I feel upset	1	2	3	4
I feel nervous	1	2	3	4
I am jittery	1	2	3	4
I feel content	1	2	3	4

The essential qualities that are evaluated by the STAI A-State scale involve feelings of tension, nervousness, worry, and apprehension. In developing the A-State scale it was discovered empirically that such feelings were highly correlated with the absence of feelings of calmness, security, contentedness, and the like. Therefore, items such as "I feel calm," and "I feel content," were included to produce a balanced A-State scale; half of the items relate to the presence of apprehension, worry, or tension, and the remaining items reflect the absence of such states. Thus, the STAI A-State scale defines a continuum of increasing levels of A-State intensity, with low scores indicating states of calmness and serenity, intermediate scores indicating moderate levels of tension and apprehensiveness, and high scores reflecting states of intense apprehension and fearfulness that approach panic.

When administered for research purposes, the STAI A-State scale may be given with instructions that focus upon a particular time period. A subject may be instructed, for example, to respond according to how he felt while performing on an experimental task that he has just completed. If the task is a long one, it may be useful to instruct the subject to respond according to how he felt early in the task, or how he felt while working on the final portion of the task. In clinical research, a patient may be asked to report the feelings he experiences in therapy interviews or how he felt while he visualized a specific stimulus situation in a behavior therapy session.

To measure changes in the intensity of transitory anxiety over time, the STAI A-State scale may be given on each occasion for which an A-State measure is needed. In research in which repeated measurements of A-State are desired during performance on an experimental task, very brief scales consisting of as few as four or five STAI A-State items may be used to provide valid measures of A-State (O'Neil, Spielberger, & Hansen, 1969; Spielberger, O'Neil, & Hansen, 1972). Responding to these brief scales does not seem to interfere with performance on an experimental task.

Multiple repeated measures of A-State may be obtained either with the same or with different instructions as to the time period for which the subject's reports are desired. For example, a subject may be asked to report how he feels immediately before he begins to work on an experimental task. Then, after he completes the task, he may be asked to indicate how he felt while he was working on it.

Correlations with other measures of A-State, such as the Zuckerman AACL, Today Form, provide evidence of the concurrent validity of the STAI A-State scale (Spielberger *et al.*, 1970). It has also been demonstrated that scores on the STAI A-State scale increase in response to various kinds of stress and decrease as a result of relaxation training (Spielberger *et al.*, 1970). Additional evidence of the construct validity of the STAI A-State scale may be found in recent studies by Auerbach (1971), Edwards (1969), Hall (1969), Hodges (1967), Hodges and Felling (1970), Lamb (1969), Lushene (1970), McAdoo (1969), O'Neil (1969), O'Neil *et al.* (1969), Parrino (1969), Spielberger *et al.* (1972), and Taylor, Wheeler, & Altman (1968).

Self-report measures such as the STAI may be criticized on many grounds. It may be argued, for example, that the items are ambiguous and mean different things to different people, or that people do not know themselves well enough to give truthful answers, or that many people are unwilling to admit negative things about themselves. Administration of the STAI A-State scale for clinical and research purposes has shown, however, that adolescents and adults with at least dull–normal intelligence are capable of describing how they feel at a particular moment in time. Most people are also willing to reveal how they feel during a therapy hour, or while performing on an experimental task, provided they are asked specific questions about their feelings, and the feelings were recently experienced. Of course, the clinician or experimenter who uses self-report scales to measure anxiety, or any other emotional state, must endeavor to motivate his patients or subjects to provide accurate information about themselves.

Toward a Trait-State Theory of Anxiety

An adequate theory of anxiety must distinguish conceptually and operationally between anxiety as a transitory state and as a relatively stable personality trait It is also apparent that a comprehensive theory of anxiety must differentiate between anxiety states, the stimulus conditions that evoke these states and the defenses that serve to avoid or ameliorate them (Spielberger, 1966a). In this section, two different anxiety constructs, state anxiety (A-State) and trait anxiety (A-Trait), will be defined. A trait-state theory of anxiety will then be proposed in which the relationship between these concepts is clarified. In setting forth this theory, we will attempt to describe some of the circumstances and conditions that appear to evoke different levels of A-State intensity in persons who differ in A-Trait, i.e. persons who are differentially disposed to experience A-States.

The Concepts of State and Trait Anxiety

State anxiety (A-State) may be conceptualized as a transitory emotional state or condition of the human organism that varies in intensity and fluctuates over time. This condition is characterized by subjective, consciously perceived feelings of tension and apprehension, and activation of the autonomic nervous system. Level of A-State should be high in circumstances that are perceived by an individual to be threatening, irrespective of the objective danger; A-State intensity should be low in nonstressful situations, or in circumstances in which an existing danger is not perceived as threatening.

Trait anxiety (A-Trait) refers to relatively stable individual differences in anxiety proneness, that is, to differences in the disposition to perceive a wide range of stimulus situations as dangerous or threatening, and in the tendency to respond to such threats with A-State reactions. A-Trait may also be regarded as reflecting individual differences in the frequency and the intensity with which A-States have been manifested in the past, and in the probability that such states will be experienced in the future. Persons who are high in A-Trait tend to perceive a larger number of situations as dangerous or threatening than persons who are low in A-Trait, and to respond to threatening situations with A-State elevations of greater intensity.

Anxiety and Stress

A major task for a trait-state theory of anxiety is to describe and specify the characteristics of stressor stimuli that evoke differential levels of A-State in persons who differ in A-Trait. Atkinson (1964) suggests that a "fear of failure" motive is reflected in measures of A-Trait, while Sarason (1960) emphasizes the special significance for high A-Trait individuals of experimental situations that arouse self-depreciating tendencies. On the basis of a review of the research findings obtained with various anxiety scales, Sarason (1960, pp. 401–402) concludes:

> the bulk of the available findings suggest that high anxious *S*s are affected more detrimentally by motivating conditions or failure reports than are *S*s lower in the anxiety score distribution . . . . It is interesting to note that high anxious *S*s have been found to be more self-deprecatory, more self-preoccupied and generally less content with themselves than *S*s lower in the distribution of anxiety . . . it may well be that highly motivating or ego-involving instructions serve the function of arousing these self-oriented tendencies.

In general, the experimental literature on anxiety is consistent with the hypothesis that situations which pose direct or implied threats to self-esteem produce differential levels of A-State in persons who differ in A-Trait. Differences in the performance of high and low A-Trait individuals on learning tasks, for example, are most often found under conditions that involve failure experiences or "ego-involving" instructions (Spence & Spence, 1966). Furthermore, circumstances that involve the risk of failure, such as academic achievement situations (Mandler & Sarason, 1952; Spielberger, 1962), or in which an individual's personal adequacy is evaluated, e.g., taking an "intelligence test" or performing on a concept attainment task, appear to be especially threatening to persons with high A-Trait (Denny, 1966; Spielberger, 1966b; Spielberger & Smith, 1966).

Experimental investigations of anxiety phenomena have produced findings that are generally consistent with Atkinson's suggestion that fear of failure is a major characteristic of high A-Trait people, and with Sarason's conclusion that ego-involving instructions are more detrimental to the performance of high A-Trait subjects than low A-Trait subjects. Apparently, failure or ego-involving instructions evoke higher levels of A-State intensity in high A-Trait subjects than in low A-Trait subjects. But whether or not a particular high A-Trait individual will show elevation in A-State in a specific situation will depend upon the extent to which he perceives the situation as dangerous or threatening, and this will be greatly influenced by past experience.

High A-Trait persons would be expected to perceive the requirement to perform on a difficult task, such as solving complex mathematical problems, as highly threatening, especially if the task were given with ego-involving instructions. Consequently, such tasks would be expected to evoke larger increments in A-State for persons who are high in A-Trait than for low A-Trait individuals. But a mathematician who is high in A-Trait is not likely to regard this task as threatening because he has the requisite skills and experience to do well on it. On the other hand, while most persons find recreational activities such as boating and swimming to be interesting and pleasurable, a low A-Trait individual who is a poor swimmer might respond to the prospect of a boat ride with a considerable elevation in A-State. Thus, while measures of A-Trait provide useful information regarding the probability that high levels of A-Trait will be aroused, in order to assess the impact of a specific situation on a particular person it will be necessary to take actual measures of A-State in that situation.

On the basis of extensive investigations of soldiers undergoing paratroop training, Basowitz *et al.* (1955) identified two different types of anxiety which they termed *shame-anxiety* and *harm-anxiety*. They based this distinction on the observation that higher levels of A-State were evoked by the anticipation of failure than by fear of serious injury or death. Basowitz *et al.* (1955, p. 93) state:

> It became clear that the anxiety generated in this situation was not a simple unitary phenomena. Despite our prior conception that the primary source of anxiety would be related to the real or phantasied dangers of jumping we found that feelings related to shame were often of greater importance. Trainees were often apprehensive not so much about the severe threat of bodily injury or death,

> but about the possibility of not measuring up to the task undertaken. This anxiety was expressed in a fear of failure; should one not "win his wings" he would be humbled before his peers and in the eyes of idealized older figures whom he was seeking to emulate.

Basowitz *et al.* theorize that "the distinction between the two different loci of anxieties is primarily a conceptual one. For the experiencer himself there may be only the unitary state of emotional stress [pp. 272–73]." This interpretation is consistent with the hypothesis that psychological threats and physical dangers may differentially influence anxiety as a unitary emotional state (A-State) because life experiences cause people to develop different dispositions to respond to these types of stressors.

Level of A-Trait would not necessarily be expected to influence the intensity of A-State responses to all stressors, but only to those that persons with high A-Trait perceive as more threatening. Since high A-Trait individuals have been described as more self-deprecatory, and as persons who fear failure, it might be expected that they will manifest higher levels of A-State in situations that involve psychological threats to self esteem rather than physical danger.

There is some evidence that persons with high A-Trait do not perceive physical dangers as any more threatening than low A-Trait individuals. It has been observed, for example, that threat of electric shock produces significant increases in both self-report and physiological measures of A-State (Katkin, 1965; Hodges & Spielberger, 1966), but the magnitude of the increment in A-State intensity produced by shock-threat in these studies was unrelated to level of A-Trait as measured by the Taylor (1953) Manifest Anxiety Scale (MAS). Similarly, Spielberger *et al.* (1970) and Lushene (1970) found that viewing a stressful movie depicting physically painful accidents in a woodworking shop evoked marked increases in A-State, and that the magnitude of change in A-State was unrelated to level of A-Trait.

In the Hodges and Spielberger (1966) study, subjects were also given a 'Fear of Shock Questionnaire" (FSQ). The FSQ, which was included among a group of tests administered two months prior to the experiment, consisted of the single item, "How much concern or apprehension would you feel about participating in a psychology experiment in which you received electric shock?" Subjects responded by rating themselves on a five-point scale from "none" to "extreme." FSQ scores were found to be positively and significantly correlated with increases in heart rate ($r = .43$) produced by threat of shock (no shock was actually given), and with level of A-State intensity as measured by the AACL-Today ($r = .49$). In contrast, the FSQ was not correlated ($r = .09$) with scores on the MAS, a measure of A-Trait, nor with changes in heart rate ($r = .05$).

Hodges and Spielberger's findings indicated that persons who reported greater fear of shock (two months prior to the experiment) showed greater increases in level of A-State intensity when threatened with shock than subjects who reported little or no fear of shock. In contrast, threat of shock failed to produce differential increases in physiological and self-report measures of A-State for persons who differed in level of A-Trait. Since the correlation between the FSQ and the MAS was essentially zero, these findings may be interpreted as providing evidence of the existence of a separate "fear of shock" trait which is unrelated to trait anxiety. In other words, individual differences in the disposition to fear shock are unrelated to individual differences in the disposition to respond to failure or threats to self-esteem with greater elevations in A-State.

It is tempting to generalize that persons high in A-Trait do not perceive physical dangers or physical pain to be any more threatening than do individuals who are low in A-Trait, but there is not yet sufficient evidence to justify this conclusion, and there is also some evidence to the contrary (Malmo, Shagass, Davis, Cleghorn, Graham, & Googan, 1948).

A Trait-State Theory of Anxiety

Trait-State Anxiety Theory provides a conceptual frame of reference for classifying the major variables that should be considered in anxiety research and suggests possible inter-relationships among these variables. The theory is especially concerned with clarifying the properties of A-State and A-Trait as psychological constructs, and with specifying the characteristics of stressful stimulus conditions which evoke differential levels of A-State in persons who differ in A-Trait. The theory also recognizes the centrality of cognitive appraisal in the evocation of an anxiety state, and the importance of cognitive and motoric processes (defense mechanisms) that serve to eliminate or reduce anxiety states.

A schematic diagram of Trait-State Anxiety Theory is presented in Fig. 2.1 which provides a cross-sectional analysis of anxiety phenomena. The theory assumes that the arousal of anxiety states involves a process or sequence of temporally ordered events initiated by either external or internal stimuli that are perceived to be dangerous or threatening by an individual. Examples of external stressors that are likely to evoke anxiety reactions are the imminent danger of injury or death that is faced by a soldier in combat, or the threat to self-esteem that is encountered when a student is called upon to recite in class. Any internal stimulus which causes an individual to think about or anticipate a dangerous or frightening situation may also evoke high levels of A-State. For example, a student who suddenly remembers that he has failed to prepare for an examination that is scheduled for the next class period would probably experience a sudden increase in A-State.

As previously noted, situations or circumstances in which personal adequacy is evaluated are likely to be perceived as more threatening by high A-Trait individuals than by persons who are low in A-Trait. It should be noted, however,

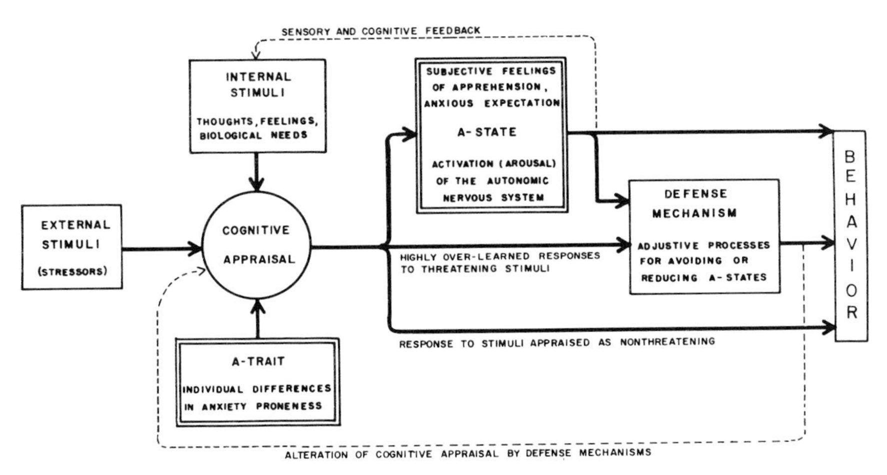

Figure 2.1. *A trait-state theory of anxiety in which two anxiety constructs, A-Trait and A-State, are posited and conceptually distinguished from the stimulus conditions which evoke A-State reactions and the defenses against A-States. The cognitive appraisal of a stimulus as dangerous or threatening evokes an A-State reaction, which may then initiate a behavior sequence designed to avoid the danger situation. An A-State reaction may also evoke defensive maneuvers which reduce A-State or alter the cognitive appraisal of the situation. Individual differences in A-Trait, along with past experience, determine the particular stimuli that are cognitively appraised as threatening. Reprinted with permission from Spielberger (1966a, p. 17).*

that the appraisal of a particular stimulus or situation as threatening is also influenced by a person's aptitude, abilities, and past experience, as well as by his level of A-Trait and the objective danger that is inherent in the situation.

Once a stimulus situation is appraised as threatening it is assumed that: (1) an A-State reaction will be evoked, and (2) the intensity of this reaction will be proportional to the amount of threat the situation poses for the individual. It is further assumed that the duration of the A-State reaction will depend upon the persistence of the evoking stimuli and the individual's previous experience in dealing with similar circumstances. Stressful situations that are encountered frequently may lead an individual to develop effective coping responses that quickly alleviate or minimize the danger and thereby immediately reduce level of A-State intensity. A person may also respond to threatening situations with defensive processes that serve to reduce the intensity of A-State reactions.

High levels of A-State intensity are experienced as unpleasant and may serve to initiate cognitive or motoric processes that have effectively reduced A-States in the past. For example, an undergraduate subject in an experiment that involved the threat of electric shock initially appraised this experimental situation as dangerous, and responded with a marked increase in heart rate. After briefly reflecting on his circumstances, the subject reasoned that either he would not be shocked (a correct assumption), or that if he was shocked it would not be very painful "because university officials would not permit this." Since the subject had no way of knowing if the experimenter would actually shock him, in effect, he used "denial" and "intellectualization" as defenses against the danger posed by the situation. Corresponding to his reappraisal of the situation there was a decline in level of A-State intensity as measured by changes in heart rate and the self-report of feelings of apprehension and tension.

It was noted previously that two important classes of stressor situations can be identified that appear to have different implications for the evocation of A-State in persons who differ in A-Trait: (1) individuals with high A-Trait appear to interpret circumstances in which their personal adequacy is evaluated as more threatening than do low A-Trait individuals, and (2) situations that are characterized by physical danger are not interpreted as differentially threatening by high and low A-Trait subjects. Accordingly, differential elevations in A-State would be expected for persons who differ in A-Trait under circumstances characterized by some threat to self-esteem, but not in situations that involve physical danger unless personal adequacy is also threatened.

The principle assumptions of Trait-State Anxiety Theory may be briefly summarized as follows:

1. In situations that are appraised by an individual as threatening, an A-State reaction will be evoked. Through sensory and cognitive feedback mechanisms high levels of A-State will be experienced as unpleasant.
2. The intensity of an A-State reaction will be proportional to the amount of threat that the situation poses for the individual.
3. The duration of an A-State reaction will depend upon the persistence of the individual's interpretation of the situation as threatening.
4. High A-Trait individuals will perceive situations or circumstances that involve failure or threats to self-esteem as more threatening than will persons who are low in A-Trait.
5. Elevations in A-State have stimulus and drive properties that may be expressed directly in behavior, or that may serve to initiate psychological defenses that have been effective in reducing A-States in the past.
6. Stressful situations that are encountered frequently may cause an individual to develop specific coping responses or psychological defense mechanisms which are designed to reduce or minimize A-State.

With regard to the origin and etiology of individual differences in A-Trait, it is assumed that residues of past experience dispose high A-Trait persons to appraise situations that involve some form of personal evaluation as more threatening than do individuals who are low in A-Trait. We may speculate that childhood experiences influence the development of individual differences in A-Trait, and that parent–child relationships centering around punishment are especially important in this regard. The fact that self-depreciating attitudes are aroused in high A-Trait persons under circumstances characterized by failure or ego-involving instructions suggests that these individuals received excessive criticism and negative appraisals from their parents which undermined their self-confidence and adversely influenced their self-concept.

In summary, the schematic representation of Trait-State Anxiety Theory that is presented in Fig. 2.1 provides a cross-sectional analysis of anxiety phenomena. In this conception, two different anxiety constructs, A-State and A-Trait, are posited and distinguished from the stimulus conditions which evoke A-State reactions and the defenses that help individuals to avoid or reduce A-States. Fig. 2.1 also provides a conceptual frame of reference for classifying the major variables that should be considered in research on anxiety phenomena, and suggests some of the possible inter-relationships among them. In addition to the constructs of A-State and A-Trait, the classes of variables that we believe to be most significant in anxiety research are: (1) the external and internal stimuli that evoke anxiety states, (2) the cognitive processes that are involved in appraising stimuli as threatening, and (3) the defense mechanisms that are employed to avoid anxiety states, or to reduce the intensity of these states once they are experienced.

Summary

Our inquiry began with the question "What is emotion?" We then proceeded to examine the history of the concept of emotion in psychology, and to discuss theoretical, methodological, and terminological issues that arise in the investigation of anxiety as an emotional state. Several general approaches to the measurement of feelings and emotions were considered and a number of specific self-report procedures for measuring anxiety as an emotional state were described. Two distinct anxiety concepts, state anxiety (A-State) and trait anxiety (A-Trait) were defined, and a trait-state theory of anxiety was outlined. The following general conclusions were reached:

1. There are a number of different kinds of emotions. While the subjective quality of the feelings experienced in emotional states seem to be their most unique and distinctive feature, emotional states also vary in intensity and fluctuate over time.

2. Anxiety was conceived of in this paper as a specific emotional state which consists of unpleasant, consciously-perceived feelings of nervousness, tension, and apprehension, with associated activation or arousal of the autonomic nervous system. This conception of anxiety is comparable in many respects to the conception originally proposed by Freud.

3. Several different measures of state anxiety were discussed, and the development of the State-Trait Anxiety Inventory was described in some detail. The STAI is a new test that provides self-report measures of both state and trait anxiety.

4. A theory of anxiety was introduced in which the concepts of A-State and A-Trait were defined and distinguished from the stimulus conditions which evoke A-State reactions and the defense mechanisms that help individuals avoid or reduce A-States.

References

Appley, M. T., & Trumbull, R. *Psychological stress.* New York: Appleton-Century-Crofts, 1967.

Arnold, M. B. *Emotion and personality.* Vol. I. *Psychological aspects.* New York: Columbia University Press, 1960.

Atkinson, J. W. *An introduction to motivation.* Princeton, New Jersey: Van Nostrand–Reinhold, 1964.

Auerbach, S. M. An investigation of the Effects of Surgery-Induced Stress on State and Trait Anxiety. Doctoral Dissertation, Florida State University, 1971.

Ax, A. F. The physiological differentation between fear and anger in humans. *Psychosomatic Medicine,* 1953, **15,** 433–442.

Ax, A. F. Goals and methods of psychophysiology. *Psychophysiology,* 1964, **1,** 8–25.

Barrett, J. E., & Dimascio, A. Comparative effects on anxiety of the "minor tranquilizers" in "high" and "low" anxious student volunteers. *Diseases of the Nervous System,* 1966, **27,** 483–486.

Basowitz, H., Persky, H., Korchin, S. J., & Grinker, R. R. *Anxiety and stress.* New York: McGraw–Hill, 1955.

Berkowitz, L. *Aggression.* New York: McGraw–Hill, 1962.

Borgatta, E. F. Mood, personality, and interaction. *Journal of General Psychology,* 1961, **64,** 105–137.

Buss, A. H. *The psychology of aggression,* New York: Wiley, 1961.

Campbell, D. T. Social attitudes and other acquired behavioral dispositions. In S. Koch (Ed.), *Psychology: A study of a science.* Vol. 6. New York: McGraw–Hill, 1963. Pp. 94–172.

Cattell, R. B. Patterns of change: measurement in relation to state-dimension, trait change, lability, and process concepts. *Handbook of Multivariate Experimental Psychology.* Chicago, Illinois: Rand McNally, 1966.

Cattell, R. B., & Scheier, I. H. Stimuli related to stress, neuroticism, excitation, and anxiety response patterns. *Journal of Abnormal and Social Psychology,* 1960, **60,** 195–204.

Cattell, R. B., & Scheier, I. H. *The meaning and measurement of neuroticism and anxiety.* New York: Ronald Press, 1961.

Clyde, D. J. *Manual for the Clyde Mood Scale.* Coral Gables, Florida: University of Miami Biometric Laboratory, 1963.

Denny, J. P. Effects of anxiety and intelligence on concept formation. *Journal of Experimental Psychology,* 1966, **72,** 596–602.

Dimascio, A., Meyer, R. E., & Stifler, L. Effects of imipramine on individuals varying in level of depression. *American Journal of Psychiatry,* 1968, **124,** 55–58.

Duffy, E. An explanation of "emotional" phenomena without the use of the concept "emotion." *Journal of General Psychology,* 1941, **25**, 283–293.

Duffy, E. *Activation and behavior.* New York: Wiley, 1962.

Edwards, K. R., Jr. Psychological changes associated with pregnancy and obstetric complications. Doctoral dissertation, University of Miami, Florida, 1969.

Eysenck, H. J. *The dynamics of anxiety and hysteria.* London: Routledge and Kegan Paul, 1957.

Freud, S. *Collected papers.* Vol. 1. London: Hogarth Press, 1924.

Freud, S. *The problem of anxiety.* New York: Norton, 1936.

Funkenstein, D. H. The physiology of fear and anger. *Scientific American,* 1955, **192**, 74–80.

Green, R. F. The measurement of mood. Technical Report, Office of Naval Research, 1964.

Green, R. F., & Nowlis, V. *A factor analytic study of the domain of mood with independent experimental validation of the factors.* Paper read at the American Psychological Association Convention, 1957.

Hall, B. Anxiety, stress, task difficulty and achievement via programmed instruction. Doctoral dissertation, Florida State University, 1969.

Hildreth, H. M. A battery of feeling and attitude scales for clinical use. *Journal of Clinical Psychology,* 1946, **2,** 214–221.

Hodges W. F. The effects of success, threat of shock, and failure on anxiety. Doctoral dissertation, Vanderbilt University, 1967.

Hodges, W. F., & Felling, J. P. Types of stressful situations and their relation to trait anxiety and sex. *Journal of Consulting and Clinical Psychology,* 1970, **34,** 333–337.

Hodges, W. F., & Spielberger, C. D. The effects of threat of shock on heart rate for subjects who differ in manifest anxiety and fear of shock. *Psychophysiology,* 1966, **2,** 287–294.

James, W. *The principles of psychology.* New York: Holt, 1890.

Janis, I. L. *Psychological stress.* New York: Wiley, 1958.

Katkin, E. S. The relationship between manifest anxiety and two indices of autonomic response to stress. *Journal of Personality and Social Psychology,* 1965, **2,** 324–333.

Krause, M. S. The measurement of transitory anxiety. *Psychological Review,* 1961, **68,** 178–189.

Lamb D. H. The effects of public speaking on self-report, physiological, and behavioral measures of anxiety. Doctoral dissertation, Florida State University, 1969.

Langer T. S., & Michael, S. T. *Life stress and mental health.* New York: Free Press of Glencoe, 1963.

Lazarus, R. S. *Psychological stress and the coping process.* New York: McGraw–Hill, 1966.

Lazarus, R. S., Deese, J., & Osler, Sonia F. The effects of psychological stress upon performance. *Psychological Bulletin,* 1952, **49,** 293–317.

Lazarus, R. S., & Opton, E. M., Jr. The study of psychological stress. In C. D. Spielberger (Ed.), *Anxiety and behavior.* New York: Academic Press, 1966. Pp. 225–262.

Levitt, E. E. *The psychology of anxiety.* Indianapolis, Indiana: Bobbs–Merrill, 1967.

Lindsley, D. B. Emotion. In S. S. Stevens (Ed.), *Handbook of experimental psychology.* New York: Wiley, 1951.

Lorr, M., Daston, P., & Smith, I. R. An analysis of mood states. *Educational and Psychological Measurement,* 1967, **27,** 89–96.

Lushene, R. E. The effects of physical and psychological threat on the autonomic, motoric, and ideational components of state anxiety. Doctoral dissertation, Florida State University, 1970.

Malmo, R. B., Shagass, C., Davis, J. F., Cleghorn, R. A., Graham, B. F., & Goodman, A. J. Standardized pain stimulation as controlled stress in physiological studies of psychoneurosis. *Science,* 1948, **108,** 509–511.

Mandler, G., & Sarason, S. B. A study of anxiety and learning. *Journal of Abnormal and Social Psychology,* 1952, **47,** 166–173.

Martin, B. The assessment of anxiety by physiological behavioral measures. *Psychological Bulletin,* 1961, **58,** 234–255.

McAdoo, W. G. The effects of success and failure feedback on A-State for subjects who differ in A-Trait. Doctoral dissertation, Florida State University, 1969.

McNair, D. M., & Lorr, M. An analysis of mood in neurotics. *Journal of Abnormal and Social Psychology,* 1964, **69,** 620–627.

Nowlis, V. Methods for studying mood changes produced by drugs. *Revue de Psychologie Appliquee,* 1961, **11,** 373–386.

Nowlis, V. Research with the mood adjective check list. In S. S. Tomkins and C. E. Izard (Eds.), *Affect, cognition and personality,* New York: Springer, 1965. Pp. 352–389.

Nowlis, V., & Green, R. F. Factor analytic studies of mood. Technical Report, Office of Naval Research, 1964.

Nowlis, V., & Green, R. F. Factor analytical studies of the mood adjective checklist. Technical Report, Office of Naval Research, 1965.

O'Neil, H. F., Jr. Effects of stress on state anxiety and performance in computer-assisted learning. Doctoral dissertation, Florida State University, 1969.

O'Neil, H. F., Speilberger, C. D., & Hansen, D. N. The effects of state-anxiety and task difficulty on computer-assisted learning. *Journal of Educational Psychology,* 1969, **60,** 343–350.

Parrino, J. J. The effects of pre-therapy information on learning in psychotherapy. Doctoral dissertation, Louisiana State University, 1969.

Plutchik, R. *The emotions.* New York: Random House, 1962.

Sarason, I. G. Empirical findings and theoretical problems in the use of anxiety scales. *Psychological Bulletin,* 1960, **57,** 403–415.

Sarason, S. B., Davidson, K. S., Lighthall, F. F., Waite, R. R., & Ruebush, B. K. *Anxiety in elementary school children.* New York: Wiley, 1960.

Schachter, J. Pain, fear and anger in hypertensives and normotensives. *Psychosomatic Medicine,* 1957, **19,** 17–29.

Schachter, S. The interaction of cognitive and physiological determinants of emotional state. In L. Berkowitz (Ed.), *Advances in experimental social psychology.* Vol. 1. New York: Academic Press, 1964. Pp. 49–80.

Schachter, S. Cognitive effects on bodily functioning: Studies of obesity and eating. In D. C. Glass (Ed.), *Neurophysiology and emotion.* New York: Rockefeller University Press, 1967. Pp. 117–144.

Scheier, I. H., & Cattell, R. B. *Handbook and test kit for the IPAT 8 Parallel Form Anxiety Battery.* Champaign, Illinois: Institute for Personality and Ability Testing, 1960.

Spence, J. T., & Spence, K. W. The motivational components of manifest anxiety: Drive and drive stimuli. In C. D. Spielberger (Ed.), *Anxiety and behavior.* New York: Academic Press, 1966. Pp. 291–326.

Spielberger, C. D. The effects of manifest anxiety on the academic achievement of college students. *Mental Hygiene,* 1962, **46,** 420–426.

Spielberger, C. D. Theory and research on anxiety. In C. D. Spielberger (Ed.), *Anxiety and behavior.* New York: Academic Press, 1966. Pp. 3–20. (a)

Spielberger, C. D. The effects of anxiety on complex learning and academic achievement. In C. D. Spielberger (Ed.), *Anxiety and behavior.* New York: Academic Press, 1966. Pp. 361–398. (b)

Spielberger, C. D., & Gorsuch, R. L. Mediating processes in verbal conditioning. Report to National Institute of Mental Health, 1966.

Spielberger, C. D., Gorsuch, R. L., & Lushene, R. E. *Manual for the State-Trait Anxiety Inventory.* Palo Alto, California: Consulting Psychologist Press, 1970.

Spielberger, C. D., O'Neil, H. F., & Hansen, D. N. Anxiety, drive theory, and computer-assisted learning. In B. A. Maher (Ed.), *Progress in Experimental Personality Research.* Vol. 6, New York: Academic Press, 1972.

Spielberger, C. D., & Smith, L. H. Anxiety (drive), stress, and serial-position effects in serial-verbal learning. *Journal of Experimental Psychology,* 1966, **72,** 589–595.

Stouffer, S. A., Guttman, L., Suchman, F. A., Lazarsfeld, P. F., Star, S. A., & Clausen, J. A. *Measurement and prediction.* Princeton, New Jersey: Princeton University Press, 1950.

Taylor, D. A., Wheeler, L., & Altman, I. Stress reactions in socially isolated groups. *Journal of Personality and Social Psychology,* 1968, **9,** 369–376.

Taylor, J. A. A personality scale of manifest anxiety. *Journal of Abnormal and Social Psychology,* 1953, **48,** 285–290.

Thorne, F. C. Theory of the psychological state. *Journal of Clinical Psychology,* 1966, **22,** 127–135.

Titchener, E. B. *An outline of psychology.* New York: MacMillan, 1897.

Wessman, A. E., & Ricks, D. F. *Mood and personality.* New York: Holt, 1966.

Wessman, A. E., Ricks, D. F., & Tyl, M. M. Characteristics and concomitants of mood fluctuation in college women. *Journal of Abnormal and Social Psychology,* 1960, **60,** 117–126.

Wilde, G. J. S. Trait description and measurement by personality questionnaires. In R. B. Cattell (Ed.), *Handbook of Modern Personality Theory.* Chicago: Aldine, 1972, in press.

Wundt, W. *Outlines of psychology.* New York: Dustav E. Stechert, 1896.

Young, P. T. *Emotion in man and animal.* New York: Wiley, 1943.

Zuckerman, M. The development of an Affect Adjective Check List for the measurement of anxiety. *Journal of Consulting Psychology,* 1960, **24,** 457–462.

Zuckerman, M., & Biase, D. V. Replication and further data on the Affect Adjective Check List measure of anxiety. *Journal of Consulting Psychology,* 1962, **26,** 291.

Zuckerman, M., & Lubin, B. *Manual for the Multiple Affect Adjective Check List.* San Diego, California: Educational and Industrial Testing Service, 1965.

Zuckerman, M., & Lubin, B. *Bibliography for the Multiple Affect Adjective Check List.* San Diego, California: Educational and Industrial Testing Service, 1968.

Zuckerman, M., Lubin, B., Vogel, L., & Valerius, E. Measurement of experimentally induced affects. *Journal of Consulting Psychology,* 1964, **28,** 418–425.

Chapter 3

ANXIETY: A VARIABLE COMBINATION OF INTERACTING FUNDAMENTAL EMOTIONS[1]

Carroll E. Izard

One of the purposes of this chapter is to attempt to bring a higher degree of order into a complex and frequently confusing subject that is of crucial importance in behavioral science, in personality and social research, and in clinical practice. After presenting an overview of the chapter, I shall clarify some aspects of my present position in relation to previous work (Izard & Tomkins, 1966). Then, I shall set the stage for the three major sections of the paper.

In the first section, I shall attempt a conceptual or substantive analysis of anxiety. First I shall present a formulation of anxiety as a variable combination

[1] I am very grateful to James Chappell for supervising computer analyses and for proofing and improving the semifinal draft, to Betty Jane Keeling, Suzanne Bichon, and Michael Potts for assisting with the preparation of the final manuscript, to Faye Weaver for her assistance with the empirical research, and to Martin Katahn and Richard Snyder, whose expertise in the subject matter led to a number of insightful and helpful suggestions that are reflected in the chapter.

of interacting fundamental emotions. Next I shall examine previous definitions of anxiety, searching especially for emotion concepts or connotations. Then I shall elaborate my pattern-of-emotions theory of anxiety by placing it in the context of a larger theory of emotion and behavior. To accomplish this, I shall present my definitions of emotion, the emotion system, and the emotion process. The complex of phenomena which I call the emotion process will be illustrated by looking at the problem of activating an emotion. Another aspect of the emotion process will be dealt with by looking at the ways that emotion and emotion components combine and interact to produce the phenomena we call anxiety and depression.

In the second section of the paper, I shall compare some of the major theories of emotion and anxiety with my own. In particular I shall compare my theory with three different versions of a cognitive theory of emotion—those of Lazarus, Epstein, and Janis. In this section I shall attempt to show how these different conceptions of the nature of anxiety and emotion have important implications for the way emotion is treated in research and in clinical practice. The two contrasting theoretical frameworks place emotion in highly different positions with respect to its importance in personality, interpersonal, and intergroup functioning.

The third section of the paper will present an empirical analysis of the concept of anxiety and of the concepts of certain fundamental emotions which I hypothesize as components of anxiety. The principal analytical tool will be a differential emotion scale, an instrument derived from my theory of emotion and partially validated through factor analytic and other research methods. A version of this differential emotion scale will be combined with a standard anxiety scale and the resulting instrument will be used in the empirical studies to be reported. The factor structure of the differential emotion scale will be compared with that of the combined emotion and anxiety scale, and then the combined scale will be used to compare an anxiety-situation with various discrete emotion situations (fear, shame, guilt, distress, interest). An analysis of the free-response descriptions of these anxiety and emotion situations will also be presented. Finally, this section will develop the concept of patterns or profiles of fundamental emotions and demonstrate its use as a means of differentially assessing the affective-motivational experiences of persons in different situations.

At the outset, I want to say something about the difference between my use of the term anxiety in the predecessor to this volume (Izard & Tomkins, 1966) and the use of this term in the present chapter. The difference calls for a new perspective and a new feeling or attitude toward the concept. In our contribution to the earlier volume, we (Izard & Tomkins, 1966) asserted that the term anxiety was something of a catchall term for all things related to negative, disruptive, or disturbing affects, and that it was also credited with facilitative effects on learning and performance. We proposed to end the confusion created by such an ambiguous omnibus by equating anxiety with fear, the latter being considered a primary or fundamental emotion that could be defined unequivocally. This tactic clearly failed.

It is true a number of investigators, apparently quite independently, have decided that they should equate anxiety with fear. But even in these cases the operational definitions of anxiety and research procedures often involve emotions other than fear. The problem may be viewed as a rigidity in conceptualizing. The term "anxiety" as an explicator of malfunction and disadaptation has acquired tremendous psychological inertia. Although some scientists have indicated that anxiety is best conceived as a single emotion (fear), neither in theoretical formulations nor in empirical research have any of these scientists clearly separated as different variables the several fundamental emotions that are typically involved in their experimentation.

In 1966 we also suggested that, aside from fear, whatever else anxiety had come to mean to different researchers and investigators should be given more specific and appropriate labels. In particular, we advocated the use of other emotion concepts such as distress and shame, emotions that were seen as frequently interacting with fear. This second tactic, which could succeed only if yoked to the first, was also doomed to failure.

To clarify the record, the Izard–Tomkins chapter in *Anxiety and Behavior* (Spielberger, 1966) must be viewed as a chapter on the emotion of fear and not as a chapter on anxiety. This is true because anxiety does not equal fear in the minds of many of those who read and write and talk about anxiety and who contribute to its definition.

In the present work, perhaps Lazarus and Averill (Vol. 2, Chapter 1) come closest to supporting our point that there are several discrete emotions that must be considered in the analysis of behavior. They speak of the need to distinguish anxiety from other fear-related emotional syndromes and of the possibility of different kinds of anxiety. Yet, their theory is not based on a clear conceptual differentiation of fundamental emotions, and they conceive of emotion as response while we view it as a process influencing and interacting with other personality and interpersonal processes.

In 1966 we argued that the intra-individual emotion process had three components–neurophysiological, behavioral-expressive, and phenomenological or subjective. This form of conceptualizing emotion (and anxiety) is now present to one degree or another in a number of theories, some of which are represented in this book. In 1966 we also argued for the need to study each of the discrete fundamental emotions. As already indicated, this idea is now being expressed in the same or similar fashion by a number of researchers and investigators, some of whom are contributors to the present volume.

In 1966 we maintained that emotion was not a response but a process capable of operating without a stimulus in the usual sense of that term. This idea, though vaguely implicit in some of the other contributions to this volume and elsewhere, remains rather esoteric—a puddle of "conceptual quicksand," if you take the view of Sarason (1967) who described our entire theory with this phrase in his review of *Anxiety and Behavior.*

In accepting the invitation to write the present chapter, I determined to analyze anxiety for whatever and what-all it is in contemporary behavioral science and in the thinking of people in general. I began by looking at the extant substantive definitions of anxiety, many of which had been collected in a recent review paper (Mallama, 1970). I found myself rather quickly reverting to the type of thinking that led to my tactical errors of 1966. For all who are willing to see, the literature on anxiety is manifestly clear on one point—anxiety is not a unitary concept. And much of the confusion in anxiety theory and research is linked to the tendency to treat it as unitary. Anxiety does not refer to a single class of antecedent conditions, or to a single class of neurophysiological, behavioral-expressive, and subjective-experiential events, or to a single class of consequent acts.

It was disappointing to find that some writers who have contributed heavily to the literature on the assessment and treatment of anxiety have contributed little to the substantive definition of the concept. Wolpe (1966), who, like many clinicians, believes that anxiety is central to most neuroses, defines anxiety as an emotional habit. He does not really give a substantive definition of anxiety but his writing leads one to believe that anxiety as an emotional habit consists of all the maladaptive emotional responses that constitute neurosis.

Many writers, particularly those inclined to controlled experimental studies in the laboratory, simply start writing about anxiety as though everyone knows what it is, but they go on to describe one or more of a wide variety of inventories or other indices to indicate that they have indeed measured anxiety. Spence and Spence (1966), who epitomize the effort to bring anxiety within the framework of *s–r* theory and into the laboratory for controlled experimentation, use the term anxiety in a rather loose way when they leave behavior theory constructs and symbols aside and speak in substantive terms. They wrote: "The Manifest Anxiety Scale (MAS) was devised as one method of selecting subjects differing in emotional responsiveness . . . [p. 294]." The test was made up of items which "describe both the physiological reactions reported by individuals suffering from anxiety reactions and the accompanying subjective reports of worry, self-doubt, anxiety, and so forth [pp. 294–5]." This contributes very little to a substantive analysis of anxiety, yet the MAS as much as any other measure has been the standard for defining anxiety operationally.

Although there are a few investigators who speak loosely of anxiety as fear or as a kind of fear, anxiety is never really treated as a single emotion, either in terms of verbal definition or in terms of the sundry operations used to measure it. Anxiety as it has been used by researchers and investigators over the years is indeed a complex of negative emotions. It now appears that our only chance of understanding this term as it has been variously used in the literature is to see it as a complex of emotions or emotion-related concepts and to abandon forever the notion that there is a unitary phenomenon of anxiety. Anxiety is not unipolar, unidimensional, or unifactor in nature.

One reason why emotion and concepts like anxiety have been treated as global, undifferentiated phenomena is due in no small measure to the fact that a chief source of data has been the maladjusted, neurotic, or psychotic individual whose behavior seemingly invited the oversimplified explanatory concept of "emotional disturbance," which implies that emotion has the character of a general, undifferentiated phenomenon. The situation has not been greatly improved in recent laboratory studies in which artificial or contrived stressors are presumed to elicit true and pure emotional states, such as "anxiety." These errors of over-simplification were enhanced and supported for more than a decade by those theorists and researchers who placed all emotion on a single dimension called activation or arousal, and by those clinically oriented theorists who viewed "anxiety" as a unitary concept that explains virtually all maladjustment and some aspects of effective adjustment. Apparently the effects of certain theorizing and evidence (Zuckerman, 1960; Sprague, Chambers, & Stellar, 1961; Tomkins, 1962; Gellhorn, 1964; Nowlis, 1965; Izard & Tomkins, 1966; Pribram, 1967) have gradually had some effect in reducing the tendency to consider all emotion on the single dimension of activation or arousal. However, the error of viewing anxiety as the central if not single source of all psychopathology remains quite common.

Indeed, the range of substantive or dynamic elements that can be found in a survey of definitions of anxiety is great enough to help account for a variety of adjustment problems and other behaviors. However, such a range of different substantive elements supports my conception of anxiety as a variable combination of fundamental emotions and their interactions.

A Conceptual Analysis of Anxiety

I maintain that all complex emotion processes such as love, hate, depression, and anxiety contain as elements two or more of the fundamental emotions or their components. In particular, I propose that anxiety involves fear and two or more of the fundamental emotions of distress, shame (including shyness and guilt), anger, and the positive emotion of interest-excitement. As already indicated, this formulation is implicitly or partially supported by almost all writers in the field—the survey of theoretical and operational definitions of anxiety showed that all the above fundamental emotions have been included by more than one author. The complete list and the a priori definitions of the fundamental emotions are presented in Table 3.1, p. 76.

Emotion Concepts in Previous Definitions of Anxiety

In his early writings, Freud did not think it necessary to give a complete description of the emotional component of anxiety since "every one of us has experienced this sensation [1917, p. 392]." Of course, Freud took special pains to point out that there is involved in this first anxiety experience an involuntary separation from the love object, mother. One of Freud's early observations is especially interesting in light of my contention that each emotion has a neuromuscular component and my conception of anxiety as a multi-variable concept. Freud stated that the phenomenological component of anxiety resulted from "perceptions of motor innervations that have occurred and direct feelings of pleasure and unpleasure [p. 395]."

Sarason, Davidson, Lighthall, Waite, & Ruebush (1960) analyzed test anxiety to be a result of the following emotional sequence. In order to avoid real danger, the child has to repress hostility toward a parent for one or more previous test-like evaluations. Next the child feels guilty for his hostility toward his usually beloved parent. The guilt has to be relegated to the unconscious as much as possible, but when it does become conscious such as in the test situation the child's negative feelings put him in a self-derogatory attitude. Ultimately the self-derogating attitude leads the child to doubt his ability in the testing situation, and to compound the uncertainty the child tends to fantasize about the parent's retaliation for the child's hostility.

In Sarason *et al.'s* analysis the anxiety experience involves the fundamental emotions of fear, shame or guilt, distress, and anger. One could reasonably account for the phenomena observed by Sarason by assuming that fear is associated with the danger of punishment and failure, shame or guilt with self-derogation and feelings of inadequacy, distress with alienation from parents or loved ones, and anger with an interpersonal situation that has demanding and apparently hostile characteristics. It would be possible to argue that all these emotions and behaviors can well be called anxiety except for the fact that experiences from other person-environment interchanges that could equally well be called anxiety might involve some, though not all, of the above emotions. Or we could have the same emotions in different sequences and different interactions. There is considerable overlap in the substance of Sarason's definition of anxiety and mine.

Grinker and Spiegel's (1945) involvement with combat-experienced soldiers was probably instrumental in convincing them that the cause of anxiety, especially in war, was a fear of losing the self, an object of love. They specify a fear component and imply a distress component in the idea of loss of loved object.

According to Sullivan (1953), anxiety can be characterized by a feeling (always unpleasant) that "all is not going so well, or a noticing of some disturbance in the activity or postural tone in one of the zones of interaction—a change in one's 'facial expression' or in one's voice, as examples—a feeling of tightening up in some skeletal muscles, a disturbance of the action of one's belly, a realization that one has begun to sweat [p. 378]." In the adult, Sullivan maintained, anxiety is a "complex" emotion, and though he claimed not to know the components, he suggested "embarrassment, shame, humiliation, guilt, and chagrin." He thought that these "emotions" were "elaborated (from anxiety) by specific early training." These component or derivative feelings add up to essentially one emotion, shame–humiliation, that in conscious experience may take the form of guilt, shyness, or shame (Tomkins, 1962).

May (1950) has defined anxiety as diffuse apprehension, differing from fear in its vagueness and objectlessness, and as a state that is associated with feelings of uncertainty, helplessness, and threat to the core or essence of personality. As Epstein (Vol. 2, Chapter 8 of the present work) suggests, this definition tends simply to redefine anxiety as a type of great and intense fear. The other substantive aspects of the definition actually appear to involve emotion-cognition interactions, i.e. feelings of uncertainty, helplessness, and threat to the essence of the personality. Certainly the latter would have to be considered an admixture of cognition and emotion. Epstein's own analysis of anxiety as reported in the present work (Vol. 2, Chapter 8) does not clearly and explicitly involve different fundamental emotion concepts. However, from experimental and illustrative situations which he uses to elucidate anxiety, one can easily infer the presence of distress and shame.

Spielberger (1966) and Levitt (1967) have essentially equated anxiety with fear. However, here again a close look at the substance of these investigators' writings and experimentation suggest that they too sometimes implicitly or explicitly include other emotions in their thinking and research on anxiety. More recently Spielberger, in the present volume (Chapter 1), refers to anxiety as "complex emotional reactions." Though still emphasizing the fear or fear-like component of anxiety, these authors seem to have allowed for the possibility of other fundamental emotions being involved.

Basowitz, Persky, Korchin, and Grinker (1955) distinguished between shame anxiety and harm anxiety. In one sense this can be seen as another way of saying that shame and fear exist as separate components of anxiety. A number of theorists and investigators have linked shame and guilt with anxiety either by including them in their definitions of anxiety or by dealing with them as overlapping concepts.

Mosher (1966) defined guilt and anxiety as related concepts that have some independence. He has developed measures of guilt that correlated only .65 with the Taylor MAS. This is a lower correlation than would be desirable if the two instruments were supposed to measure the same construct. It is considerably lower than the correlation between two anxiety measures such as the MAS and the Spielberger–Gorsuch–Lushene (1970) anxiety scale, STAI.

Katz and Zigler (1967) discuss guilt as a parallel condition to anxiety. With chronological development the individual becomes more capable of self-derogation and of experiencing a wider disparity between real and ideal self concepts. This increases the capacity for guilt and anxiety.

Maher (1966) saw guilt as a particular instance of anxiety, namely fear of loss of love and other punishments for one's own deeds. Spielberger (1966) alluded to "that special form of anxiety which is guilt [p. 3]."

Punishment may be seen as a common factor tending to link guilt and fear. Wrong-doing can lead to guilt and to the anticipation of punishment or to real punishment. Such punishment can evoke fear. This notion is consonant with some of the thinking of Unger (1962) and Sarason (1966).

Gottschalk and Gleser (1969) have classified anxiety, as they observed it in clinical experience, into six subtypes: death, mutilation, separation, guilt, shame, and diffuse or nonspecific anxiety. In these category terms we can see most of the emotion concepts which I have included in my definition of anxiety.

In his factor-analytic framework, Cattell (1966) views anxiety as a second order factor. He has specified the first-order components of anxiety as: ego weakness, ergic tension, guilt proneness, defective integration of the self-sentiment, and protension or suspicion (Cattell & Scheier, 1961). In this analysis Cattell has clearly recognized anxiety as a complex of primary factors. My conception is somewhat similar in form, but there are several important differences. I believe factor analysis provides a useful tool in studying the conceptual phenomenology of the emotions, but I doubt that it can specify a fixed set of primary factors that constitute anxiety. My own factor analytic research has supported the position that what we call anxiety is an unstable and variable set of fundamental emotions, which can sometimes be identified statistically as primary factors. Substantively, some of Cattell's primary factors seem to correspond or overlap with my fundamental emotion concepts; e.g., guilt proneness with shame-humiliation, protension or suspicion with fear. However, such factors as ego weakness and defective integration of self-sentiment might relate to more than one fundamental emotion and to different emotions for different individuals. Finally, I see fundamental emotions as both structures and processes, and it is their process-nature that makes them somewhat elusive when one tries to pin them down in terms of factor structure. Emotions are highly active and flexible in nature. Human experience is much more frequently characterized by two or more fundamental emotions in a complex interaction than by any pure single-emotion state or experience.

Variableness and Interactions among the Emotions in Anxiety

No single author has included all the posited five fundamental emotions in his definition of anxiety nor has anyone conceptualized them as discrete yet systemic components of anxiety. It appears to me that all five considered as variable components of a system are necessary for an adequate theory of anxiety, even though all experiences that are described as anxiety may not include all the possible component fundamental emotions.

The way the emotion components interact may also vary from individual to individual. A prominent distress component may amplify the fear component in some individuals and the shame component in others. An interest-excitement component may oscillate with fear or shame or inhibit distress.

The Emotion System and the Emotion Process in Relation to Anxiety

My conception of anxiety derives from a more general theory of emotion and behavior. Let me state briefly the aspects of the general theory that are most pertinent to the conception of anxiety as a variable combination of fundamental emotions.

Definition of Emotion

Emotion is a complex concept that has neurophysiological, motor-expressive, and phenomenological aspects. At the neurophysiological level emotion is defined primarily in terms of patterns of electrochemical activity in the nervous system, particularly in the hypothalamus, the limbic system, and in the facial and trigeminal nerves. The cutaneous nerve supply in the face and the proprioceptors in the facial muscles also participate in emotion at the neurophysiological level. At the motor level emotion is primarily facial activity and facial patterning, and secondarily it is bodily (postural-gestural, visceral, and sometimes vocal) activity. At the phenomenological level emotion is essentially motivating experience and/or experience that has immediate meaning and significance for the person.

My contention that any fundamental emotion has a motor or neuromuscular component and the fact that this component is of crucial importance in the feed-back and component interactional processes of emotion and behavior are supported by the research of Malmo (1966) and his colleagues. Among other things, their research points very strongly to the fact that measures of striate muscle activity are better for differentiating between anxiety patients and controls than the GSR, long considered by many as the best physiological measure of anxiety. Malmo's research has shown that psychiatric patients tend to have somewhat higher muscle tension levels than normals. Following stimulation calculated to startle, patients showed a mean rise in muscle tension similar to that of normals, but while the normals returned to prestimulus level between .2 and .6 of a second, the patients' mean muscle tension level remained elevated significantly higher than that of normals for a period longer than three seconds. Thus, neuromuscular changes occur in emotion for normals and for anxiety patients, and the evidence indicates that these changes in the motor component of emotion may serve as an index of maladjustment.

When neuro-chemical activity via innate programs produces patterned neuromuscular responses of the face and body and the feedback from these responses is transformed into conscious form, the result is a discrete fundamental emotion that is both a motivating and meaningful cue-producing experience. Phenomenologically, positive emotions have inherent characteristics that tend to enhance one's sense of well-being and to instigate and sustain approach toward and constructive interactions or relations with the involved persons, situations, or objects. Negative emotions tend to be sensed as noxious and difficult to tolerate and to instigate avoidance and/or nonconstructive interactions or relations. While certain emotions tend to be positive and others negative in import, these terms cannot be applied rigidly to the various emotions without considering other factors.

The emotion system consists of the nine major emotions and their inter-relationships. The emotions are: interest, enjoyment, surprise, distress, disgust, anger, shame (including shyness and guilt), fear, and contempt. As I have indicated, five of these may be components of anxiety--fear, shame (–shyness–guilt), distress, anger, and interest.

The Emotions as a Personality Subsystem

The concept of emotion system is important for my analysis of anxiety. While I think it is important to conceive of the fundamental emotions as a system of interacting and mutually influencing components, I would like to caution against thinking of the emotion system as having all the characteristics of any known type of system. I would be particularly careful in considering it as a hydraulic system, a digital system, or as any other kind of computer or electronic system. Perhaps the most important point here is that by conceiving of the emotions as constituting a system, we accept the principle that each of the fundamental emotions can interact with and influence other fundamental emotions within the system. Further, as any separate fundamental emotion is in itself a system (or sub-system) having its three basic components (neurophysiological, behavioral-expressive, and experiential), we can also assume that one or more of the components of a given emotion may interact with one or more of the components of another or several other fundamental emotions. It is the assumption of a highly flexible and interactive system of emotions and emotion components that renders feasible my present conception of anxiety.

The bases for describing the emotions as a system have been detailed elsewhere (Tomkins, 1962; Izard & Tomkins, 1966; Izard, 1971) so I shall merely summarize some of the main points. Various emotions are interrelated in dynamic and relatively stable ways on the basis of both their innate and learned characteristics. Some emotions are organized in hierarchical relationship with respect to the gradients of neural stimulation that activate them (see Tomkins, 1962, 1970).

Certain emotions have been considered by various theorists (Darwin, 1872; Plutchik, 1962) as existing in polar relationships. For example, joy and sadness, anger and fear, and other pairs are often considered as polar opposites. Again, I would caution against analogy to an oversimplified model such as the actions and interactions of positive and negative poles in a magnetic field.

Certain emotions tend to have fairly regular relationships under certain circumstances. For example, interest may oscillate with fear as an organism explores some unknown object or situation, and contempt may oscillate with enjoyment to produce some of the heinous effects observed in interracial and intergroup conflicts.

All the emotions tend to have great generality and flexibility as well as other common characteristics such as their noncyclical nature. Any emotion can influence or regulate other personality systems, frequently acting as amplifiers or attenuators of homeostatic, drive, cognitive, and motor processes.

The emotion system interacts with other personality systems. The brain stem reticular system serves as a regulator or control for the neural component of emotion, acting either as amplifier or as attenuator. The glandular-visceral system helps prepare the body for determined and directed action and helps sustain the emotion or emotion-related phenomena. The cardio-vascular and respiratory systems also interact in important ways with emotion. The major personality systems of cognition and motor activity typically interact with the emotion system in almost all organismic endeavors, and effective personality functioning depends on balance and integration of the activities of these systems.

The Emotion Process and the Activation of a Fundamental Emotion

An appreciation of the complexity of the emotion process and its activation is important in understanding the analysis of anxiety as a variable combination of interacting fundamental emotions. An effort toward a complete analysis of the highly complex neurophysiology and phenomenology of the emotion process has been detailed elsewhere (Izard, 1971). Here I shall simply illustrate its complexity and something of its nature by considering the problem of initiating or activating an emotion. (The various forms of the verb "activate" and the noun "activation" are used here in their more generic sense and not in reference to specific functions of any neural mechanism such as the brain stem reticular system.)

In addition to certain innate releasers and Tomkins' (1962) principle relating to density of neural firing, there are three other principles that may help explain how the different emotions are activated and how it happens that there is some patterning in emotion-related person-environment interactions. First, there is the possibility of innate pathways or neural programs which may be characterized by a selective sensitivity to certain inputs or environmental conditions. The positive emotional responses of infants are more consistently triggered by human than nonhuman stimulation. This principle of selective sensitivity may operate somewhat differently at different ages or stages of development. With increasing maturity, input patterns or environmental conditions can be psychologically simulated through cognitive processes such as dreams and imagination. Producing a particular fundamental emotion by activating an innate neural program subserving (or constituting the neurochemical component of) that emotion would seem to call for selective neural stimulation more than for intensity of neural stimulation.

As I have shown elsewhere (Izard, 1971), socio-cultural phenomena constitute another factor influencing emotion processes. Cultural differences in attitudes toward certain emotions are incorporated during socialization and result in different relationships among the emotions and between the antecedents, concomitants, and consequences of a given emotion.

Another principle that helps explain some of the patterning or consistencies between particular antecedents and particular emotions is learning and idiosyncratic experience. Distress may elicit fear in one individual and shame in another, due to differences in personal experience.

Any of these principles—selective sensitivity of innate neural programs, changes in density of neural firing, idiosyncratic experience, and socialization—may activate or influence the activation of an emotion and play some role in the emotion process and in emotion-related person-environment interactions.

Elsewhere (Izard, 1971) I have specified several types of person-environment interactions and several types of intra-individual processes that can initiate or activate emotion. These processes include perceptual, hormonal, and skeletal-motor activity as well as memory, imagination, and proprioception.

After the initial activity in the emotion process, the order and loci of second and subsequent steps or phases of the process are partially a function of the site and nature of the initial activity. The emotion process is not a lock-step sequence of cortical, facial, postural, motor, RAS, ANS, neural, glandular, and visceral activities. There is no fixed number of such activities that is required for activation of any or all of the components of emotion. The emotion process can begin with memory or imagination in the ideation centers of the brain or with perception of, or excitation of receptors by, an external emotion-effective object or event. (The term perception is used here to signify stimulation input—the selective or demanded energizing, excitation, of receptors or sense organs. It does not refer to a central, cognitive-interpretive activity.)

Although the problem of emotion activation is quite complex, the complete emotion process is obviously of still greater complexity. The activation of emotion is only the beginning of the process, but it illustrates the intricacy of emotion and its interactions with other personality and person-environment processes.

How Emotions and Emotion Components Combine and Interact

Each of the fundamental emotions has distinct components. The components of emotion are largely interdependent, but they also have a degree of independence, especially under certain conditions. A feedback or interaction mechanism is necessary for the integration of the components in the process that produces a complete and discrete emotion. Concomitantly, the integration of emotion components into a particular individual emotion is a fundamental part of the process whereby the discrete emotions are differentiated. Without such integration of components we can have incomplete or undifferentiated emotions. We can have facial patterning without the phenomenological existence of emotion in conscious experience. We can have undifferentiated or nonspecific emotional experience without a particular facial pattern. Finally, we might have facial activity innervated by the seventh nerve but interruption of feedback from the face via the fifth nerve or failure of such feedback to achieve awareness. Emotional experience would then have to be based on the slower and grosser feedback from the viscera and/or from postural activity. Such emotion would be gross and vague and lack the character of a discrete emotion.

Components of two or more emotions may make simultaneous or rapidly alternating demands on neurophysiological mechanisms and on consciousness. Such a combination of the interacting and alternating components of different fundamental emotions could help account for the vagueness and undifferentiated character so frequently attributed to such nebulous and elusive concepts as anxiety and depression.

I view the emotion component of facial-postural activity (neuromuscular patterning) as crucially important in determining whether we experience an unambiguous fundamental emotion such as fear or a complex combination-interaction of emotions such as anxiety. In infancy and childhood, facial expressions clearly communicate emotions to others. The proprioceptive patterns of these expressions determine or significantly influence the brain processes that generate the subjective experience of a discrete fundamental emotion. In American culture, as well as in many other cultures, socialization processes typically lead to a diminution or suppression of facial patterning as the individual moves toward later childhood and adolescence. However, the emotion system and the emotion process can still function in essentially the same way as in infancy and early childhood because of developmental changes in the psychoneurological mechanisms which underlie the development of certain cognitive abilities. When an individual has learned a given facial pattern or pattern of proprioception and is capable of retrieving it from memory, the image of the pattern can operate in a reafferent or inner loop in an analogous fashion to the motor pattern in the afferent or outer loop through the face. The memory image may substitute for or complement the actual motor pattern or a diminished and micromomentary pattern in the face.

The pattern of facial activity or the image of the corresponding pattern of proprioception is a chief determinant of the specific quality of any felt emotion. If the pattern is that of an innately programmed fundamental emotion there will be a corresponding specific emotional experience. A fundamental emotion will be felt. If the pattern combines elements of two or more innate programs or consists of two or more fundamental patterns in rapid sequence or alternation, the experience will consist of "mixed emotions." Such is the case with "state anxiety." It's a mix-up! It has no fixed neurophysiological structure. It has no characteristic face.

The various emotions that constitute anxiety may oscillate in awareness or move back and forth across several levels of awareness. Likewise, at the neurophysiological level elements of one emotion may interact in various ways with elements of another.

However, two or more fundamental emotions that are mixed frequently may produce over time a relatively stable, well defined emotional experience that may be considered a complex of emotions strongly influenced by learning and experience. If there are certain prevailing conditions which regularly elicit this combination of emotions, this complex and its related cognitive-motor behaviors may take on the nature of a personality characteristic or trait. One possible result would be a combination that could be called "trait anxiety," a complex trait subserved by a relatively consistent pattern of emotions. However, the anxiety trait, as the anxiety state, must be conceived as a variable combination of interacting fundamental emotions. There is the possibility that the more fixed and stable the combination of emotions in state or trait anxiety the more likely we are to have psychopathology.

I use the terms "state anxiety" and "trait anxiety" with a high degree of tentativeness. In my view any meaningful analysis of anxiety calls for a statement of the particular profile or pattern of emotions characteristic of the individual or experience under consideration. The particular fundamental emotions and emotion interactions involved in what is called anxiety have to be considered as something that varies with individuals and situations. However, as already suggested, it may be possible to delineate certain types or groups of individuals as characterized by an anxiety that is defined as a particular pattern of emotions and emotion interactions that tend to prevail under specifiable conditions.

This formulation of anxiety has implications for psychodiagnostic assessment and psychotherapy and for the analysis and management of interpersonal and intergroup problems. For one thing, therapy or any therapeutic behavior change program dealing with anxiety might best begin with an attempt to analyze the anxiety into its component fundamental emotions, assessing the degree to which each is present and selecting appropriate treatment or management procedures that take each emotion, its interactions, and its motivational-experiential properties into account.

Some Differences among Theories of Emotion and Anxiety

To help clarify the position I am taking in this chapter, I shall draw some distinctions between my theory and that presented by Lazarus and Averill (Vol. 2, Chapter 7 of the present work), that of Epstein (Vol. 2, Chapter 8 of the present work), and that of Janis (1969). I see these authors as representing somewhat different versions of a cognitive theory of emotion. Thus, the differences in the positions of these authors and my own will also distinguish my position from that of a number of other contributors to this volume.

Emotion and Behavior as a Result of Cognition

Lazarus and Averill imply that emotion must follow from the purely cognitive process of appraisal. They assume that a person or animal proceeds through processes described as primary appraisal, secondary appraisal, and reappraisal, all presumably cognitive functions, without experiencing any emotion. That is quite a bit of cognition to have to occur in the face of threat or provocation prior to any emotion or emotion-related activity. Yet, if cognitive theorists admit that some emotion may follow immediately after primary appraisal and before the other steps in the appraisal process, then the notion that cognition is the sole mediator of emotion appears untenable. Once on the intrapsychic scene, it seems highly probable that emotion will influence the subsequent stages of appraisal and all other organismic processes and activities. It seems highly unlikely that a person can complete an appraisal without some interaction between emotion and cognition.

A weakness in Lazarus and Averill's dependence on cognitive processes as the basis for emotion differentiation in experience and behavior is exemplified in their efforts to distinguish between separation distress and separation anxiety as experienced by the infant and young child. They are undoubtedly correct in arguing that separation distress is more closely related to grief than to fear or anxiety. (See also Averill, 1968.) I see distress, as defined in Table 3.1 (p. 76), as the central emotion in grief, but I do not believe that we can look to cognitive processes as the sole means of mediating the experience of distress. Lazarus and Averill acknowledge that the infant can experience separation distress as early as six months. Many observers would agree that infants experience distress of some sort almost from the beginning of life, as witnessed by the cry of distress and its ubiquity at birth and in the early weeks following birth. No one would argue that distress in infancy is accompanied by the same symbolic processes as distress in adulthood, but some would agree that infantile distress is a valid distress experience, having psychological structure and significance similar to that of later distress experiences.

If we accept the fact that the infant does experience distress at birth and in the first days of life, then it seems to render untenable the notion that this experience is mediated by symbolic processes. As Tomkins (1962) has so well stated, one does not learn how to feel distressed or how to feel afraid. One does eventually associate certain stimuli and certain actions with distress and other stimuli and actions with fear, but this learning process does not mean that the individual learns the meaning and significance of the emotion-experience itself. It is the failure to recognize the utility of conceptual distinctions between the intra-individual emotion process, on the one hand, and antecedent and consequent person-environment or social processes on the other, that has created so much confusion in emotion theory and research.

Lazarus and Averill see appraisal and subsequent cognition as the activators of emotion. Further, they maintain that the ebb and flow of emotion as well as subsequent coping behavior is a result of changing cognitive activity which arises from new input and from feedback from reaction and reflection, all of which alter the appraisal. The fundamental question which Lazarus and Averill have not answered is what motivates and sustains cognitive activity. They cannot answer this by simply saying inputs or feedback from reaction and reflection, for this is circular and an overly mechanistic *s–r*-like formulation. They might say that life itself guarantees cognitive activity, but this would leave unanswered even more critical questions. What guides perceptual-cognitive activity? What determines the selection of sensory data and the focusing of input? Obviously a person or animal does not react to all data available to the sensory systems and the feedback mechanisms. I propose that the emotions play a crucial role in selecting sensory data and guiding the processing of these data and subsequent activities. As I have argued previously (Izard, 1971), meaningful or purposive perceptual-cognitive processes are initiated and in part sustained and guided by the emotion of interest.

The principle of the primacy of cognition in organismic functioning also runs counter to general principles underlying phylogeny and evolution. It implies that in the evolutionary process animals had to be able to "think" before they could "feel." The opposite case seems much more plausible. The principle of the primacy of cognition as elaborated by cognitive theorists also requires that cognitive processes generate and guide the coping or problem-solving efforts that an individual makes when the demands he faces are highly relevant to his survival and welfare. I believe with Jolly (1966) and Hamburg (1963) that emotions and emotion processes preceded higher order intelligence. In evolutionary perspective, it seems highly probable that emotion played a vital role in problem-solving and survival efforts of animals and man. Lack of the experience of anger in the face of a need to defend one's physical self or one's integrity, the lack of fear in the face of imminent danger, or the lack of interest in the face of a need to perceive and sort out relevant data may well have proved a fatal deficiency in a coping or survival effort.

Of course, cognition plays a great role in influencing emotion and emotion-related behaviors, but this role develops through conditioning, learning, and idiosyncratic experience built on a foundation of evolutionary-hereditary mechanisms. In essence, the individual does not learn how to be afraid (an hereditary given), but he learns some of the things to be afraid of and what to do in the face of these things. Putting it another way, an individual expands his flexibility and adaptability as a living organism as he generates more and more cognitions or cognitive mechanisms for influencing emotion and emotion-related behaviors. This is made possible through the acquisition of language and the skills of symbolizing. As required by the innumerable man-made dangers of our era, an individual learns efficiently to rule in or rule out certain situations as fear-worthy and as requiring responses appropriate to fear. In this way cognitive processes increase man's freedom by increasing his power to differentiate between situations worthy of increased emotion and action and those that are not.

As I have noted elsewhere (Izard, 1971) the position developed by Lazarus and his associates (Averill, Opton, & Lazarus, 1969) contains many points of similarity with Arnold's system. In turn, Arnold drew some of her concepts from St. Thomas Aquinas. I refer especially to the Thomistic notion that organisms' responses follow from and are guided by cognitive processes. In the fourth article of the *Summa Theologica,* Aquinas (c. 1266, transl., 1948) observed that animal motion and action follow apprehension. He defined the estimative power as one of the four interior sensitive powers which constitute part of the soul, designated as the intellect. He pointed out that it is the estimative power that enables the animal to apprehend something as harmful or beneficial. Such apprehension may be based on the perception of intention, a process which may be independent of the form or color of the object.

Actually, Aquinas leaned more toward innate (as opposed to environmental) determinism than do contemporary cognitive theorists. He gave as an example of the estimative power the sheep's apprehension of the wolf as dangerous. The apprehension, according to Aquinas, is not based on the color or shape of the wolf but based on the fact that the wolf is a natural enemy and intends harm. Aquinas pointed out that this natural estimative power in animals is referred to as the cogitative power of man, the power which enables him to discover intentions that define things as harmful or beneficial.

Aquinas defined apprehension as a power or function of intellect which in turn is a power of the soul. Arnold, Lazarus and Averill, and other cognitive theorists follow essentially the same logic, making emotion dependent upon apprehension and recognizing apprehension as an intellective or cognitive function. In this system the soul or, in more contemporary psychological terminology, cognition and such cognitive functions as estimation and appraisal, tend to take on the quality of an entelechy or autochthonous process which operates without "motivation" or influence from other processes. Therefore, Arnold and Lazarus and Averill are essentially in agreement with the 13th century rationalism of St. Thomas Aquinas. I see no useful distinction between the central thesis of the cognitive theorists and Aquinas' proposition that emotions are strong and transient affections, reactions of the sensory-rational being to things apprehended or known.

In contrast to Lazarus and Averill, and by way of summary of our differences with respect to the role of cognition, I assume that emotion may be mediated or elicited and influenced not only by cognition but by innate releasers, homeostatic processes, drives, and other emotions or emotion components. I believe that these other emotion activators and regulators can, under certain conditions, operate completely independently of cognition and that they frequently operate with some degree of independence, particularly of conscious cognition. In turn, emotion enjoys the same kind of independence, yet it is continually interacting with and influencing cognition and action.

The rational-man ideology, brought to sharp focus by Aquinas and represented in contemporary behavioral science by cognitive theories of behavior, holds that processes like primary and secondary appraisal and reappraisal and subsequent cognition determine the quality and degree of every emotional response. Further, it maintains that the coping processes are also set in motion by appraisal and cognition. This vitiates or drastically limits the significance of emotion and its role in other important psychological and behavioral processes.

Emotion as Response or Response Syndrome

Cognitive theorists have maintained that emotion is really not very important. They see emotion primarily as response, as a result of things rather than as a cause of things. Lazarus and Averill go so far as to describe emotion as a syndrome, a term typically applied to a set of symptoms resulting from a disease.

Lazarus and Averill describe as the basic components of the emotion response syndrome cognitive appraisal, physiological reaction, expressive behavior, and instrumental acts. This breakdown bears some similarity to Izard and Tomkins' (1966) analysis of the components of emotion as neurophysiological, behavioral-expressive, and phenomenological or experiential. However, this similarity between the two theoretical models is more superficial than real in view of the other fundamental differences in conception. Lazarus and Averill emphasize the response quality of emotion and fail to distinguish between intraperson and person-environment activities at the conceptual level. Again and again Lazarus and Averill underscore the point that the essential determinant of behavior is cognition and that emotion is a kind of by-product of cognition and a concomitant of instrumental behavior. This is diametrically opposed to the position of Izard and Tomkins and a number of other theorists who see emotion as having very important motivational characteristics including guidance and cue-producing functions and also the function of giving meaning and significance to life itself.

In elaborating the concept of emotion as response, Lazarus and Averill actually draw an analogy between emotion and disease. I see this as an unfortunate comparison. There are so many characteristics of disease that have no counterpart in emotion that the analogy seems far more misleading and harmful than enlightening and helpful. Perhaps the greatest contrasting characteristic between disease and emotion is the very fact that disease is considered an abnormal process, typically involving invasion of the organism by foreign bodies with consequent disruption and dysfunction of various organs and systems. Emotion, on the other hand, is a natural and normal subsystem of the person or organism. It requires no invasion of foreign bodies and no stimulation or input from the outside in order for the process to be initiated and to proceed through its course.

Serious conceptual problems result from the over-inclusion of relatively independent subsystems in the Lazarus–Averill definition of the emotion response syndrome. They maintain that an emotion syndrome includes instrumental acts and other coping responses. To say that an emotion includes instrumental motor activities reflects Lazarus and Averill's tendency to fail to differentiate between the intraperson emotion process, and the activities related to and subsequent to the emotion process.

In my view it would be more nearly correct to say that any emotion such as fear or anger involves a neuromuscular component. This neuromuscular component results in certain patterning of the muscular-skeletal system. This neuromuscular patterning may take on the appearance of a bodily attitude consonant with withdrawal or movement away from objects, when indeed there are externally perceived objects. But, in fear, or, certainly, in anxiety as defined by Lazarus and Averill, there is not always an externally perceived object. There is, in effect, nothing external to the person to escape from.

The point at issue is that the neuromuscular patterning inherent in the intra-individual emotion process should be conceptually distinguished from instrumental acts or person-environment interaction which, for example, involve the gross movement of the organism toward or away from a person or object. Of course, the neuromuscular patterning inherent in each emotion normally facilitates adaptive action on the part of the person or organism. Nevertheless, the connections between the neuromuscular patterning and the specific motor activities and person-environment interactions that follow must be conceived as being variable and flexible. This conception is necessary in order to explain adequately the degree of flexibility and freedom which the individual has in acting in relation to his emotions. To suggest an invariable connection between emotion and instrumental response, as implicit in Lazarus and Averill's formulation, is to make the kind of mistake made in early *s–r* psychology and early instinct psychology. It amounts to conceiving man as far more mechanistic and automatic than he really is.

Another problem with Lazarus and Averill's over-inclusive definition of emotion or the emotion response syndrome is pointed up by the contention that "most emotions cannot be defined without reference to their objects." They note that Freud used distinctions between sources (objects) of threat as a means of distinguishing between objective anxiety (fear), social anxiety (shame), and moral anxiety (guilt). This is another way of saying that emotion is to be understood as response and that the response cannot be understood without specifying and understanding the stimulus. This takes us back to the search for the stimulus and to an inexorably oversimplified *s–r* psychology. It is a denial of the crucial importance of emotion, an experience defined not by a stimulus but by evolutionary-hereditary processes. It is like saying that the infant does not know how to feel distressed until it can conceptualize the distressing situation or that an individual does not know how to feel angry until he can specify the nature of the provocation. This formulation flatly contradicts the concepts of free-floating anxiety or objectless fear. The concept of objectless fear has long been viable in common sense and clinic. One of the basic types of fear situations is one in which the object is unknown, or at least unfamiliar and undefined. If the unknown or mysterious quality is sensed as dangerous, the individual may experience fear, but if it is not sensed as dangerous he may only experience excitement or heightened interest.

In the individual case, it is sometimes important to know what elicits fear, but what elicits fear in a particular individual may tell us nothing about the intra-individual emotion process. It may tell us nothing about the neurophysiology of fear, nothing about the behavioral-expressive component of fear, and nothing about the experience of fear and its meaning and significance for the individual. This suggests that there is a place for the study of intraperson emotion per se. The understanding of emotion or emotion process can contribute to an understanding of the person and his social interactions, with or without the specification of a particular stimulus and a particular response that might sometimes be associated as an antecedent or as a consequence of the emotion.

Emotion Response Syndrome versus Intraperson Emotion System

Lazarus and Averill's version of cognitive theory devalues the role of emotion in personality and behavior. Perhaps it is because of this that they have difficulty in accepting the fundamental emotions of human experience as discrete and scientifically useful concepts. It may also explain their failure to deal with the intraperson processes of emotion as a relatively independent subsystem of personality rather than as part of a syndrome that includes cognition and instrumental acts.

After summarizing their theoretical orientation Lazarus and Averill raise the question as to whether the common sense emotion categories represent unitary syndromes. They think not, and there are two reasons why they could easily have reached this conclusion. First, in their examples of common sense emotion categories they include such disparate terms as anxiety, fear, anger, depression, and love. As we have shown elsewhere (Izard, 1970a; 1971), two of these, fear and anger, are fundamental emotions which can be represented at the phenomenological level by a single and unique concept; whereas, depression and love, like anxiety, represent variable combinations of fundamental emotions which cannot be represented phenomenologically by a single or unitary emotion concept. The other reason why Lazarus and Averill did not recognize discrete emotions is their over-inclusive definition of the emotion response syndrome which fails to disentangle antecedent processes, emotion processes, and consequent processes.

Lazarus and Averill raise the question as to whether there is more than one kind of fear; this question, too, reflects their tendency to confound emotion and emotion-related activities. There is only one emotion process which generates the experience of fear, but there are many stimuli which can touch off this process and many behaviors which may be learned as adaptive or maladaptive responses to the fear experience.

With respect to the problem of classifying or categorizing emotions or emotional reactions, Lazarus and Averill propose that this be done by examining the response topographies of the emotion. By response topographies they mean the motor or instrumental acts, the subjective manifestations, the patterns of physiological arousal, and the patterns of motor expression. Here again we can see the lack of a clear conceptual separation of emotion process on the one hand and the antecedents and consequences of the emotion process on the other. Experiential emotion, its guidance and cue functions, interact with the cognitive and motor systems, but they also enjoy a significant degree of functional independence.

In my view we can most readily find a high degree of consistency in topography of human functioning if we look at the neuromuscular component of the emotion process itself. This component is manifested in the expressive features of higher animals and children, and to some extent in the spontaneous expressions of adults. But as we move out into the realm of instrumental responses, as opposed to the emotion process per se, we shall find great variety. We need to acknowledge the fact that there is such a thing as an emotion proper and that the intra-individual emotion process itself has a motor or behavioral-expressive component as well as a neurophysiological and a subjective-experiential component. Using such a framework we can expect to find consistencies among emotion processes on the one hand and to understand the varieties of emotion-related responses on the other.

Anxiety as Anticipatory Reaction or Arousal

Epstein's explanatory paradigm for anxiety is similar to that of Lazarus and Averill.

> Given a crisis it is important that the organism rapidly assess the situation and take rapid action. The first step has to consist of perception of danger. This is followed by a state of heightened diffuse arousal that prepares the animal non-specifically for fright or flight. Normally a rapid assessment will be made, and the arousal will support a differentiated motive state, such as fear, and its corresponding action, in the case of fright. . . . [p. 34]

Epstein's theorizing leads him to suggest the desirability of substituting the term arousal for anxiety. He does not do this because the experimental literature uses the term anxiety to refer both to "anticipatory reaction to noxious stimuli and to certain levels of arousal [p. 35]." The substitution of arousal for the term anxiety would seem to be a step backward in the development of an adequate conceptual framework for the study of the emotions. There is now substantial support both in theory and empirical evidence (Sprague, *et al.*, 1961; Tomkins, 1962; Gellhorn, 1964; Izard, 1971) to indicate that arousal or activation is clearly separate and distinct from emotion.

Epstein interprets May's (1950) interpretation of Kierkegaardian anxiety as support for his hypothesis of a complex relationship between expectancy and anxiety. In our chapter in *Anxiety and Behavior* (1966) we gave an analysis of Kierkegaard's (1844) thought on anxiety and showed how this brilliant philosopher's presentation was an insightful precursor of a theory of discrete emotions (Izard & Tomkins, 1966, pp. 122–123). Kierkegaard linked anxiety to the concepts of choice and possibility, and in particular to the possibility of freedom. These concepts have somewhat broader meaning in Kierkegaardian and existential philosophy than does expectancy in Epstein's controlled laboratory studies. Kierkegaard saw these latter concepts as the cognitive framework that facilitated creativity. A careful study of Kierkegaard shows that his concept of anxiety is clearly multidimensional and, as we indicated earlier (Izard & Tomkins, 1966), it clearly involves an oscillation between the negative emotion of fear and the positive emotion of interest-excitement.

Most of the empirical research which Epstein reports in his chapter in this volume are framed in terms of manipulating expectancy as the independent variable and using heart rate and skin conductance as dependent variables. Since heart rate and skin conductance are known to vary with a number of other emotions, conditions, and situations, he does not claim that these are studies of anxiety.

Epstein has attempted to measure changes in physiological indices during a period in which the subject awaits some noxious and presumably threatening stimulus. The fact that he undergoes changes in physiological functioning in such a period is no surprise to anyone. The fact that these changes fluctuate or vary at different points in the time interval during expectation or waiting should be no more surprising. As has been shown elsewhere (Tomkins, 1962; Izard & Tomkins, 1966; Izard, 1971), pure emotions are rare and difficult to obtain in the laboratory. If one is obtained, it is probably only a matter of seconds before that emotion elicits other emotions and interacts with cognition. Indeed, such is the nature of anxiety. The first emotion elicited in an "anxiety situation" may be fear, but fear may quickly elicit some distress, shame, or guilt. The variations and the physiological responses might be better explained not in terms of the concept of expectancy and changes in expectancy over time, but in terms of changes in emotions and emotion interactions elicited while waiting for a noxious stimulus in a contrived and artificial situation.

Similarly, the variation in intensity of the noxious stimulus, from which Epstein infers variation in threat expectancy, could easily lead to changes at the physiological level for more than one reason. One explanation equally plausible to that of Epstein's is that a group threatened with a highly noxious stimulus might first feel some fear, while a group threatened with a mildly noxious stimulus might in fact feel the annoyance and irritation of mild anger.

Epstein, Lazarus, and Averill, and other cognitive-theory oriented investigators seem to assume that once a particular emotion is elicited, this emotion state remains in pure form for a substantial period of time. This appears to be a naive and untenable assumption. One emotion can almost instantaneously elicit another emotion which amplifies, attenuates, inhibits, or interacts with the original emotional experience. When a person begins cogitating the situation which has evoked the emotion and as he waits in anticipation for some noxious stimulus, other emotions are almost certain to be elicited. For example, as a subject contemplates the possibility that the experimenter is playing games with him by manipulating the painful event that may or may not happen to him, he may get angry instead of afraid even though the coming event is presumably threatening and anxiety- or fear-producing.

Interestingly, some of the informal investigations which Epstein reports are similar to the systematic studies to be reported in the empirical section of this chapter. Epstein has described certain situations to students and asked them to indicate whether they would feel fear or anxiety. While it is unfortunate that Epstein limited the student's choices to these two concepts (fear and anxiety), he did obtain results somewhat similar to my own. He summarized the results as follows: "Some situations are almost unanimously recognized as fear, some as anxiety, and for some there is a division of opinion, suggesting that there is a mixture of the two." The problem with his approach is that we have no basis for knowing exactly what students mean when they use the label of anxiety.

Epstein found that knowledge of the source of threat did not serve as a distinguishing factor between what students labeled as fear and anxiety. He thought that all the anxiety situations had one thing in common: "an inability to direct the arousal produced by threat into an action tendency." This type of evidence and reasoning led Epstein to define fear as "an avoidance motive supporting directed action" and anxiety as "unresolved fear." Alternatively, he defined anxiety as "a state of undirected arousal following the perception of danger."

There is an alternative to Epstein's conceptualization. What he terms "undirected arousal" may more accurately be seen as the presence of more than one fundamental emotion, each having its own cue and guidance functions. When the different emotions constituted different and opposing or conflicting motivations, the "anxiety state" would appear to be undirected and unresolved.

Some of the situations which Epstein gave his students for labeling as anxiety or fear could also be the source of emotions other than these. Let's look at one example closely.

> Now imagine that you have been sent by your mother to buy something at the store. You have heard that there is a vicious dog who lives around the corner and you have often seen him straining at his chain to get you. Usually he is kept in the house but sometimes he gets free. Will he be there when you round the corner? You are approaching the corner and will soon find out. What is your feeling now?

Epstein said his students labeled the feeling in this situation as anxiety. His students' choice would confirm my conception of anxiety if it could be demonstrated that several fundamental emotions would obtain in this situation. Let's look at the possibilities. The individual may feel some distress (discouragement, downheartedness, etc.) over his inability to cope with the threatening situation. This may cause him to recognize some weaknesses or inadequacies in himself as an individual. Such recognition of inadequacy and the possibility of defeat could lead to a feeling of shame. The notion that he may not be able to complete the mission may lead to feelings of guilt. If this trip has been made a number of times with success, there is even the possibility that the individual approaching the corner may feel some interest and excitement at the possibility of grazing danger without actually being physically harmed or psychologically debilitated. Fear certainly may be the most prominent of the fundamental emotions in this situation, but the possibility that it might oscillate with interest-excitement has been described elsewhere (Izard, 1970b; Izard & Tomkins, 1966), and certainly there is no reason to discount the possibility that any of the other fundamental emotions mentioned (distress, shame–shyness–guilt) could also be present. These are the emotions I have hypothesized as components of anxiety.

Anxiety as a Concept That Includes Fear, Shame, and Guilt

Although Janis (1969) has been strongly influenced by the work of Lazarus and Epstein, his ideas come closer to the sense of my conception of anxiety than other cognitive theorists. Janis concluded that anxiety is a concept that "most theorists use as a generic term that includes fear, shame, and guilt [p. 111]." Janis was assuming, and to a large extent correctly so, that most theorists have been strongly influenced by Freud's description of objective anxiety (fear), social anxiety (shame), and conscience or moral anxiety (guilt).

Janis introduced the concept of reflective emotion as a tool for differentiating between normal and neurotic emotional reactions. His concept of reflective emotion is in one sense an extension of Freud and in part a confirmation of Schacter's (1964) and Lazarus' (1966; Chapter 4, this volume) positions. It also contains a clearly original contribution to the analysis of anxiety and of emotion in general. Janis considers reflective emotion as generally normal but he recognizes that the distinction between reflective and nonreflective, and between normal and abnormal, is sometimes thin and tenuous. An emotional state is reflective if it can be influenced by thoughtful reflection. Since reflective emotion is mediated by conscious verbal responses it tends to be directly correlated with changes in signs of external threat. "In other words, the emotion reflects like a mirror the environmental changes [p. 114]." Reflective emotion tends to increase vigilance and a somewhat conflicting need to seek emotion-alleviating reassurances. These changes lead to changes in cognition and action. Finally, reflective emotion increases the likelihood that the "person will develop a new attitude constituting a compromise between vigilance and reassurance tendencies [p. 115]."

After noting that anxiety is a generic term that includes fear, shame, and guilt, Janis, unlike Lazarus, Epstein, and others, proceeds to deal with fear, shame, and guilt as separate phenomena. However, like others, Janis tends to confuse antecedent conditions, emotion, and consequent emotion-determined or emotion-related actions.

Janis does not clearly recognize the influence of emotion on cognition and action, but he implicitly acknowledges the principle of cognition-emotion interaction with his concept of reflective emotion. More importantly, he does not recognize the principle of emotion-emotion interactions—the power of one emotion to elicit, inhibit, attenuate, or amplify another.

Empirical Analysis of "Anxiety"

I undertook a series of studies in search of empirical confirmation of the central thesis of this paper: anxiety is an unstable and variable combination of interacting fundamental emotions. I say combination primarily to indicate that more than one discrete emotion is involved. Certain fundamental emotions or their components may interact so closely and so regularly as to give the appearance of a unity with distinct characteristics and functions, but I suspect the search for such unity will be futile, as was our historical search for a unitary concept of anxiety. The combination is described as unstable and variable because it is susceptible to change in relation to time, persons, and situations, and because the fundamental emotions of the combination may vary in quality and intensity. That is, anxiety may be an interaction of strong fear, moderate distress, and mild guilt or shame, or it may be an interaction of fear, anger, and interest, and so on through many possible combinations and interactions.

It should be helpful in understanding the framework for these studies to take a look at the list of fundamental emotions and their definitions. These are presented in Table 3.1. In general, the first term following the number in the left hand margin of the table corresponds to a relatively lower intensity of the emotion while the second term indicates a higher intensity of the emotion. The adjectives or phrases following the emotion category label are defining terms selected primarily on the basis of synonymity. These are essentially a priori definitions though some of the defining terms were added as a result of empirical studies. The fundamental emotions as labeled and defined in Table 3.1 have been

TABLE 3.1
The Fundamental Emotions; A Priori Definitions

1. Interest–Excitement (I–E):	Concentrating, attending, attracted, curious
2. Enjoyment–Joy (E–J):	Glad, merry, delighted, joyful
3. Surprise–Startle (S–S):	Sudden reaction to something unexpected, astonished
4. Distress–Anguish (D–A):	Sad, unhappy, miserable, feels like crying
5. Disgust–Revulsion (D–R):	Repugnance, aversion, distaste, sickened
6. Anger–Rage (A–R):	Angry, hostile, furious, enraged
7. Shame–Humiliation (S–H):	Shy, embarrassed, ashamed, guilty
a. Guilt	
b. Shyness	
8. Fear–Terror (F–T):	Scared, afraid, terrified, panicked
9. Contempt–Scorn (C–S):	Disdainful, sneering, derisive, haughty

used in a variety of studies, both in the laboratory and in cross-cultural research (Ekman, Sorenson, & Friesen, 1969; Izard, 1971; Snyder & Katahn, 1970).

The list of fundamental emotions requires one further explanation. We consider shame–humiliation, number 7, to be a fundamental emotion, but as will be evident from data to be presented later, factor analyses of emotion terms representing all fundamental emotions often divide the terms used in the a priori substantive definition of shame–humiliation into two primary factors. The terms of one factor correspond rather well to the concept of guilt (7a of Table 3.1) and those of the other correspond to a concept of shyness (7b of Table 3.1). Tomkins (1962) maintains that there is one innate neural program for the fundamental emotion of shame–humiliation that may be represented in conscious experience as shame, shyness, or guilt. I have tended to agree with Tomkins and, since the factor analyses that separated shyness and guilt were based on self-reports (of conscious experience), this neither confirms nor rejects the hypothesis of a single underlying mechanism for these three different emotional experiences. Of course, if I had obtained only one factor for shame–shyness–guilt, this would not have proven anything about the neurological basis of the phenomenon, and I want to make it clear that I am not making such an inference in those instances where the statistical factors matched the a priori definitions. Such matching does strengthen our theoretical postulate of discrete fundamental emotions as useful scientific concepts at the phenomenological or experiential level.

The central aim of the empirical studies was to delineate the components (discrete emotions) of anxiety at the phenomenological level. To accomplish this aim two things were necessary—a technique for measuring the emotions of subjective experience and an "anxiety situation." Our approach to the measurement problem was to develop a set of adjective scales that would enable subjects to indicate the degree to which each of the fundamental emotions is present in experience. This instrument will be described in the next section.

The second thing that was needed was a situation that would elicit anxiety in all subjects. Previous research (Allport, 1924; Izard, Wehmer, Livsey, & Jennings, 1965; Tomkins, 1962) suggested that few if any contrived laboratory situations would do the job well. Taking a lead from behavior therapy (desensitization procedures) and some pilot research comparing emotional experiences induced by hypnosis and waking suggestion, I decided simply to instruct subjects to visualize or imagine a situation in which they had personally experienced strong anxiety. The specifics of this procedure will be described later.

The Differential Emotion Scale

The Differential Emotion Scale (DES) (Izard, 1968) is based on premises derived from the theory just presented. In particular, the DES assumes that separate and discrete emotions exist and that each has measurable experiential and motivational properties. Thus, a major aim (ideal) in the construction and refinement of the DES was to develop relatively independent scales or factors corresponding to each of the fundamental emotions.

Development of the DES

The Differential Emotion Scale (DES) is also based on the assumption that for each subjective experience corresponding to a fundamental emotion there is a corresponding facial pattern or expression. From cross-culturally obtained free responses to the facial expressions of the fundamental emotions, at least six adjectives were selected to represent each one of the nine fundamental emotions. The resulting group of 67 items was given to 622 freshmen students during a session of placement and personality tests at Vanderbilt University in September, 1968. DES instructions and sample items are presented in Table 3.2. The students were given the DES and asked to indicate their present feelings or emotions by using the five-point scale by each of the 67 emotion terms. Table 3.3 presents the primary factor loading of each adjective listed by factor.

TABLE 3.2
Instructions and Sample Items for the 67 Item Differential Emotion Scale

This scale consists of a number of words which describe different emotions or feelings. Please indicate the extent to which each word describes the way you feel at the present time.

Record your answers by circling the appropriate number on the five-place scale following each word. Presented below is the scale for indicating the degree to which each word describes the way you feel.

1	2	3	4	5
Very slightly or not at all	Slightly	Moderately	Considerable	Very strongly

In deciding on your answer to a given item or word, consider the feeling connoted or defined by that word. Then, if at the present moment you feel that way very slightly or not at all, you would circle the number 1 on the scale; if you feel that way to a moderate degree, you would circle 3; if you feel that way very strongly, you would circle 5, and so forth.

Remember, you are requested to make your responses on the basis of the way you feel at this time. Work at a good pace. It is not necessary to ponder; the first answer you decide on for a given word is probably the most valid. You should be able to finish in about five minutes.

1. Downhearted	1	2	3	4	5	26. Guilty	1	2	3	4	5
6. Astonished	1	2	3	4	5	35. Afraid	1	2	3	4	5
18. Attentive	1	2	3	4	5	44. Joyful	1	2	3	4	5
20. Ashamed	1	2	3	4	5	61. Angry	1	2	3	4	5

TABLE 3.3

Promax Factor Rotation of 67 Item Differential Emotion Scale[a]

Factor	Loading	Item
I. Interest–Excitement		
	.85	Attentive
	.80	Concentrating
	.74	Alert
	.72	Engaged in thought
	.67	Interested
	.53	Contemplative
II. Enjoyment–Joy		
	.88	Joyful
	.88	Enthusiastic
	.86	Delighted
	.82	Happy
	.78	Excited
	.70	Energetic
	.68	Warmhearted
	.66	Blissful
III. Surprise–Startle		
	.81	Surprised
	.78	Amazed
	.77	Startled
	.75	Astonished
	.74	Shocked
IV. Distress–Anguish		
	.77	Sad
	.75	Downhearted
	.73	Lonely
	.73	Discouraged
	.72	Upset
	.67	Distressed
	.59	Emotional
V. Disgust–(Mixed)		
	.69	Feeling of revulsion
	.66	Sickened
	.60	Contemptuous
	.58	Quarrelsome
VI. Anger–Disgust–Contempt		
	.80	Irritated
	.79	Scornful
	.79	Angry
	.77	Mad
	.77	Feeling of distaste
	.75	Bitter
	.74	Disdainful
	.73	Disgusted
	.72	Annoyed
	.71	Hostile
	.68	Provoked
	.67	Loathing
	.65	Feeling of aversion
	.64	Defiant
	.62	Rebellious
	.61	Enraged
	.50	Haughty
VII. (Shame)–Guilt		
	.81	Guilty
	.75	Ashamed
	.69	Blameworthy
	.69	Repentant
VIII. (Shame)–Shyness		
	.91	Bashful
	.88	Shy
	.71	Sheepish
IX. Fear–Terror		
	.91	Afraid
	.91	Scared
	.89	Fearful
	.87	Frightened
	.78	Jittery
	.66	Shaky
	.52	Anxious
	.52	Inadequate
X. Contempt–Scorn		
	.74	Sarcastic
	.67	Mocking
XI. Fatigue–Sleepiness		
	.82	Sluggish
	.81	Fatigued
	–.72	Awake

[a] Data from 1968 Freshman Testing, $N = 622$.

These were taken from the promax rotation of a principal components factor analysis. The factor names were assigned on the basis of the a priori expectations. These results offer strong support for some aspects of my theory, though some items did not factor quite as expected.

A slightly modified list of 72 five-point emotion-adjective scales (a revised DES) was administered to the next entering freshman class (Fall, 1969, $N = 1182$). The factor analysis of the revised DES closely paralleled and confirmed the results shown in Table 3.3. The eight factors of interest, enjoyment, surprise, disgust–(mixed), anger–disgust–contempt, guilt, shyness, and fatigue emerged with very similar content. However, most of the fear and distress words mixed on a single (fear-distress) factor. Three words were added for the fatigue factor in the 72 item DES, and all three had high primary loadings on the intended factor. (The title fatigue was chosen over arousal or activation to avoid the confusion that might arise from the surplus and erroneous connotations sometimes associated with the latter terms.) On the whole, the similarity of factor structure on the two occasions was quite substantial.

A third factor analysis was computed from data on 163 black college students who were participating in a study to be described in more detail below. In this study the students were asked to say how they felt in three emotion-eliciting situations–two real and one hypothetical. Again, the factor structure was substantially similar to that obtained in the two previous analyses, but again there were some minor differences.

I suspect that some degree of variation in factor structure might reasonably be expected when a state measure is given on different occasions to different samples. In situations or conditions where one or two emotions may be prominent and two or three notably absent, discrimination among the remaining emotions may not be as fine. In establishing the psychometric properties of state measures, our present concepts of reliability and validity may have to be further delineated or complemented by some new concepts.

A DES "Validity" Study

Izard, Chappell, and Weaver (1970) gave the 72 item DES to black college students. They were asked to describe the emotions characterizing the experience of being the recipient of race prejudice in one hypothetical (imagined) and two actual (remembered) situations. The order of presentation of the three situations was balanced so that effect of order could be evaluated. Pilot interviews with several black college students revealed that their first clear memory of prejudice occurred somewhere around age five to seven. Most recent incidents were likely to have occurred during the past few months.

We expected that the first instance of prejudice and the most recent instance would be characterized by different emotions or different emotion factor scores.

Since the first instance usually occurs during the more vulnerable childhood years and probably in an adult–child relationship, and since prejudice can be both accusatory and threatening, we thought the scores on the guilt, shyness, and fear-distress factors would be higher than for the other situations. We thought the child's naivete with respect to prejudice and his lack of expectation of racial discrimination would cause the scores on the surprise factor to be higher than for the other situations. We expected that the most recent and the hypothetical situations, occurring during college years when the subjects have greater understanding of prejudice and civil rights, would produce higher scores on the anger–disgust–contempt factor. We thought the hypothetical situation would be more like the most recent experience with prejudice than like the first encounter. Scoring was based on the factors of the 72 item DES, which contained seven identifiable emotion factors.

A separate analysis of variance was computed for each emotion factor, with situation and order as the main effects. Order was significant in only one instance, on the enjoyment factor. As was expected, the variance in emotion factor scores due to situation was significant. For five emotion factors—surprise, anger–disgust–contempt, guilt, shyness, fear–distress—p was less than .001. For interest, p was .004 and for enjoyment, .036. Also, as expected, the situation of the first encounter with prejudice elicited higher scores on surprise, guilt, shyness, and fear–distress. The hypothetical situation elicited a higher score on anger–disgust–contempt than either of the other two situations, and the most recent encounter elicited a considerably higher score on this factor than did the first encounter. These results generally confirmed our expectations and furnished evidence for one kind of validity for the DES.

Emotional Connotation of DES "Anxiety" Items

In studying the factor analyses of the DES for possible indications of the hypothesized nature of anxiety, I discovered that several items (concepts) which are frequently included on anxiety scales had factor loadings that tended to be consonant with my conception of anxiety. These DES items and their factor loadings are presented in Table 3.4.

Interestingly, the term anxious had its primary loadings on fear, but it had fairly substantial loadings on shyness, distress, surprise, and enjoyment–joy. Most of the other terms which are typically considered to be anxiety terms also have their primary loadings on fear, with their next highest loadings on distress, guilt, and shyness. These data tend to confirm my conceptual analysis of anxiety.

Combining the DES and an Anxiety Scale

The next step in the analysis of anxiety in terms of fundamental emotions was to combine the DES with a standard anxiety scale. In order for the combined instrument to be of reasonable length the DES was abbreviated. I selected three words or terms to represent each of ten emotions and three to represent the nonemotional factor of fatigue. Insofar as possible the selection of these items was based on the factor loadings determined by previous analyses.

TABLE 3.4
Factor Loadings for "Anxiety" Words on DES Emotion Factors[a]

		"Anxiety" words			
	Emotion factors	Anxious	Jittery	Shaky	Inadequate
I.	Interest–Excitement	.24	.13	.15	.12
II.	Enjoyment–Joy	.42	.18	.10	.10
III.	Surprise–Startle	.38	.29	.24	.32
IV.	Distress–Anguish	.35	.53	.51	.47
V.	Disgust–(Mixed)	−.01	.03	.19	.08
VI.	Anger–Disgust–Contempt	.01	.10	.11	−.03
VIIA.	(Shame)–Guilt	.19	.42	.41	.37
VIIB.	(Shame)–Shyness	.33	.49	.37	.49
VIII.	Fear–Terror	.52	.78	.66	.52
IX.	Contempt–Scorn	.17	.07	.01	.08
X.	Fatigue–Sleepiness	.01	.14	.24	.19

[a] $N = 622$; Condition–Freshman Testing.

The state form of the Spielberger–Gorsuch–Lushene (1970) State Trait Anxiety Inventory (STAI) was chosen as the anxiety scale for combining with the DES. The STAI is brief (only 20 items), its scale format is similar to the DES, it has good psychometric properties, and it correlates very well with other well accepted anxiety measures. For example, correlations between the STAI A-Trait Scale and the Taylor Manifest Anxiety Scale have ranged from .79 to .83.

The STAI items were condensed to match the form of the DES items. This was easily done since each STAI item refers to only one feeling (concept), usually represented by a single word. The conversion of STAI items to DES-type items is shown in Table 3.5. Items 7 and 17 both seemed to be represented reasonably well by the term worried, and the term joyful is identical to one of the DES items. Thus, 18 independent STAI items were added to the 33-item DES to form the 51-item DES + A.

The DES + A represents ten emotion concepts, one nonemotion concept, and an anxiety scale. The DES + A will be used in all subsequent studies reported in this chapter.

TABLE 3.5

Conversion of Spielberger–Gorsuch–Lushene STAI Items to DES-Type Items

1. I feel calm	Calm
2. I feel secure	Secure
3. I am tense	Tense
4. I am regretful	Regretful
5. I feel at ease	At ease
6. I feel upset	Upset
7. I am presently worrying over possible misfortunes	Worried
8. I feel rested	Rested
9. I feel anxious	Anxious
10. I feel comfortable	Comfortable
11. I feel self-confident	Confident
12. I feel nervous	Nervous
13. I am jittery	Jittery
14. I feel "high strung"	"High strung"
15. I am relaxed	Relaxed
16. I feel content	Content
17. I am worried	Worried
18. I feel over-excited and rattled	Over-excited and rattled
19. I feel joyful	Joyful
20. I feel pleasant	Pleasant

DES+A as a Tool for Analyzing the Experience of Anxiety

As the first phase of the empirical analysis of experiential anxiety, the DES + A was administered to four classes of introductory psychology students ($N = 297$). On the first occasion the subjects were asked to visualize a situation which made them anxious and, while recalling that experience, to fill out the DES + A. The specific instructions for the administration of the DES + A in the anxiety-situation and the items of DES + A are presented in Table 3.6.

The factor analysis of the DES + A is presented as Table 3.7. The items marked with an asterisk are the anxiety terms from the STAI.

As can be seen, the factor structure and factor content of the DES + A as administered in the anxiety situation are quite similar to what was obtained for the 67 item DES (Table 3.3) as administered during freshman testing. The obtained factor structures correspond rather well with the aprioristically defined fundamental emotions. Without the STAI items, the contents of the statistically derived factors and the contents of the aprioristically defined emotions are perfectly matched for interest, enjoyment, surprise, shyness, and fear. All the a priori terms for distress and all those for guilt combined into a single factor in this study. Similar combinations have occurred in previous studies. In the factor analysis of the data from the 1969 freshman testing study, distress combined

TABLE 3.6

Instructions for the Anxiety Situation and the DES + A

Our era has been called the Age of Anxiety. Whether or not this is the best name for our age, all of us experience anxiety from time to time.

Each of us has our own idea as to the meaning of anxiety and the feelings that go with it. We would like for you to use the scales below to describe your personal experience, your own feelings, when you are anxious.

Please try to recall a time or situation in which you were anxious. Without revealing any names or personal information you do not wish to disclose, identify below the situation or type of situation you are recalling.

Situation:______________________________

Now, keeping the anxiety situation in mind, complete the scales below, circling the appropriate scale number to indicate the degree to which each word describes your feelings while you are experiencing anxiety.

1	2	3	4	5
Very slightly or not at all	Slightly	Moderately	Considerably	Very strongly

1. Comfortable	1	2	3	4	5	27. Relaxed	1	2	3	4	5
2. Repentant	1	2	3	4	5	28. Angry	1	2	3	4	5
3. Calm	1	2	3	4	5	29. Sad	1	2	3	4	5
4. Delighted	1	2	3	4	5	30. Guilty	1	2	3	4	5
5. "High strung"	1	2	3	4	5	31. Anxious	1	2	3	4	5
6. Feeling of distaste	1	2	3	4	5	32. Bashful	1	2	3	4	5
7. Downhearted	1	2	3	4	5	33. Nervous	1	2	3	4	5
8. Surprised	1	2	3	4	5	34. Disgusted	1	2	3	4	5
9. Confident	1	2	3	4	5	35. Joyful	1	2	3	4	5
10. Fatigued	1	2	3	4	5	36. Feeling of revulsion	1	2	3	4	5
11. Contemptuous	1	2	3	4	5	37. Over-excited & rattled	1	2	3	4	5
12. Sheepish	1	2	3	4	5	38. Disdainful	1	2	3	4	5
13. Jittery	1	2	3	4	5	39. Upset	1	2	3	4	5
14. Attentive	1	2	3	4	5	40. Blameworthy	1	2	3	4	5
15. Scared	1	2	3	4	5	41. Tense	1	2	3	4	5
16. Secure	1	2	3	4	5	42. Astonished	1	2	3	4	5
17. Enraged	1	2	3	4	5	43. Alert	1	2	3	4	5
18. Happy	1	2	3	4	5	44. Worried	1	2	3	4	5
19. Scornful	1	2	3	4	5	45. Mad	1	2	3	4	5
20. Pleasant	1	2	3	4	5	46. Rested	1	2	3	4	5
21. Concentrating	1	2	3	4	5	47. Discouraged	1	2	3	4	5
22. Content	1	2	3	4	5	48. Shy	1	2	3	4	5
23. Amazed	1	2	3	4	5	49. Regretful	1	2	3	4	5
24. Fearful	1	2	3	4	5	50. Sleepy	1	2	3	4	5
25. At ease	1	2	3	4	5	51. Afraid	1	2	3	4	5
26. Sluggish	1	2	3	4	5						

TABLE 3.7
Factor Analysis of DES + A (DES-33 + STAI Items)[a]

Factor	Loading	Item
Factor I Interest	.75	Alert
	.75	Attentive
	.72	Concentrating
Factor II Enjoyment + "Negative of Anxiety"	.83	Happy
	*.81	Pleasant
	*.79	Joyful
	*.78	Content
	.78	Delighted
	*.71	Secure
	*.68	Confident
	*.67	Relaxed
	*.66	At ease
	*.60	Rested
	*.43	Comfortable
Factor III Surprise	.85	Amazed
	.84	Astonished
	.79	Surprised
Factor IV Distress–Guilt + "Anxiety"	*.84	Regretful
	.84	Blameworthy
	.84	Guilty
	.71	Repentant
	.71	Downhearted
	*.71	Upset
	.70	Sad
	.65	Discouraged
Factor V Anger–Disgust–Contempt	.86	Mad
	.85	Angry
	.83	Disgusted
	.82	Enraged
	.81	Scornful
	.80	Contemptous
	.80	Feeling of revulsion
	.77	Disdainful
	.74	Feeling of distaste
Factor VI Shyness	.84	Shy
	.82	Bashful
	.64	Sheepish
Factor VII Fear + "Anxiety"	*.83	Nervous
	*.82	Tense
	*.81	Jittery
	.80	Fearful
	.78	Afraid
	*.77	Worried
	.77	Scared
	*.65	Over-excited and rattled
	*.60	Anxious
	*.54	"High strung"
Factor VIII Fatigue	.71	Sleepy
	.68	Fatigued
	.63	Sluggish
Factor ?	*.55	Calm

[a] $N = 297$; Subjects were visualizing an anxiety-situation of their own choosing; STAI items are marked by asterisk.

with fear, and for the black students in the prejudice study, shyness combined with fear. Such combinations of fundamental emotions into single first order statistical factors may reflect an instability of factor structure that would characterize any state measure, or some of them may be seen as relatively good descriptions of anxiety as defined by one or more of the theorists discussed in this chapter. Viewed in this way, we have another illustration of the instability and variability of anxiety as a concept.

All the a priori terms for the three emotions of anger, disgust, and contempt combined into a single first order factor. These emotions have combined in this way in most of the DES factor analytic studies, though occasionally some disgust terms emerge as a separate factor, as do some contempt terms. Other studies using other research approaches and measurement techniques have presented strong evidence as to the existence of anger, disgust, and contempt as discrete emotions. The strongest such evidence has come from cross-cultural and developmental studies of the recognition and labeling of facial expressions of emotions (Ekman *et al.,* 1969; Izard, 1971). The DES's greater dependence on cognitive report of the phenomenological or experiential component of emotion may help explain the frequent emergence of anger–disgust–contempt as a single DES factor. It is possible that these three emotions are not always clearly differentiated at the level of conceptual experiencing, at least in some situations or conditions.

Considering both the DES and STAI items, the factor content shown in Table 3.7 gives some support for my formulation of anxiety as a combination of certain fundamental emotions. The DES fear factor (represented by the words fearful, afraid, and scared) was the factor on which most of the negative items of the STAI loaded. This is quite as expected since Spielberger emphasizes the emotion of fear in his substantive definition of anxiety.

In the present factor analysis, distress (aprioristically defined by the terms downhearted, sad, discouraged) and guilt (aprioristically defined by the terms blameworthy, guilty, and repentant) came together in a single statistical factor. Two of the STAI items loaded on this distress–guilt factor.

One of the items of the STAI (calm) emerged as a separate factor. Our present data do not make it possible to say much about the meaning of this possibly chance factor.

All other STAI items loaded on the enjoyment factor of the DES. This seems somewhat unexpected in terms of our conceptualization of anxiety, but it apparently is not inconsistent with Spielberger's theorizing (Chapter 1, this volume). In selecting these terms for the STAI scale, Spielberger was hypothesizing that the absence of security, confidence, comfort, relaxation, joy, etc., was, in effect, an indication of anxiety.

In summary, various STAI items had primary loadings on factors representing three of the five fundamental emotions hypothesized as components of anxiety—fear, distress, and guilt. The failure of any STAI items to load on the shyness factor could be due to the sample of DES items selected to represent this factor or, more likely, to the way the STAI defines anxiety. The loadings of anxiety terms on the DES factor representing enjoyment–joy may also be more a function of the particular substantive qualities of STAI than of anxiety measures in general. The fact that no STAI items loaded on the DES factor of interest may be due simply to the lack of interest-affect content on the STAI.

DES+A Applied to the Emotions That Constitute Anxiety

The next step in the empirical analysis of experiential anxiety was to use the DES + A as a tool to study each of the fundamental emotions that I have hypothesized as a possible component of anxiety. The same psychology classes who visualized an anxiety situation and took the DES + A were used as subjects. Three of the classes were subdivided randomly into four groups. The first subgroup was asked to visualize a fear situation, the second a guilt situation, the third a distress situation, and the fourth a shyness situation. The fourth class, tested as a whole, was asked to visualize a situation in which they experience a high degree of interest and excitement. In all classes except the last the anxiety situation and one of the emotion situations were stapled together and administered in the same session, making it possible to compare a given group of subjects' DES + A scores derived from the anxiety situation with their scores derived from an emotion situation. All subjects remained anonymous, having been told at the beginning of the session that they need not put their names on the test forms. [The role of anger in anxiety will be reported in a forthcoming publication (Izard, in press).]

Instructions for visualizing or imagining the fear situation and for the subsequent completion of the DES + A are presented as Table 3.8. (To simplify things for the subjects, I referred to the DES + A as the DES, a name with which they were already familiar.) Corresponding instructions were used for the distress situation, the guilt situation, the shyness situation, and the interest situation.

As already indicated, there were four groups for which we could collate the subjects' performance on the DES + A in the anxiety situation with their performance on the DES + A in one of the emotion situations—fear, distress, guilt, or shyness. For each of these four groups we performed two kinds of analyses. First, for a given group we compared DES + A anxiety scores from the

TABLE 3.8
Instructions for Visualizing the Fear-Situation and Subsequent Completion of the DES + A

Emotions in Life-Situations

All individuals experience fear in certain situations. Different individuals experience fear in different kinds of situations. We would like for you to describe below a situation or condition that you have been in, may be in again, and in which you experience fear. Please be careful to indicate a situation in which *fear,* not some other negative feeling, is the dominant emotion.

Fear Situation:____

Now use the attached Differential Emotion Scale (DES) to describe your feelings in that situation. We would like for your responses to be as true as possible to the real-life situation you have listed above. Visualize the situation again, or recall it as vividly as you can, while you complete the attached DES.

anxiety situation with DES + A anxiety scores from the particular emotion situation that this group visualized. Thus, for the group that imagined a fear situation, we could compare DES + A anxiety scores based on the recall of their experience in an anxiety situation with DES + A anxiety scores based on their recall of their experience in a fear situation. The anxiety scores were based on the 19 scales of DES + A which were derived from the items of the STAI. Since there were 19 five-point scales, the minimum anxiety score would be 19 and the maximum anxiety score 95. (The corresponding minimum and maximum scores for the 20 four-point items of the STAI are 20 and 80.) As would be expected, the mean scale scores of all the emotions hypothesized as components of anxiety were higher in the anxiety situation than the corresponding mean scale scores obtained during the placement and personality testing session for the 1969 entering freshmen.

Second, we compared the DES + A factor scores (emotion profiles) from the anxiety situation with the emotion profiles from the particular emotion situation visualized by the group being considered.

To illustrate the first kind of analysis, let us consider the group who completed the DES + A while imagining an anxiety situation and then later completed the DES + A while imagining a fear situation. The treatment (situations) x subjects, analysis of variance of the anxiety scores from the anxiety and fear situations is presented in Table 3.9.

TABLE 3.9

Analysis of Variance of DES + A Anxiety Scores from the Anxiety Situation and the Fear Situation

Source	*df*	*MS*	*F*	*p*
Situations (Anxiety versus Fear)	1	62.6250	.6880	.5828
Subjects	37	227.6419	2.5009	.0035
Situations x Subjects	37	91.0236		

The significant *F* due to Subjects is as expected, simply reflecting inter-subject variability in anxiety scores. The term of most importance is the variance due to situations, which was far from statistically significant. Thus, anxiety as measured by the STAI items on the DES + A did not differ in the fear situation and the anxiety situation. This is pretty much as expected in view of STAI's emphasis on fear in defining anxiety.

Similar analyses were performed for each of the other groups. The variance due to subjects was highly significant in all analyses except in the comparison of the anxiety situation and the guilt situation, where $p = .0586$. As in the comparison of the anxiety and fear situations (Table 3.9), the variance in anxiety scores due to situations was not significant for the comparison of the anxiety and distress situations or for the anxiety and guilt situations.

The difference in mean anxiety scores from the anxiety situation and each of the four negative emotion situations was significant only for the shyness situation. The analysis of variance for this comparison is presented in Table 3.10. Inspection of the means, presented in Table 3.11A, revealed that the average DES + A anxiety score from the shyness situation was significantly lower than the anxiety score from the anxiety situation. Thus, the experience of shyness as imagined by these subjects did not produce as much anxiety as measured by the STAI items of the DES + A as did the imagined experience of the anxiety situation or any of the other negative emotion situations—fear, guilt, distress—all

TABLE 3.10
Analysis of Variance of DES + A Anxiety Scores from the Anxiety Situation and the Shyness Situation

Source	*df*	*MS*	*F*	*p*
Situations (Anxiety versus Shyness)	1	776.8750	8.9669	.0050
Subjects	37	189.0777	2.1824	.0100
Situations x Subjects	37	86.6385		

TABLE 3.11A
Anxiety Score Means and SD's of the Five Groups in the Different Emotion Situations and in the Anxiety Situation

Situations	$\bar{x}$	*SD*
Group 1:		
Anxiety	76.32	12.07
Fear	78.13	12.83
Group 2:		
Anxiety	77.42	10.11
Guilt	76.25	12.46
Group 3:		
Anxiety	79.21	12.74
Distress	75.69	12.36
Group 4:		
Anxiety	75.29	10.78
Shyness	68.89	12.34
Group 5:		
Anxiety	75.35	11.90
Interest	52.31	12.24

TABLE 3.11B

Analysis of Variance of Anxiety Scores Considering all Emotion Situations at Once (Fear, Guilt, Distress, Shyness, and Interest)

Source	*df*	*MS*	*F*	*p*
Between emotion situations	4	4435.453	27.9001	.001
Within emotion situations	189	158.976		
	193	247.608		

of which produced approximately equal mean anxiety scores. The imagined shyness experience probably produced the lowest anxiety score of all the negative situations because the shyness concept is not represented on the STAI.

The final step in studying the anxiety scores of the several groups was an analysis of variance considering all situations at once. In this analysis it was possible to include the group who imagined the interest situation. The overall analysis of variance is presented in Table 3.11B. The variance in anxiety scores due to emotion situations is highly significant, as would be expected from the relatively low mean anxiety score in shyness and the even lower mean for interest. This analysis gives a statistically derived confidence level for what had already become obvious; namely, that anxiety as measured by the DES + A STAI items, which emphasize the fear component of anxiety, varies among the five emotion situations. This significant variance is due mainly to the relatively low means for the shyness and interest situations. Since STAI items loaded on the DES factors representing fear, guilt, and distress, it is quite reasonable that these three emotion situations yielded higher anxiety scores than did shyness and interest. Also, as expected, the mean anxiety score in the four negative emotion situations were all substantially higher than the anxiety score from the one positive emotion situation, interest. The rank order of the mean anxiety scores speaks well for the efficacy of the experimental procedure of imagining or visualizing emotion eliciting situations. For example, the subjects who imagined the fear situation had the highest mean anxiety score while those visualizing the interest situation had the lowest. The argument is further supported by the highly significant F for the first term in Table 3.11B, between emotion situations.

The shyness and interest situations were not altogether anxiety-free. Remember, the minimum mean anxiety score would be 19.00, whereas that obtained in the interest situation is 52.31. This corresponds to a mean scale score of 2.70 on a five-point scale. The corresponding mean scale score derived from the state form of STAI taken under instructions to assume a calm state was 1.75 on a four-point scale (Spielberger *et al.*, 1970). For both the DES + A and the STAI the minimum obtainable mean scale score is 1.00. The finding that the

STAI anxiety mean in the least anxious situation of interest is considerably above the obtainable minimum and somewhat higher than that reported for a calm state provides further support for my formulation of anxiety. This argument is strengthened by the fact that the STAI items do not measure all the fundamental emotions hypothesized as possible components of anxiety.

The foregoing analyses generally support the hypothesis that anxiety is a combination of fundamental emotions. Subjects describing their experience in imagined emotion situations of fear, guilt, and distress produce anxiety scores equally as high as subjects describing their experience while imagining or visualizing an anxiety situation. The mean anxiety scores in the fear, guilt, distress, and anxiety situations were significantly higher than the mean for shyness which was higher than the mean for interest. Yet, even in the interest situation the anxiety scores were well above the minimum obtainable and apparently higher than those reported for subjects asked to describe their feelings (on the STAI) in a calm state.

Put another way, the foregoing empirical analyses suggest that anxiety as a concept and anxiety scales as measurement techniques do not constitute an adequate means for the study of discrete human emotions. The STAI is a carefully developed instrument with well above average psychometric properties; yet, as used in the DES + A, it failed to differentiate between a visualized anxiety situation and a fear, distress and guilt situation respectively. This may be viewed as a reasonable and expected outcome rather than a failure in discriminatory power, if we view the STAI as a measure of a complex concept, which has certain fundamental, discrete emotion concepts as constituent elements.

In the interest of refining instruments for use in planning treatment and intervention programs, it would be well for STAI and all other anxiety scales to specify the extent to which they measure fear, distress, guilt, or other discrete emotions. The assumption that the different fundamental emotions have different antecedents, different existential and motivational properties, and different consequences is rapidly achieving the status in science that it has long enjoyed in folk wisdom.

Pure Emotions versus Emotion Profiles

This topic will be treated in more detail in a later work, but a few observations and comments are in order here. Most theories that treat discrete emotions have suggested that existence of a pure emotion such as pure fear or pure guilt is probably fairly rare in day-to-day living and virtually impossible to obtain in the laboratory or any research setting. I share this position, particularly if the dimension of time is considered. I believe we experience pure emotion from time to time but, since any emotion is one of the principal activators of itself and other emotions, the pure emotion or one of the constantly changing elements of the perceptual-experiential field quickly elicits a second or third emotion.

The original pure emotion may dominate the scene for a while, with other emotions alternating, interacting, or possibly combining in some way. There was evidence from the present studies that suggested something like this obtained as the subjects visualized or imagined the five different emotion situations. In three out of the four negative emotion situations the factor most closely corresponding to the imagined emotion had the highest mean of any DES + A factor (see Table 3.12). In the shyness situation, the shyness factor had by far the highest mean. The next highest mean was for the factor of distress–guilt. Tomkins has suggested that shame, shyness, and guilt are different conscious experiences of the same fundamental emotion. If we look at the guilt situation, column 2 of Table 3.12, we find a parallel and consistent pattern. In the guilt situation, the highest mean was on the distress–guilt factor, with shyness having the second highest score. In this situation the mean factor score for anger–disgust–contempt was virtually the same as that for shyness, but this too makes some sense in terms of theories of emotion dynamics. Psychoanalytic theory posits a relationship between guilt and hostility in explaining the dynamics of grief (Janis, 1969), and Tomkins (1962) maintains that distress (an emotion component of grief) and anger are activated by a similar condition of neural activation—a relatively high and steady level of neural stimulation.

The exception was the fear situation in which the mean for the factor representing the functionally related emotion of surprise was slightly higher than the mean for the fear factor. However, in the fear situation the fear factor mean may be artificially low and the range of mean factor scores restricted, because fear is a prominent component of anxiety, and the T-scores used to compute the means in Table 3.12 were based on the means and *SD*'s derived from the data of the anxiety situation in which fear was elevated. That is, it was a fairly high raw score mean for fear that was converted to the T-score mean of 50. Within the restricted range of means for the fear situation it is still possible to find a pattern that fits reasonably well with our hypothesis with respect to the activation of a dynamically related cluster or profile of emotions. Three of the four highest factor means were those representing fear, surprise, and interest, long thought to be functionally and dynamically related (Darwin, 1872; Tomkins, 1962).

The case is not quite as clear for the interest situation. Here, the interest factor had the second highest mean, enjoyment the highest. However, even in this case, the factor scores for the positive emotions and for surprise are clearly higher than all of the factors representing negative emotions.

In summary, there was a tendency for an imagined emotion situation to yield an elevated mean on the DES factor representing that emotion. Factors representing emotions that relate and interact dynamically with the imagined

TABLE 3.12

DES + A Factor Means for each Emotion Situation Imagined by the Subjects[a]

DES + A Emotion-Factors	Emotion-Situation Imagined: Fear	Guilt	Distress	Shyness	Interest
	$N = 38$	$N = 40$	$N = 39$	$N = 38$	$N = 38$
Interest	52.13	43.41	45.89	44.43	55.59
Enjoyment + "Negative of Anxiety"	47.45	48.25	47.28	52.73	71.15
Surprise	55.33	50.63	56.70	52.07	52.16
Anger–Disgust–Contempt	52.70	56.40	60.24	52.02	44.14
Distress–Guilt + Anxiety	48.64	61.50	61.62	53.32	39.10
Shyness	48.66	56.44	51.35	63.72	43.98
Fear + Anxiety	54.28	46.66	46.33	42.75	36.01
Fatigue	47.31	50.44	54.62	49.36	44.25

[a] Means are reported in terms of T-scores, with the factor means and standard deviations for the total sample in the anxiety condition arbitrarily fixed at 50 and 10, respectively. Since the T-scores were based on the data from the anxiety-situation in which negative emotions were elevated, we would expect those emotions most predominantly involved in anxiety to show relatively less elevation than others. Remembering how STAI defines anxiety we can see that this is rather precisely what happened. According to STAI, fear is the predominant negative emotion in anxiety, followed by distress and guilt, with shyness not represented. Consistent with this reasoning, the mean Fear + Anxiety score in the fear situation is the lowest of the four negative mean emotion factor scores in their respective emotion situations. The means for the Distress-Guilt + Anxiety factor in the distress situation and guilt situation are in the middle, and the mean shyness factor score in the shame situation is highest.

emotion also tended to be elevated. Thus, it is quite conceivable that the imagined situations followed real life situations true to form. Fear, guilt, or shyness may come first in a given situation, quickly followed by dynamically related and interacting emotions. In measures depending on verbal self-report, the dominant as well as the related emotions show relatively elevated means.

Relationships among Free-Response Descriptions of the Anxiety-Situation and the Discrete Emotion-Situations

On occasions when the subjects were asked to visualize the anxiety situation and the different fundamental emotional situations they were also asked to give a brief description of the scene they were visualizing or imagining (see Tables 3.6 and 3.8). I was highly impressed by the apparent candidness of the subjects. The situations which they listed had a great deal of face validity for the type of situation they were asked to visualize.

The chief use made of these data was to determine the degree to which the content of the free-response descriptions of the anxiety situation overlapped with the content of the free-response descriptions of the various discrete emotion situations. Two judges independently determined the number of anxiety situation descriptions that were identical to descriptions of one or more of the five discrete emotion situations. These data, summarized in Table 3.13, offer some of the strongest support for my conception of anxiety. Here we have the subjects' free-response descriptions of situations they consider as anxiety situations. We also have subgroups of the same subjects giving their free-response descriptions of what they consider to be a fear situation, distress situation, a guilt situation, a shyness situation and an interest situation. As my conception of anxiety would predict, we have a rather substantial overlap in these free-response descriptions between the anxiety situation and each of the fundamental emotion situations.

Consider the first block of Table 3.13, the anxiety situation. It can be seen that there were 86 free-response descriptions of anxiety that were identical to one or more responses given in one or the other of the discrete emotion situations. These 86 responses represent 150 *S*s. Consider next the second block of that table, the distress situation. There were 23 free-responses given in the distress situation that were identical to responses given in the anxiety situation. Thirteen of the 30 different free-responses given by the 40 subjects in the guilt situation were identical to free-responses that could be found among the free-response descriptions of the anxiety situation. Somewhat similar proportions hold for the situations of shyness and interest–excitement. The distress situation had the highest number of responses that were identical with anxiety responses, and the fear situation had the second highest number of identical responses. In summarizing the data presented in Table 3.13, we can say that the population of events and situations (perceptions) that people see as

TABLE 3.13
Comparison of Subjects' (Ss') Free-Response Descriptions (Rs) of the Anxiety Situations with Their Descriptions of Fundamental Emotion Situations

Situation	Type of Responses		
	Identical	Nonidentical	Total
Anxiety			
Rs	86	103	189
*S*s	150	147	297
Distress			
Rs	23	6	29
*S*s	23	16	39
Guilt			
Rs	13	17	30
*S*s	15	25	40
Fear			
Rs	15	11	26
*S*s	21	17	38
Shyness			
Rs	15	16	31
*S*s	18	20	38
Interest–Excitement			
Rs	12	17	29
*S*s	12	20	32

"causes" of anxiety overlap considerably with what they see as "causes" of distress, guilt, fear, shyness, and interest–excitement. This overlap in perceived causes furnishes another kind of evidence that anxiety is a combination of fundamental emotions.

Can Anxiety Be Considered a Second Order Factor?

One way of viewing the results of the analysis of the substantive components of the concept of anxiety as presented in the first section of the chapter is to assume that the various theorists and investigators have tacitly accepted the fact that emotion has a number of different elements or components. Some theorists have attempted to put this in more rigorous mathematical or statistical language. As we have already noted, Cattell has argued that anxiety is a second order factor and he has specified certain primary factors as its constituents.

If I were to follow the form of Cattell's argument, I would say that anxiety is a second order factor in which the discrete fundamental emotions are the primary factors. To test the reasonableness of this formulation we computed the second order factors for the data obtained on the 297 subjects who took the 51 item DES + A while imagining an anxiety situation. The second order factors and the primary factors composing them are shown in row 1 of table 3.14. As we can see, there is no second order factor which contains all of the hypothesized emotions of anxiety. Second order factor II contains most of the fundamental emotions of anxiety.

In all, we have looked at the second order factors from four different investigations involving the DES. The factors shown in row 2 of Table 3.14 were derived from the data obtained by means of a summer mailout of the 72 item DES to incoming Vanderbilt freshmen. The mailout included a letter which, in effect, told them that their previous letter of acceptance to Vanderbilt was a mistake and that they actually could not be admitted to the university. The instructions told them that the "delayed rejection" letter was a hoax, but they were to respond to it as though it were true, using the DES to describe their emotions. As can be seen in row 2, the second order factors do not correspond very well with those in row 1. Again there is no single order factor which contains all of the emotions hypothesized as components of anxiety. Row 3 of Table 3.14 shows the second order factors for the 72 item DES which was administered to freshmen during the on-campus placement and personality testing of orientation week. The second order factors in this case are quite similar to those for the DES + A as shown in row 1.

The second order factors shown in row 4 were obtained during the placement and personality testing session for entering freshmen in 1968. These data conform most closely to what I would predict if I viewed anxiety as a second order factor. Second order factor II contains separate primary factors for all four of the negative emotions hypothesized as components of anxiety.

The data of Table 3.14 suggest that anxiety cannot be considered as a second order factor with fixed and stable primary factors as its component first order factors. However, in some analyses second order factors contained most of the components of anxiety, as defined by differential emotion theory.

Patterns of Fundamental Emotions

The theory I have presented suggests that a particular individual in a particular situation typically experiences more than one emotion, interactions among emotions, and possibly a combination of emotion elements. Perhaps the development of the science of emotion would be facilitated by using the concept of patterns or profiles of emotions. This would mean viewing any significant social or person-environment interaction as one that is characterized by a pattern of emotions rather than by a single discrete emotion. When students were asked to imagine a fear situation, scores were elevated on the factor representing fear and also on the factor representing surprise and the factor representing interest. When they were asked to imagine a distress situation, their scores on the factor

TABLE 3.14

Second Order Factors for the DES + A and Other Forms of the DES

	Factor I	Factor II	Factor III
DES + A (51 items) 1970; $N = 297$	.62 Interest −.58 Enjoyment	.77 Distress–Guilt + Anxiety .72 Fatigue .69 Anger–Disgust–Contempt .61 Fear + Anxiety .54 Surprise	.58 Shyness
DES (72 items) 1969; $N = 823$	.50 Interest .79 Contempt .64 Anger–Disgust–Contempt	.79 Distress .49 Disgust .78 Fear .62 Surprise	.67 Shyness .68 Guilt .66 Enjoyment .51 Fatigue (a) .48 Fatigue (b)
DES (72 items) 1969; $N = 1189$	.61 Interest .77 Enjoyment	.74 Fear–Distress .75 Guilt .63 Anger–Disgust–Contempt .58 Surprise	.58 Shyness .57 Fatigue .75 Mixed
DES (67 items) 1968; $N = 622$	−.77 Interest −.76 Enjoyment .64 Fatigue .52 Mixed	.79 Distress .64 Guilt .83 Fear .76 Shyness	.79 Contempt .77 Anger–Disgust–Contempt .58 Surprise

representing distress were elevated, but so were their scores on the factor representing anger–disgust–contempt and on the factor representing surprise. The picture was similar for the other emotion situations. (It is interesting to note, as shown in Table 3.12, that the nonemotional factor representing fatigue had its highest mean in the distress situation. Clinically, sad or bereaved clients often appear fatigued, and there is a similar loss of muscle tone in certain types of depression and fatigue.)

The question arises as to whether or not the patterns or profiles of emotion factor scores vary significantly among the imagined or visualized situations: This question was answered by a series of three way (subjects x DES + A factor scores x situations) analyses of variance. Using the factor structure derived from the data of the 297 subjects visualizing the anxiety situation, we obtained for each individual in each situation eight factor scores, seven factors representing emotions and one representing fatigue. (Raw scores were converted to T-scores so that factors containing different numbers of items would be comparable. The mean factor scores for the different emotion situations were presented in Table 3.12). First, a separate analysis of variance compared the profile of emotions in each of the emotion situations with the anxiety situation. One of these analyses, the one comparing the anxiety situation with the fear situation, is presented in Table 3.15. The variance due to factors was significant at the .02 level. The variance attributable to situation approached significance at the .05 level; the variance for situations was attentuated since all factor means from the anxiety situation tended to approach 50, the T-score value assigned the factor means of the total sample in the anxiety situation.

The term of greatest importance, the interaction of factors by situations (A x B), was highly significant. This F-ratio indicates that the pattern of scores on the several emotion factors was quite different for the fear situation and for

TABLE 3.15

Subjects x DES + A Factor Scores x Situations Analysis of Variance: Anxiety Situation versus Fear Situation

Source	*df*	*MS*	*F*	*p*
Subjects	37	392.4863		
DES + A Factors	7	242.7143	2.3434	.0243
Situations (B)	1	334.0000	3.6846	.0596
A x B	7	237.2857	3.6134	.0013
A x subjects	259	103.5753		
B x subjects	37	90.6486		
A x B x subjects	259	65.6680		
	607	107.7496		

the anxiety situation. The factors by situation (A x B) interaction was significant in every comparison between the anxiety situation and a discrete emotion situation. Remember, when the anxiety scores based on the STAI items of the DES + A were compared for the anxiety situation and the fear, guilt, and distress situations, there were no significant differences. There was a significant difference for anxiety scores only between the anxiety situation and the shyness situation. However, when we compared the pattern of factor scores from the anxiety situation and each of the emotion situations we got consistent and highly significant differences in every instance.

In addition to the comparisons between the anxiety situation and each of the fundamental emotion situations, we did an overall analysis which compares the emotion factor profiles, considering all emotions situations at once. This analysis is presented in Table 3.16. As shown in the table, the variance due to situations and the variance due to emotions were both highly significant. Again, the term of greatest importance, the interaction of situations by factors, was also highly significant. The comparisons of the profiles of factor scores between all possible pairs of discrete emotion situations will be the subject of a later work.

In reviewing our thinking and research on patterns of emotions or factor profiles, two important points emerge. In the first place, it appears from the data in Table 3.12 that when subjects visualize or imagine a situation which they perceive as most closely related to a particular fundamental emotion such as fear or guilt, they not only experience an elevation in the particular emotion of fear or guilt but in other emotions which are functionally or dynamically related to it and which frequently interact with it. Further, as demonstrated by the analyses presented in Tables 3.15 and 3.16, the patterns of emotions or factor profiles tend to vary significantly and in a logically consistent fashion from situation to situation.

TABLE 3.16

Analysis of Variance of Emotions (DES + A Factor Scores) Considering All Emotion Situations at Once

Source	*df*	*MS*	*F*	*p*
Subjects	193	212.222		
Situations	4	932.547	4.7343	.0015
Between error	189	196.977		
Within subjects	1358	123.760		
Emotion (DES + A) Factors	7	1863.161	24.7431	.0000
Situations x Emotion Factors	28	1978.627	26.2765	.0000
Within error	1323	75.300		
	1551	134.768		

Patterns of Emotions in a Highly Threatening Real-Life Situation

The study using the 72-item DES to analyze the emotions involved in black–white encounters characterized by race prejudice was extended to a predominantly black institution, Jackson State College, during a highly stressful and threatening time. (The original study, discussed on pp. 80–81, was conducted in February, 1970, at predominantly black institutions in Nashville, Fisk and Tennessee State Universities, during a normal time.) The experiment was conducted in Jackson on June 30, 1970, after the May 14th police–student encounter which resulted in the killing of two students and the injury of more than ten other students.

Some students were still very much concerned over the May 14th incident. Student rallies and rap sessions focusing on the event and how to deal with it were being held periodically. The content and atmosphere of these meetings and material obtained in interviews with individual students suggested that mean scores would be elevated for certain emotions—the emotions associated with a highly threatening situation. In particular, I expected that the Jackson State students would have higher means on some of the DES factors representing the emotions related to the concept of anxiety—fear, distress, shame (including shyness and guilt), and interest. I also expected that the recent tragedy on the Jackson State campus would result in significant Cities x Situations interactions for the emotions of anxiety, with the Jackson students' scores on the most recent situation yielding higher means than those of black college students in Nashville.

A two-way (cities, situations) analysis of variance was performed for each of the seven emotion-factors and for the nonemotional factor of fatigue. An example of these eight analyses of variance, that for the fear–distress factor, is presented in Table 3.17.

TABLE 3.17
Two-Way Analysis of Variance (Cities, Situations) for the Fear-Distress Factor Scores

Source	*df*	*MS*	*F*	*p*
Subjects	270	158.821		
Cities	1	2843.188	19.1021	.0001
Between error	269	148.842		
Within subjects	542	52.584		
Situations	2	2610.312	62.1801	.0000
Cities x situations	2	347.447	8.2765	.0005
Within error	538	41.980		
	812	87.909		

I shall summarize the results most relevant to the present work and reserve the detailed presentation of the findings for a later work.

The statistical analyses confirmed the expectation that some of the factors representing the emotions related to the concept of anxiety would be elevated. The means for the Jackson students were higher than those for the Nashville students on all but one of the hypothesized emotions, that for shyness, on which the two group means were about the same. Jackson students had a higher mean on interest, though the difference considered separately was not statistically significant ($p = .20$). The means of the Jackson State students were significantly higher on fear–distress ($p = .0001$), and on guilt ($p = .0048$). The Jackson and Nashville students were different on only one other emotion-factor; Jackson students were significantly higher on surprise ($p = .0039$), an emotion which may be dynamically related to fear.

The high mean on the fear–distress factor is readily understood. Many students continued to fear for their lives; this was particularly true for a sizable number who, at the time the study was conducted, were participating in a boycott of white businesses on the main street of Jackson. Most students were afraid that anything they did which could be interpreted as a sign of disorder would result in another police invasion of the campus and more deaths. Of course, they were also distressed and saddened by the death of their fellow students. Many felt helpless to do anything about what they saw as unprovoked and needless killings.

The high mean on guilt may not appear so immediately understandable, but there are several reasonable explanations in terms of emotion–emotion interactions and the actual events. Some students reported in interviews with the author that they were ashamed that they were scared. Many students may well have felt guilty about leaving campus after the official closing of the college immediately after the tragedy, though few could see a feasible alternative. Only about ten students remained on campus and on the "case." Most of these became members of the Committee of Concerned Students, and in some of the rallies they made speeches which unequivocally placed blame on their fellow students for running scared and leaving the scene.

The analyses also tended to confirm the expectation of significant cities x situations interactions, with higher DES factor means for Jackson students responding to their most recent black–white prejudice encounter. These interactions were significant in the analyses for fear–distress, guilt, interest, and surprise. For each of these four analyses, the Duncan range test indicated that Jackson students had significantly higher means for the most recent situation than did the Nashville students. The meaningfulness of this finding is increased by the fact that in the free-response descriptions of the most recent situation, approximately one-third of the Jackson State students described the tragic night of May 14th when white police fired upon them, killing two and seriously injuring several others.

There is the possibility that some of the differences between Jackson and Nashville black students for the most recent encounter could be attributed to regional socio-cultural differences (deep south versus border state) or to time of testing (winter versus summer). If these possible sources of uncontrolled variance were responsible for these differences, there should be as many differences for the hypothetical situation as for the most recent encounter. These are comparable situations in that both involve experiences at the same age level, young adulthood. However, for the hypothetical (experimenter-defined) situation, there were no significant differences between Jackson and Nashville students. This does not mean that there are no important socio-cultural differences for the regions represented by the two groups of students. There probably are some and it is reasonable to expect their influence to be greater in childhood than in adulthood, and somewhat more repressive for Jackson students, most of whom come from rural Mississippi or elsewhere in the deep South. The results confirmed this expectation. For the earliest encounter, Jackson students had significantly higher mean scores on the factors representing fear–distress and guilt.

Summary and Conclusions

The theory presented in this chapter defines anxiety as a variable combination of fear and two or more of the fundamental emotions of distress, anger, shame (including shyness and guilt), and interest–excitement. In different persons and in different situations, anxiety may be any combination of these fundamental emotions and they may exist and interact at any level of intensity. Anxiety is always a complex of fundamental emotions and their interactions. It cannot be adequately conceptualized and understood or effectively assessed and treated when considered as a unitary concept.

The theory was supported by a substantive analysis of anxiety definitions in the literature. Many of these definitions, ranging from those of Freud to those of the most contemporary theorists and investigators, clearly connoted two or more of the fundamental emotions hypothesized as possible components of anxiety.

I compared my theory of differential emotion patterns with three versions of a cognitive theory of emotion and anxiety. The contrast is between a theory that explains certain key processes of personality and human functioning on the basis of the patterning and interactions of fundamental emotions and a theory that uses cognitive processes to explain behavior, including emotional responses. The crucial questions for the two approaches are these: Are our thoughts and actions determined more by what we know (perceptual data or information), or by how we feel (emotion or, typically, a pattern of emotions)? Are the dynamic and functional relationships between cognition and behavior more fundamental than those between the emotions and behavior?

A crucial deficiency in cognitive theory is its failure to explain the highly important and ever-present phenomena of selectivity and purposiveness or directionality in perceptual-cognitive functioning. I maintain that the person's pattern of emotions subserves selective perception and cognition, with the emotion of interest–excitement normally playing a critical role. An emotion or pattern of emotions may be activated or changed as a function of numerous intra-person, social, and person-environment processes.

Following a Thomistic-rationalistic ideology, cognitive theory views perceptual and thought processes as the key determinants of behavior, including emotional behavior. Thus, emotion is viewed as response, often unwanted response, to a troublesome and undesirable stimulus. The emphasis is on the maladaptive–maladjustive emotional response to stressful and frustrating stimuli. This line of reasoning is taken to its logical extreme by Lazarus and Averill who view emotion as a syndrome analogous to a disease process. In virtually complete opposition, I see the emotions as the most important motivating and meaningful experiences of human life, and as having inherently adaptive functions.

I believe the differences between differential emotion theory and cognitive theory have implications of great importance to future developments in this area. The single most important implication relates to the place of emotion in the science of man. Generally, cognitive theory relegates it to a relatively insignificant role. In contrast, I see emotion as crucially important in providing motivation and guidance for critical aspects of personality, interpersonal, and intergroup functioning.

The empirical studies yielded additional support for the theory. "Anxiety words" loaded on emotion factors representing the fundamental emotions that constitute anxiety. A modified standard anxiety scale failed to differentiate between an anxiety situation and the emotion situations of fear, guilt, and distress. In contrast, the patterns or profiles of emotions derived from the Differential Emotion Scale were significantly different for the anxiety situation and each of the emotion situations.

The 72 item Differential Emotion Scale was administered to Jackson State College Students during a highly stressful and threatening time. The resulting pattern of emotions or DES emotion profile was quite close to what was expected under the prevailing conditions. Most of the factors related to the concept of anxiety had elevated means. These high means, particularly those for the fear–distress and guilt factors, were apparently quite consistent with independently reported experiences and with actual events.

A particular individual in a particular situation typically experiences more than one emotion, interactions among emotions, and emotion components. To name these intra-personal processes "anxiety" probably leads to more difficulties than solutions. This is particularly so if anxiety is viewed as a unitary concept and the operations used to measure the intra-personal processes take on the nature of unidimensional measures. The scientific usefulness of the term anxiety has been rendered highly questionable. To use it intelligently we need to have certain understandings about its complexities and its constituents. Each time we use the term we shall need a series of subscripts or qualifications specifying the qualities and intensities and probable interactions of the constituent fundamental emotions.

It is certainly premature to propose a conceptual and measurement panacea. However, I believe we can move forward in the development of a science of emotions and behavior with emphasis on the person and interpersonal and intergroup relations, if we use a framework like differential emotion theory and instruments like the Differential Emotion Scale to search for patterns or profiles of emotions that characterize human experience.

References

Allport, F. H. *Social psychology.* Cambridge, Massachusetts: Houghton–Mifflin, 1924.

Aquinas, St. T. *Summa theologica.* Transl. by A. C. Pegis. New York: Random House, 1948. (Written circa 1266).

Averill, J. R. Grief: its nature and significance. *Psychological Bulletin,* 1968, **70,** 721–748.

Averill, J. R., Opton, E. M., Jr., & Lazarus, R. S. Cross-cultural studies of psychophysiological responses during stress and emotion. *International Journal of Psychology,* 1969, **4,** 83–102.

Basowitz, H., Persky, H., Korchin, S. J., & Grinker, R. R., Sr. *Anxiety and stress.* New York: McGraw–Hill, 1955.

Cattell, R. B. Anxiety and motivation: Theory and crucial experiments. In C. D. Spielberger (Ed.), *Anxiety and behavior.* New York: Academic Press, 1966. Pp. 23–62.

Cattell, R. B., & Scheier, I. H. *The meaning and measurement of neuroticism and anxiety.* New York: Ronald Press, 1961.

Darwin, C. *The expression of the emotions in man and animals* (with a preface by Konrad Lorenz). Chicago: The University of Chicago Press, 1965. (First edition, 1872).

Ekman, P., Sorenson, E. R., & Friesen, W. V. Pan-cultural elements in facial displays of emotion. *Science,* 1969, **164,** 86–88.

Epstein, S. The nature of anxiety with emphasis upon its relationship to expectancy. Chapter 5, this volume.

Freud, S. *Introductory lectures on psychoanalysis.* London: Hogarth Press, 1917.

Gelhorn, E. Motion and emotion: The role of proprioception in the physiology and pathology of the emotions. *Psychological Review,* 1964, **71**(6), 457–472.

Gottschalk, L. A., & Gleser, G. C. *The measurement of psychological states through the content analysis of verbal behavior.* Los Angeles, California: University of California Press, 1969.

Grinker, R. R., Sr., & Spiegel, J. P. *Men under stress.* Philadelphia, Pennsylvania: Blakiston, 1945. [New York: McGraw–Hill, 1963 (paperback).]

Hamburg, D. A. Emotions in the perspective of human evolution. In P. H. Knapp (Ed.), *Expression of emotions in man.* New York: International Universities Press, 1963. Pp. 300–317.

Izard, C. E. The emotions and emotion concepts in personality and culture research. In R. B. Cattell & R. M. Dreger (Eds.), *Handbook of modern personality theory.* In preparation.

Izard, C. E. On understanding and promoting human effectiveness. *The Human Context,* 1970, in press.

Izard, C. E. *Patterns of emotions.* New York: Academic Press, in press.

Izard, C. E. *The face of emotion.* New York: Appleton–Century–Crofts, 1971.

Izard, C. E. *Differential Emotion Scale.* Unpublished test, Vanderbilt University, 1968.

Izard, C. E., Chappell, J. E., & Weaver, F. Fundamental emotions involved in black–white encounters characterized by race prejudice. *Proceedings, 78th Annual Convention,* APA, 1970.

Izard, C. E., & Tomkins, S. S. Affect and behavior: Anxiety as a negative affect. In C. D. Spielberger (Ed.), *Anxiety and behavior.* New York: Academic Press, 1966. Pp. 81–125.

Izard, C. E., Wehmer, G. M., Livsey, W., & Jennings, J. R. Affect, awareness, and performance. In S. S. Tomkins & C. E. Izard (Eds.), *Affect, cognition, and personality.* New York: Springer, 1965. Pp. 2–41.

Janis, I. L. Part one, stress and frustration. In I. L. Janis, G. F. Mahl, J. Kagan, & R. R. Holt (Eds.), *Personality: Dynamics, development, and assessment.* New York: Harcourt, Bruce & World, 1969.

Jolly, A. Lemur social behavior and primate intelligence. *Science,* 1966, **153,** 501–506.

Katz, P. K., & Zigler, P. K. Self-image disparity: A developmental approach. *Journal of Personality and Social Psychology,* 1967, **5**(2), 186–195.

Kierkegaard, S. *The concept of dread.* Transl. by W. Lowrie. Princeton, New Jersey: Princeton University Press, 1944. (Originally published in Danish, 1844.)

Lazarus, R. S. *Psychological stress and the coping process.* New York: McGraw–Hill, 1966.

Lazarus, R. S., & Averill, J. R. Emotion and cognition: With special reference to anxiety. Chapter 4, this volume.

Levitt, E. E. *The psychology of anxiety.* Indianapolis, Indiana: Bobbs–Merrill, 1967.

Maher, B. A. *Principles of psychopathology.* New York: McGraw–Hill, 1966.

Mallama, A. D. Substantive definitions and descriptions of anxiety. Unpublished manuscript, Vanderbilt University, 1970.

Malmo, R. B. Studies of anxiety: Some clinical origins of the activation concept. In C. D. Spielberger (Ed.), *Anxiety and behavior.* New York: Academic Press, 1966. Pp. 157–177.

May, R. *The meaning of anxiety.* New York: Ronald Press, 1950.

Mosher, D. L. Differential influence of guilt on the verbal operant conditioning of hostile and "superego" verbs. *Journal of Consulting Psychology,* 1966, **30**(3), 280.

Nowlis, V. Research with the mood adjective check list. In S. S. Tomkins & C. E. Izard (Eds.), *Affect, cognition, and personality.* New York: Springer, 1965. Pp. 352–389.

Plutchik, R. *The emotions: Facts, theories, and a new model.* New York: Random House, 1962.

Pribram, K. H. Emotion: Steps toward a neuropsychological theory. In D. C. Glass (Ed.), *Neurophysiology and emotion.* New York: Rockefeller University Press, 1967. Pp. 3–40.

Sarason, I. G. Anxious words. Review of C. D. Spielberger (Ed.), *Anxiety and behavior. Contemporary Psychology,* 1967, **12**(12), 601–602.

Sarason, S. B. The measurement of anxiety in children: Some questions and problems. In C. D. Spielberger (Ed.), *Anxiety and behavior.* New York: Academic Press, 1966. Pp. 63–79.

Sarason, S. B., Davidson, K. S., Lighthall, F. F., Waite, R. R., & Ruebush, B. K. *Anxiety in elementary school children.* New York: Wiley, 1960.

Schacter, S. S. The interaction of cognitive and physiological determinants of emotional state. In L. Berkowitz (Ed.), *Advances in experimental social psychology,* Vol. 1. New York: Academic Press, 1964. Pp. 49–81.

Snyder, C. R., & Katahn, M. The relationship of state anxiety, feedback, and ongoing self-reported affect to performance in complex verbal learning. *American Journal of Psychology,* 1970, **83,** 237–247.

Spielberger, C. D. Theory and research on anxiety. In C. D. Spielberger (Ed.), *Anxiety and behavior.* New York: Academic Press, 1966. Pp. 3–20.

Spielberger, C. D., Gorsuch, R. L., & Lushene, R. L. *State Trait Anxiety Inventory Test manual for Form X.* Palo Alto: Consulting Psychologists Press, 1970.

Spence, J. T., & Spence, K. W. The motivational components of manifest anxiety: Drive and drive stimuli. In C. D. Spielberger (Ed.), *Anxiety and behavior.* New York: Academic Press, 1966. Pp. 291–326.

Sprague, J. M., Chambers, W. W., & Stellar, E. Attentive, affective, and adaptive behavior in the cat. *Science,* 1961, **133,** 165–173.

Sullivan, H. S. *The interpersonal theory of psychiatry.* New York: Norton, 1953.

Tomkins, S. S. Affect as the primary motivational system. In M. Arnold (Ed.), *Feelings and emotions.* New York: Academic Press, 1970. Pp. 101–110.

Tomkins, S. S. *Affect, imagery, consciousness.* Vol. I. *The positive affects.* New York: Springer, 1962.

Unger, S. M. On the development of guilt reactivity in the child. Doctoral paper, Cornell University, 1962. (Courtesy of Dr. R. Gorsuch, Peabody College.)

Wolpe, J. The conditioning and deconditioning of neurotic anxiety. In C. D. Spielberger (Ed.), *Anxiety and behavior.* New York: Academic Press, 1966. Pp. 179–190.

Zuckerman, M. The development of an affect adjective check list for the measurement of anxiety. *Journal of Consulting Psychology,* 1960, **24,** 457–462.

COMMENTS ON DR. IZARD'S PAPER

Silvan S. Tomkins

Let me say a few general things about the strategy of Izard's research. Needless to say, I believe the message in this research is of rather fundamental significance. I have felt for a long time that if we had treated drives as we now treat affects, we would have statements like, "A person had a good time last night," meaning by this to refer conjointly to a good meal and drink. Now the fact of the matter is we often do eat and drink at the same time. We do many things together and there are words in our language to indicate that totality. If we were to take such words seriously, it would lead investigators to assume that we were dealing with unitary phenomena.

The heritage of this particular word, anxiety, is somewhat paradoxical. It comes, of course, from Freud, and it reflects Freud's inadequate and incomplete analysis of affects. He had only two—aggression and anxiety. The paradox of Freud is that even anxiety, in his later work, was not an affect. It was a signal. Freud was a cognitive theorist in the anxiety domain, which is incredible considering that Freud taught us to be concerned about affects. He was the man in the twentieth century who put the finger on our feelings and, yet, conceptually he didn't recognize this, either in terms of the definition of anxiety, or in examining very carefully the range of affects. And, so, superego or conscience for Freud is intra-aggression because he only had these words. You have to kill yourselves, in a sense, in order to have a conscience in Freudian theory.

The fact that one can have contempt for himself, the fact that one can have shame for himself, the fact that one can cry about what one has done, and so on, or the fact that one can be without excitement about what one is doing, all these things have no place because the language isn't there. It's as simple as that. So I take a dim view about any systematic research based on this heritage. It is, in one sense, a bad heritage, not because we don't experience fear, we clearly do, but we also experience so many other things, both at the same time and in sequence. The word anxiety has really become an omnibus word, and that's what Cal's message is, and I think his research provides some support for this view.

Now there are some special reasons, I believe, for this kind of confusion. One of them is that you can have fear about other affects, not only about other objects. You can be afraid of automobiles, you can be afraid of men, or women, or children, and you can also be afraid of any other feeling or set of feelings. Indeed, as you know, you can become afraid of having the experience of fear and will do anything in order to avoid this. But you can also be terribly afraid of the contempt of others. People go to their death on the battle field so that they won't experience the imputation of cowardice. That's fear about the contempt of the other, because one has shown fear.

Now, there are two points here. One is that you can be afraid of any other affect and these tend to coalesce so that the experience you have is not simply fear. It is fear, for example, lest you lose control of your anger, fear lest you show sexual excitement, fear lest you become disgusted at your own behavior. An obsessive is afraid lest he do something unclean. These affective mixtures are felt usually as a package. They are pretty hard to pull apart, and that's why anxiety scales are always mixing things up. In one sense, they are being faithful to the nature of our experience, but there are two questions to be raised here. One is the nature of our experience and the other is what our theoretical posture should be.

There is no question but that fear is a very flexible response which may accompany, precede, or follow any experience. It can either be sequential or simultaneous, and that's another source of confusion. We may be afraid that we will get more afraid, or that we will feel distressed, or that we will feel excitement if we happen to be puritanically raised. That's one kind of fear.

The other kind of fear is the one that is experienced simultaneously with some other affect. This is a different kind of fear and will be experienced differently than one where the fear is sequential. If the sequence is stretched out in time, it can very easily happen that we get what is sometimes called anxiety, namely, what is called objectless fear. What we are afraid of right now we don't know. There is something we're afraid of, but we don't know it because that sequence has been pulled apart, and we intend to pull it apart and keep it apart as long as possible because even though we pay a price in present fear, or anxiety, what we are afraid of appears to be even worse.

Now, let me give you another example of a concept that has similar properties, that doesn't arise from Freud, and which I think illustrates the kinds of problems we face here. That is the concept of depression. It has never been adequately conceptualized, at least from my point of view, in an affect way. What is a person like who is depressed? We all know what that word means. We've all been depressed, we've seen others depressed. But the fact of the matter is that the word is used just as anxiety is used.

I submit that depression has three components which can be readily pulled apart and shown to vary in exactly the same way that Cal is talking about here. One is the distress response. A depressed person, among other things, may weep a lot. He may cry. Or if he doesn't cry, his mouth is turned down and he looks sad. If you show his picture to anyone they will say he looks sad. That's one thing. Quite orthogonal to this is the shame response. He hangs his head and casts his eyes down. This is quite separate from sadness. One can be ashamed without being sad and one can be sad without being ashamed. In depression, however, they often go together. Third, in depression, there is also contempt or disgust. You look at the face of a depressed person and he looks like he is smelling something bad. The world is sour for him. It leaves a bad taste in his mouth. That's also in depression. It varies, it comes, and it goes.

Finally, there is what I call a reduction in amplification–what others might call a reduction in energy. Objective evidence through moving pictures shows that the depressive, if you take a picture of him when he walks, or talks, or uses his hands or arms, does so with reduced amplitude. His energy is down. It's as though he is walking in his sleep. That's part of being depressed. Now if you're talking about agitated depression, you have to add fear to this complex. And it can get to be quite a complicated thing.

Depression is much like anxiety in its structure in that these components go up and down. They can also be felt at the same time, and although such a combination is a perfectly real phenomenon, that doesn't mean we shouldn't be analytic about it. Some depressions have more of one component than another, and that is the argument that is being made here by Dr. Izard. And I am in sympathy with him. What I am not so much in sympathy with is the limitation upon our posture which I think Cal's position partly imposes on us. If what I have said is true, you would have to expand that list and talk about components where the major negative affects have very little fear in them, and yet there would be scales that would properly be regarded as having something to do with anxiety. Let me give you a rather trivial example. You and I cross the street every day. Are we afraid when we cross the street? You say no, and I agree with you. Most of us don't have a panic every time we cross the street. Yet if we step out into the street, or we see somebody take a step out into the street, especially a child of ours, and we see a car coming, suddenly there is a panic.

This is "as if" behavior, that is, behavior whose history originally involved massive affect, usually fear, fear of being killed by an automobile. But we have learned techniques sufficiently skilled so that it squeezes that affect out of that total complex, only to reemerge if certain conditions are now seen as stressing the adequacy of our avoidance response. If we thought it was safe and we moved out into the street, and there is a car suddenly that we didn't see, we are quite anxious. We are always prepared for this anxiety response. It is not, as Richard Solomon has suggested, "conserved." I think it is better to say it is an "as if" organization in which there is a potential for the reemergence of the original affect which was used to create the highly skilled successful avoidance of anxiety.

So I am arguing that perhaps we might give thought to a more radical suggestion than Cal is making. We might be better off in the long run if we didn't insist that anxiety is a finite, definable entity. However, I do think that these components that Cal talked about can be found in one or another scale as he had demonstrated. Should we be governed by the heritage of Freud, by the heritage of phenomenology, and by the heritage of investigation over a long number of years, is the question I am raising. In the long run, will this be as profitable as naming more specifically and precisely what it is that we are involved in? In drive research, for example, it would be better if we said even though a person can eat and drink at the same time, it would be important to be clear about the fact that he can also drink separately and eat separately. There are also special appetites when just any old food won't do. These are physiologically known to be quite specific and we will find the same specificity in the affect domain if we look.

With regard to Cal's data on the responsiveness of blacks to fear, we have some interesting evidence which was produced by Burt Karon in a study using my representative sample on the PAT, plus a rather large sample from a rural southern community. This was quite a large sample, and indicated, back in 1955, that the black community was struggling with the fear of loss of control of anger, indicating that this concern is not all that recent. No one believed this evidence then but I believe that it was very substantial. The sample certainly was very adequate.

On the matter of shame–guilt, I don't have a doubt in my mind that the empirical findings are as Cal described them. There is no question that the feeling of guilt feels different from the feeling of shame. I have no doubt about that at all. The only question I have concerns whether these two phenomenologically different things should be called different fundamental emotions.

I argue against this on the grounds that we are dealing with a difference in a set of other things in which the same affect is coassembled. I would not make a distinction, for example, between fear and anxiety. If you are afraid of snakes and you have free-floating anxiety, I cannot believe that the nervous system is endowed with a set of mechanisms which have evolved in order to permit the luxury of feeling afraid of snakes on the one hand or girls, or free-floating anxiety on the other. I cannot believe that it is anything but the same affective mechanism, the same response, but coassembled with quite different things.

To take a very simple example, consider anorexia, the loss of appetite or fear of the consequences of eating, and bulemia, the fear of the consequences of over-eating. Now these go in exactly opposite directions. In one instance the patient starves to death because he is afraid to eat. In the other case he kills himself by overeating, because he is afraid of starving to death. I can't believe that a different affect is involved in these two cases. It may be, but biologically it seems to me it would have been extremely wasteful for any organism to evolve in such a way so that every time one of these very high powered response mechanisms was triggered, it had to be triggered differently for every other thing that went on at that time.

I could make up a test that would show just as clearly, I believe, that shyness is quite different from shame, and that both are quite different from the kind of discouragement you feel when you have been working and working and you hang your head down and say "I'm beat, I can't do it, I'm discouraged." Discouragement is not felt the same way as shyness, but I am suggesting that it is basically the same response. It is a simple reduction in excitement which is symbolized in man by the lowering of the eyelids, the lowering of the head. Indeed, it is not just found in man. If you talk in a way your dog doesn't like, he will also hang his head.

This concept has been extremely difficult for psychologists to take very seriously, and I don't quite know why. It seems very evident to me that one should be as parsimonious as possible in postulating fundamental mechanisms. To give an analog in the realm of taste, if I said there were sweet, sour, and salty tastebuds and you said no, there's vanilla ice cream taste buds and chocolate ice cream taste buds, I couldn't argue with you if you made up a test on which, in fact, people distinguish these. But this is a different question from evidence which would compel us to postulate these as different fundamental response mechanisms.

On the contempt anger, disgust mix-up, there was a similar problem. Cal Izard and Paul Ekman have been able to show recently that one can pose photos in such a way that the characteristic misrecognition of anger, disgust, and contempt do not occur. You have to pose them in an extremely specific way. They frequently go together, and whether they go together is to some extent class linked. That is, if as a parent I say to a child "damn it, why did you do that? I'm disgusted with you," then the affects of anger, contempt, and disgust go together. It's not very puzzling why, when you show a face that is either angry or sneering, it may be regarded as representing anger or disgust, because they have, in fact, gone together.

There is nothing to prevent any two affects from going together and being learned as a unit so that later you can't pull them apart. And that's what I think is going on here. I think that we can show that for different classes in different societies where heavy hands are laid on a child, but without an overload of disgust, people might clearly separate these affects. Or, taken the other way around, I believe that we could show that in middle class socialization, you will have disgust or contempt quite free of any mixture of anger. The typical middle class parent doesn't lay heavy hands on his child. He may say I'm ashamed of you, or I'm disgusted with you, but without hitting the child. In the lower class one might expect much more of the mixture of anger with contempt, and in some lower class families no contempt, but just anger. "You do that once again and I'll push your teeth in." Persons from such families would also be able to distinguish anger from contempt. They would not mix them up.

In conclusion, my argument is not against the study of complex affect combinations. I simply advocate a little more analytical attitude toward what's going on.

COMMENTS ON DR. IZARD'S PAPER[1]

Eugene E. Levitt

I want to talk about the question of what correlation coefficients show. Remember, the things we are dealing with are just words, like distress, or shame, or guilt. What does it mean to find that they are correlated to the extent of .20, .40, or .80? Does it mean that we are talking about two different phenomena that cofluctuate? Does it mean that we are talking about one thing which is a component of another thing? Or, finally, when the coefficient is very high (allowing for attenuation by unreliability of measures) maybe we are not actually talking about two different things at all.

[1] In the anxiety symposium, Dr. Tomkins discussed Dr. Izard's paper, and then presented his own paper entitled, "Affect Theory, the Role of the Vascular Facial Response and Its Inhibition." Dr. Levitt served as discussant for Dr. Tomkins' paper at the symposium, but spontaneously decided to comment on Izard's paper as well. It was not possible for Dr. Tomkins to edit and revise his symposium presentation in time for it to be included in this volume. Consequently, Levitt's comments have been edited and discussion pertaining exclusively to Tomkins' paper has been eliminated.

Remember the research on the authoritarian personality in which the correlations ran around .80 between the *E* and *F* Scales. The question is, do you have two different factors, one of which is called "ethnocentrism" and the other, "fascism?" The answer to this question involves nonstatistical considerations. Take the factor loadings that Izard has presented. In themselves they do not demonstrate that guilt is part of anxiety, or that anxiety is different from guilt, or that guilt is a component of anxiety. These are interpretations that are made on the basis of value judgments regarding the size of the coefficients.

It is also important, I think, to keep in mind that words are not isomorphic with emotional states. This was a question brought up yesterday by someone in the audience after my talk. When you say to a person, look at this face, what does it show, and he says "distress," the person has applied a word and that is all that we know for sure. If someone else applies the same word it does not necessarily follow that they mean the same state. There is absolutely no way to tell whether each of you means the same thing when you say "distress" or "anxiety."

Many years ago, Allport and Odbert went through Webster's International Dictionary and found that there were 18,000 adjectives that were used to describe human characteristics. Izard used only 67 in his studies. If he had used a different set of 67, or if he had used 134, his results would very probably have indicated that there are other words that people apply to feelings. But that's still not the same as the reality of what people feel. It is well to keep in mind words and experienced feelings are not isomorphisms.

The point was raised by Izard about fears of different things. I want to go back to one of the points that Tomkins made about what Izard said. It's true that there are such things as fear of snakes, or fear of women, or fear of high places, and many other specific fears, but it is highly improbable that the body's reaction is different for each of these fears. There is almost an infinity of different phenomena that could be feared, and there is simply not enough physical reaction parameters to permit a different reaction to each one. The value of studying specific fears, of going down into micro-components, as both Tomkins and Izard suggest, remains to be demonstrated in psychological research. We do not yet know much about test anxiety, which is, after all, a major macro-anxiety.

In effect, at the present moment, Izard has a fascinating study in semantics, but not necessarily in the measurement of emotion. It remains for him to demonstrate that he can predict better by the kinds of words he uses, or by separating out components if you want to look at it that way, then can be predicted otherwise.

Chapter 4

THE NATURE AND GENESIS OF MOOD STATES: A THEORETICAL MODEL WITH EXPERIMENTAL MEASUREMENTS CONCERNING ANXIETY, DEPRESSION, AROUSAL, AND OTHER MOOD STATES

Raymond B. Cattell

Introduction

The student who is reading these pages will be more strongly concerned, and rightly so, with psychological findings rather than methodological points, which tend often to finish in dry abstractions about the philosophy of method. Nevertheless, if he has pursued the background history of the present topic at all he must have been appalled by the amount of running around in circles and the backtracking from apparent gains that have resulted from failure to make a sound conceptual and therefore operational distinction between anxiety, depression, effort stress, arousal, etc. Along with this has gone the perennial and age old tendency of excited theorists to theorize without due statement regarding the behavioral referents by which their theories may be tested.

It is an unhappy state of affairs, and yet the student will save himself much discouragement if he watches for the hallmarks of good method in the contributions he reads, and builds his thinking only on a firm basis. Furthermore, despite his eagerness to get to psychological conclusions, I am suggesting in the present chapter that he patiently give thought to abstract issues of method and conception before he begins to draw conclusions about the data. For example, there is talk about anxiety as a trait and anxiety as a state, but except for Spielberger, Beck, Sarason, Lazarus, and one or two others, it must be bluntly said that some contributors to this volume have either ignored the question, or discussed it without any reference to the need for a precise model which has concerned the third section (p. 138) of this chapter.

In this and the previous volume on anxiety it has been Dr. Spielberger's laudable but difficult aim to get diversified leading contributors to the field (1) to interact on their methodological standards, and (2) to attempt replication of experimental results across different laboratories. The latter is difficult, for research support is short, and it is only right and proper that each investigator should pursue his own line of development so long as it is rewarding in terms of consistent results. But the first is not an unreasonable demand, and it is precisely here that the student sees the field cut in two by an academic wall, the reality of which is hard to believe unless one knows something of research history and present teaching practices. I refer to the difference of methodological standards between the traditional bivariate and newer multivariate experimental methods.

To grasp the full significance of this the student must be referred to a comparison of the *Handbook of Multivariate Experimental Psychology* and the *Handbook of Experimental Psychology* (which was titled before consciousness of the need for the adjective "bivariate" was born). But within the present domain we may recognize that in dealing with the question "What is anxiety?" the bivariate experimenter takes a measure, say "low electrical skin resistance" and another, say, "pulse rate," and tries to show by analysis of variance that they are jointly expressions of what he theorizes as "anxiety." The multivariate experimenter, on the other hand, takes perhaps twenty variables that people have suspected to be measures of anxiety (such as are shown in Tables 3.2 and 3.3) and by correlating and factoring them, discovers whether a single general factor *or* two or three distinct conceptual influences underly them. The multivariate approach has at least three advantages:

1. It is more economical and likely to be thoroughly executed. Twenty variables require $20 \times 19/2 = 190$ separate paired experiments by the bivariate experimenter to cover the same evidence, and the simple historical answer is that he does not cover them.

2. Neither analysis of variance nor correlation in successive pairs will answer the question of whether a unitary concept or a cluster of concepts are required,

but factor analysis will deliver us firm unitary concepts on which to proceed to good manipulative experiment.

3. Experimenters sometimes talk as if concepts were pulled out of thin air. It is unfortunately true that a lot of bivariate concepts are pulled out of verbal air. But concepts that avoid the staggering infantile death rate of verbal concepts (Darwin's evolutionary concept would be a multivariate case in point) are based on multivariate observations. One should not be deceived by the writer's claim that he has a right to start with any theory. A man has a right to jump out of an airplane, but the wiser one will take careful account of all available aerodynamic information about parachutes.

The best basis for a theory of anxiety, for example, as developed below, is a precise factor pattern description of all the known affected variables, and of how much their variance is so affected. Actually many bivariate studies do not even define anxiety or arousal by as much as two variables. They start, as in Epstein's chapter, with the assumption that what Epstein calls arousal is measured by high skin conductance (low resistance), and then proceed to make generalizations about the course (the plot) of arousal, in relation to this and that, from this single measurement. It is not surprising that curious anomalies occur when these results are compared with others in which the same or a different experimenter relates "arousal" to something using pulse rate as a measure of arousal.

The fact is that both skin conductance and pulse are determined about as much by anxiety and effort stress as they are by arousal, so that the error in estimating arousal is systematic, not random, that is, results could just as easily be due to effort stress. To measure arousal it is necessary (Tables 3.9 and 3.10) to measure at least half a dozen and preferably ten different subtests, just as we measure intelligence by several different subtests. When this is done, a precise validity coefficient can be worked out for the measurement against the factor concept. Moreover, the wider basis is, of course, the true foundation from which the essence of the theoretical concept is derived.

If the bivariately trained experimenter were called upon to do all the basic and complex factor analytic work himself before beginning his manipulative type of experiment one could sympathize with, if not condone, his attempt to "beat the gun," methodologically. But the fact is, as set out below, that twenty-five years of painstaking multivariate experiment and attention to all kinds of methodological advances in factor analysis have long made available (1) replicated, checked, uniquely-determined, state-expression factors as a firm basis on which to develop theory, and (2) batteries or scales of determinable validity for as many as half-a-dozen distinct concepts (Nesselroade, 1971; Cattell & Scheier, 1961; Cattell, 1971).

The more the school-uninvolved psychologist looks at this situation, the more palpable becomes this academic wall, which, like the Berlin wall, severs what should be a common, functional road system. And the more credible, if not creditable, becomes the initially incredible situation.[1] The root of the problem is actually a very simple one. Only perhaps ten percent of American university psychology graduate departments require that graduate students learn multivariate factor analytic techniques as well as analysis of variance, designed for the traditional experimenter. Both are obviously essential, and for the psychologist who has to deal with patterns as his central concepts, the factor analytic understanding is absolutely indispensable.[2] However, the stale past is perpetuated in a changing world because teachers tend to teach what they were taught. In the country of the blind the one-eyed man is certainly still king, and the two-eyed man is an unfortunate deviate best kept beyond the wall.

The rest is clinical. If students are brought up unfamiliar with a methodology (somewhat difficult to learn later, on their own) they will find reasons for not learning it later, which will consist in "profound doubts as to its advisability." For example, despite evidence that linear analyses will sufficiently approximate curvilinear ones, they claim to reject factor analysis because it is linear, or because "You can only get out relations among what variables you put in it," (fortunately for our sanity, this is true of all experiments) or because "factor patterns change with age, and time of measurement, so that what is positively correlated at one time is negatively related at another," (this is what factor analysis and any other method is interested to find out). And so, ad infinitum. Multivariate methods like any others have their known limitations. Inapplicability to the problems here studied is not among them. The honest objection that appeared in discussion from one member of this symposium was "I simply do not have time to do a whole battery of measurements for anxiety." It is as honest as that of the European sociologist who said "Alas, I had not time to stop off and check my observations in America, but I did fly over it."

The reaction of the symposiasts to a dozen slides (in tables below) summarizing twenty years of strategically planned research on the separation of states, their unique identification and measurement, by such consistent contributors as Baggaley, Bartlett, Connor, Cross, Curran, Delhees, Hundleby, Luborsky, Nesselroade, Pawlik, Scheier, Sweney, Van Egeren and Williams, was

[1] The most systematic attempt to remedy this situation has been made in the last decade by the Society for Multivariate Experimental Psychology and its journal, *Multivariate Behavioral Research.* The former is an organization of leading psychologists devoted to broadening the methodology of experimental psychology. The latter, both in its editorials and its special substantive issues on clinical (Cattell, 1968) and other areas, has clarified the gains, especially conceptual gains, from approaching such "pattern" problems as those of state analysis through multivariate designs of experiment.

[2] This is often perceived by the enterprising graduate student who then asks in vain for a decent training in these methods in his own university.

an uneasy silence.[3] There are both successes and failures in this work, and discussion of both would be highly enlightening for the kind of manipulative experiment now being planned in our own laboratories and in those of several other symposiasts. Factor analytic identification is only a preliminary, though a practically indispensable preliminary, to manipulative and often bivariate experiment. (See the *Handbook of Multivariate Experimental Psychology,* 1966, for elaboration of this general strategy.) Both eyes have to be used.

If there are any systematic errors in this taxonomic ground work they should be attacked forthwhile. In the appropriate sections below I propose to indicate what may in fact be considered the strong and the weak points of the present definition of states–the points where we have far more definite concepts and measurements than many investigators are availing themselves of, and the points where decidedly more systematic research is still needed. The former I propose to state as clearly, unambiguously, and challengingly, as possible. It is my hope, indeed, to knock a hole in the wall that now divides these citizens of what should be a common scientific enterprise.

The plan of presentation will therefore be as follows:

1. A discussion of the conceptual status of states and traits.
2. The model for interaction of states and traits.
3. The technical procedures in separating states and traits.
4. Technical necessities in the measurement of states and traits.
5. Further developments of theory in the concepts of *liability* and *modulation.*
6. Checking the model by a systematic analysis of variance.
7. A review of findings over twenty-five years.
8. Theoretical developments and the analysis of state processes.

Thus the beginning student in this area must be encouraged to brace himself for some rather abstract discussion of methods and models before the substantive findings and the broader theoretical issues can be reached. However, he may rest assured that nothing unnecessary to the understanding of the experimental field will be dragged in as wanton pedantry.

[3] Moreover, subsequent inventions of personal concepts of arousal, anxiety, depression, etc., proceeded without help from or criticism of this massive evidence of what patterns exist in this field. (What we choose to call them can be personal and is almost irrelevant, so long as we index them and recognize their invariant identities, as scientists in other fields had the sense to do with vitamins, bacteria, etc.

That I am not altogether a voice crying in the wilderness–or at least not a voice out of touch with reality–is evidenced by comments, of which Irwin Sarason's in reviewing the last symposium volume is an expression with high fidelity: "Virtually all references to Cattell (and the work of his many associates) . . . direct one to Cattell's (present) chapter. References to Malmo (and the work of his many associates) are almost always to the pages of his chapter." (I have added what is in parentheses to convey the sense of the context.) Desegregation is obviously an urgent priority in the state study field.

The Basis for Differentiating the Concepts of States, Traits, and Trait Change Factors

Whatever particular state or trait we use as a concept it must first meet the test of unitariness. Talking about, say, a conglomerate of three different things, unevenly mixed as if they were a single pure concept, will not advance clarity of conception, as chemistry realized when it advanced from alchemy. As mentioned above, there are two experimental ways of showing that some twenty behavior manifestations belong together—the bivariate way, which is tedious, chancy, and, in the end, downright impotent for this particular purpose, and the multivariate way, which divides again into two: the finding of correlation clusters ("surface traits"), and the finding of factors ("source traits" or unitary influences). These methods are as applicable to states as to traits, for, if our theory asserts that responses a, b, g, and h, but not c, d, e, and f express state X, then the first four but not the last four should correlate positively together when measured over time, and over changing stimulus circumstances. By contrast, in a trait unity, any theory of a trait requires that the measures should correlate positively over people, that is, in terms of individual differences, and stay at a fixed level in any one individual.

Let us return to these matters with greater precision in a moment and meanwhile sketch in the context verbally. The débâcle in state measurement among those who have not paused to pursue clear models of this kind has, at last, forced a salutary recognition that a science of moods—or states as they may be more generically designated—will appear only when we examine mathematical models and evaluate them by appropriate experiment. The ruins of a Tower of Babel in state names and theories now litter the scenery; yet most of us are hopeful that behind the popular use of such terms as anxiety, arousal, depression, and so on, there exist some truly distinct and distinctly measurable entities, and some not too complex models for leading to rational ways of measuring their changes and interactions. From the history of science we have also reason to hope that if such models are found they will in turn lead to novel concepts and means of control at present beyond our ken.

One comparatively simple model, which has shown already a very satisfactory fit to the data in research over the last twenty-five years (Cattell, Cattell, & Rhymer, 1947), is that which recognizes a state by a factor pattern in what will soon be described as P-technique and dR-technique in factor analysis.

This model views the mood state as a temporarily persisting condition which is itself a response pattern to some broad ,internal or external stimulus. Operationally it is to be recognized as a set of behavioral and physiological changes coordinated in time. Since this description would also cover both a surface state, that is, an actually observed correlation cluster from correlating manifestations over time, and a source state, that is, the correlations due to a single abstracted simple structure factor, let it be said at the outset that only the source state model has proved successful in attempting to define unitary states. The reasons for abandoning the surface state have been fully set out elsewhere (Cattell, 1957a, 1966a) in regard to the exactly corresponding issue of surface traits versus source traits.

Logically tied to this choice of the source state as the true state definition is the postulate that the unitariness of the state is an innately given unitariness of response pattern (or, possibly, in cases not yet investigated, a common human pattern due to a common culture). This latter might apply particularly to the social gestures and facial expressions of mood, such as Izard (1973) has investigated. The idiosyncrasies of human learning experience may cause one and the same response pattern, such as anxiety, to be triggered in different people by different stimuli. This means that our definition of a state must rest more on the recognizable repetition of a response pattern, than on our claiming to know: "This is an anxiety stimulus," "That is a depression stimulus," and so on. In other words, the initial naming of a response state as, say, anxiety, must rest on the questionnaire items or autonomic physiological responses found in the patterns being of that character to which the term "anxiety" has traditional semantic claim. However, we must be prepared for factor analytic outcomes that will tell us there are, perhaps three or more entities where we have expected semantically to find one, that is, where the behavior is popularly covered by a single word. If that occurred we should have to designate them as anxiety I, anxiety II, etc.

This recognition of the underlying unitary factor dimension of response as the true identifier of a particular state enables us exactly to designate in turn all kinds of mixed common states, appearing as individually-experienced unique states. The composite experienced states that actually appear are thus to be considered as combinations of the pure unitary states, and what seem to the individual to be uniquely repeating state patterns are likely to be idiosyncratic habits of responding with particular mixtures of unitary states. This notion that the spectrum of human moods can be reconstituted from a limited number of primary colors is quite an old one (see McDougall's sensitive but nonfactorial analysis of "secondary emotions" into "primary instinctual emotions," 1932), but it is now in the process of being demonstrated, with location of the particular ingredient patterns.

In suggesting that an innately given pattern of simultaneous response in several behavioral and physiological manifestations is the core definition of a state, we are not overlooking that: (1) all the elements in any discovered common source state may not be innate; in a highly uniform culture certain acquired elements may be attached from an early age to the innate core, and (2) the unity of the common state response, initially most effectively recognized in cross-sectional measures of change patterns, for example, dR-technique, needs to be supplemented by longitudinal studies of process, as expanded upon in the section below (p. 127).

In this connection, it will be seen that there is no need to interpret the data, either of our own experiments or of those of Lacey and Lacey (1958), in the way that the latter have done, namely, to conclude that there are real differences of state response pattern among (1) individuals and (2) occasions of stimulation. Of course there are surface differences in the surface state pattern, but these can be resolved into source states which differ only in their differing magnitudes (not patterns) due to differences in the stimuli to which the persons are reacting, and the situations to which learning has attached the standard response. That is to say, the more economical explanation first deserving consideration is that the source states are the same, but their combinations are different (see Equation (1), p. 126). I have yet to see any experimental or statistical demonstration that anything more complicated than this is necessary.

What we may thus most briefly designate descriptively as the Source Response State, or SRS model of states, has given consistent replication over dozens of researchers over the last twenty years (see section, p. 153) for distinctive patterns for anxiety, stress, depression, arousal, fatigue, adrenergic response, and various motivation states. Some of these twenty source states have been found in questionnaire material, henceforth Q-data, some in objective and physiological measures, henceforth T-data, and some in both. Examples of state dimensions cross checked as to their appearance both in Q- and T-data are anxiety (indexed as the T : S.U.I. 9 pattern–T for objective tests, and QII-second order questionnaire factor II.1), arousal (indexed T : S.U.I. 1), three distinct depression factors, the stress response pattern (T : S.U.I. 4), and some not so well replicated as these.

The prospect of simplification so far looks good, in that the Q- and T-media of observation are increasingly converging on the same concepts, and the replication across the different methods has been carefully set out in more extensive tables from which those set out here are illustrative excerpts. However, a complication has appeared in the apparent need for a third concept, beyond those of state and trait, namely, that of a trait change pattern. This need for a further concept is now best clarified by proceeding in the next section to the more precise and less "misconstruable" mathematical statement of the general trait and state model just stated verbally.

The Expansion of the Traditional R-technique Specification Equation to Incorporate States and Trait-Change Factors

For many years psychometricians have proceeded effectively in a wide variety of prediction situations using trait scores and factor weights in linear and additive equations. As we enter on the study of states we encounter the same basic argument for the linear, additive form, namely that science should proceed with the simplest formulation of relations unless and until forced to a more complex model. Its use for states is, in short, reinforced now by its success with traits. To this relation between traits and between states we now add the assumption that the relations of traits and states are additive, and that the relation between the level of behavioral expression and the level of the state concept is approximately linear.

What precisely are the R-, dR- and P-techniques, to which only general reference has so far been made? They are the three primary experimental techniques from which additive, linear equations of the above type can be derived. In R-technique, which is the most traditional, we can study individual differences on a given occasion of measurement, resolving each of the given variables (specific behaviors) into a set of underlying predictors, arbitrary or factorial, according to mathematical choice. Here one starts with correlations among variables over people. This has long been called R-technique among factor analytic designs of experiment, and the term can appropriately cover all kinds of correlational and co-variance analysis of absolute, single occasion measures. The concept of intelligence and such measurement scales as Thurstone's primary mental abilities are products of this approach.

Second, we can measure many people each on two occasions, perhaps with some experimental influence in between, and analyze the change scores, that is, the differences of occasion one and two. This has been called differential R-technique, or dR. What one is actually factoring here are the response *change* scores. In a special development of this—the Condition-response factor design (Cattell & Scheier, 1961)—the different stimulus magnitudes and the response changes are factored together, thus handling the familiar bivariate manipulative design in multivariate terms. However, ordinary dR-technique suffices for finding the dimensions of state response change in themselves.

Third, we can take one person and measure him on the same kind and set of variables over, say, a hundred or more occasions. By factoring these correlations over time we find what coordinated patterns of state expression exist. This has been called P-technique or single person factoring. Incidentally, it is an ideal design for putting the clinician's intensive single case study approach on an objective scientific basis.

Now, although ordinary R-technique has long been used as a means of identifying traits, that is, fixed and steady structures accounting for individual differences in behavior, the little recognized fact is that such experiments must also yield states. People stand, at the given moment of measurement, at different levels on, for instance, their anxiety state response, and the immediate statistical analysis is quite incapable of distinguishing between a trait structure and this instantaneously "frozen" state, just as a person who had never seen the sea might interpret a photo of big waves as mountains. The ratio of trait to state variance could of course be increased by measuring each person several times and averaging the scores. However, the only way to knock the trait variance out altogether is to use dR or P-techniques. Since these use scores which are the differences (or deviation) of scores for each individual, whatever is stably characteristic of such individuals, that is, whatever repeats itself from occasion to occasion, cannot enter into the measurements. The dR- or P-technique domain of measurement is thus purely concerned with the process of state change—the flow of mood in response to changing occasions.

Until comparatively recently the traditional division of the variance into contributions from trait structure and state pattern factors would have been considered an adequate model. But since about 1960 evidence has been piling up in both dR- and P-techniques that among the patterns first considered to be states there are some that parallel known traits, to a quite uncanny degree, in their loading patterns. For example, (as shown in Table 4.1) corresponding to the well known extraversion–introversion trait pattern, as a second order factor in Q-data (QI), there is found in dR-analyses a state-like dimension of extraversion–introversion variation. In exact work, to escape many unwarranted elaborations in the popular conception of extraversion-versus-introversion, both the trait and state dimensions have been systematically named exvia-versus-invia, and we shall adhere to this in precise references, that is, to exvia-trait and exvia-state. As so defined operationally by the A+, F+, H−, L−, Q_2- pattern in the primaries, it has since been replicated many times in other studies.

Indeed, in every investigated instance where a known source trait has been examined by dR-technique—including even Horn's recent studies (1968) of fluid and crystallized intelligence—a change factor has been found mimicking the trait factor. Of course, this first step in analysis does not show whether the "trait change" in question represents a briefly reversible fluctuation or some steady, slighter growth through maturation and learning. That must be determined separately as discussed below.

Naturally such an absolutely regular apparent reflection of the trait rock in the lake of mood excites the suspicion that some as yet unknown artefactual statistical effect is accounting for the reproduction. As a result of an investigation to clear this issue, I pointed out two real possibilities by which a "reflection" factor could arise: (1) through a gross difference of reliability of the measurements of the same variables on the two occasions, and (2) through systematic differences of the variance on the before and after measurements on all variables involved. Although these deserve further consideration by experts, the examination of present data is reasonably convincing for the conclusion that these trait change factors are real (Cattell, 1966a). In strong support of this are the initial findings that the same "trait change" factors also appear

TABLE 4.1

Similarity of R and dR Patterns Illustrated in Q-data (for Second Stratum Factors)[a]

First-order factor	Second-order factor I; introversion–extraversion or invia–exvia			First-order factor	Second-order factor II; anxiety			First-order factor	Second-order factor III; pathemia (affectivity) versus corticalertia			First-order factor	Second-order factor IV; promethean will versus resignation		
	Adult trait	Adult state	Child trait		Adult trait	Adult state	Child trait		Adult trait	Adult state	Child trait		Adult trait	Adult state	Child trait
A–	–42	–38	–49	Q_4+	+67	+44	+44	I+	+44	+50	+19	N+	+32	+21	
F–	–40	–22	–44	O+	+60	+20	+50	N–	–37	–50		E+	+28	+52	+28
H–	–35	–12	–43	Q_3–	–53	–51	–33	A+	+28	+18	+60	Q_1+	+27	+12	
Q_2+	+32	+39	+06	C–	–49	–53	–40	Q_3–	–21	–04	–02	J–			–37
M+	+26	+36		L+	+45	+08		C–	–17	–08	–05	F+	+14	+17	+20
Q_1+	+19	+20		H–	–32	–06	–57	O+	+17	(–13)	+07	Q_3–	–01	–07	–24
L+	+14	+12		M+	+30	+18						D+	+43		+09
				Q_2+		+30						C–	–15	(+02)	–01
				D+			+43								

[a] Several studies have shown that this second order pattern of anxiety in the 16 PF holds with high constancy across other cultures (Cattell, 1965).

independently in P-technique, where these artificial effects could not possibly arise.

Accordingly, we are forced to admit to the state and trait model a third term—the trait change factor—indicating a pattern of change which parallels the pattern of trait. Elsewhere I have reasoned that the growth change in a trait might be expected on general psychological grounds to take one of two forms, according to circumstances: (1) the uniform organic growth form, in which the numerical loadings on the change factor (dR-technique) will very closely parallel those on the corresponding individual difference (P-technique) pattern, as just discussed. This would occur according to factor analytic principles where the trait has grown in a quite uniform way from zero, as a fir tree grows from a seed, that is, measures of trunk height, trunk thickness, branch length would correlate as change scores in the same pattern, as they do in individual difference scores. (2) The phased growth form, where, as in the growth of an insect or a house, different growth phases affect quite different elements. In this case, though perhaps attaining a generic resemblance, the actual parallelism of trait and trait-change loading pattern could be virtually absent. If there should exist some kind of simple, small reversible fluctuation in trait level, one would expect it to take the first or "uniform" form. The pattern of change due to trait learning and maturation, on the other hand, could be either phased or uniform. These two change or growth pattern factor entities are symbolized respectively as T_u and T_p (for "uniform" and "phased") below, with the understanding that the first will by hypothesis exactly replicate the trait pattern (except for experimental error).

The three term model (four-term if we consider *both* kinds of trait change forms) will now be as follows (omitting here and later the specific and error factors as irrelevant to present purposes):

$$a_{ijk} = \sum_{w=1}^{w=s} b_{jkw}T_{wi} + \sum_{x=1}^{x=t} b_{jkx}T_{uxi} + \sum_{y=1}^{y=u} b_{jky}T_{p\cdot yi} + \sum_{z=1}^{z=v} b_{jkz}S_{zki} \quad (1)$$

Here a_{ijk} is a measured act (response) of individual i to focal stimulus j in a background, ambient situation k, the latter being the stimulus for the mood state. T_w is any trait, S_z any state, and T_{ux} and T_{py} are any trait change factors (uniform and phased respectively). There are s traits, t uniform trait change factors, u phase trait change factors, and v states.

The b's are, as usual, behavioral indices, obtainable as factor loadings, showing how rapidly the particular response measure (sub-b indexed) changes with change in the trait or state level. Apart from the novelty of (1) introducing state and trait change terms and (2) having two subscripts, u and k, instead of one for each piece of behavior, this is the ordinary, familiar specification equation. These represent respectively the specific focal stimulus, j (to which there is only one associated response, a, so that no separate designation of the response is necessary), and the ambient stimulus situation, k, which is involved both in affecting the magnitude of the response, a_i, and, (as we shall see in the modulation theory, later,) in directly affecting the level of a state.

In passing, it should be noted that this formulation asserts that the nature of a state is to be understood both from (1) the behaviors which it directly produces, such as a physiological reaction, and by (2) the modification of behavior which it produces in reactions to familiar focal stimuli. The reaction a_{ij} of individual i to focal stimulus j is modified according to the ambient situation k_1 so that it is different from what it would be in another ambient situation, k_2, which affects the state level and the meaning of the global situation $(j + k)$. For example, the focal stimulus, j, "Hurry" in an ambient situation, k_1, "House on fire" brings quite a different response from the same remark uttered in the same house when it is not on fire (k_2).

Despite the developments in splitting the global situation into two dimensions, j and k, and in recognizing that both state and trait change factors rightly belong in the behavioral equation, the latter remains formally the same as the traditional factor specification equation. That is to say, as far as calculation is concerned (as distinct from the formal design of the experimental, data-gathering situation), we are using the usual model, succinctly expressible in matrix terms as:

$$R_v = V_{fp} R_f V'_{fp} \tag{2}$$

where R_v and R_f are the correlation matrices respectively among variables (reduced) and factors (unreduced), and V_{fp} is the factor pattern matrix. The specific signature of any state is therefore the pattern constituted by its column of loadings in the V_{fp} matrix. It is by this set of effects on a strategically chosen set of variables that we recognize each recurrence of the given state response pattern in various experiments. And it is by a weighted total of the standard scores on a subset (the salient, nonhyperplane variables) among those variables that we assign individuals their appropriate individual scores on that state at that time.

The Use of Coordinated R-, dR-, and P-technique Experiments to Effect Separation and Identification of Trait, Trait Change, and State Structures

When a series of experiments with mutually coordinated variables has replicated the main V_{fp} patterns, thus establishing the stable individualities of the patterns, the question still remains "Which of these patterns are traits and which are states?" It may seem an obvious and sufficient procedure to decide which of the V_{fp} columns express traits, on the one hand, and states or trait change factors on the other, by giving individuals their scores and waiting to see which scores remain steady and which change radically between the present and another occasion. Presumably, the stability coefficients will distribute themselves bimodally—those for traits approaching unity and those for states approaching zero—though I know of no thorough experimental check on this—and the patterns could thus be sorted into two groups. Conceivably, and this is where our model can get greater closure only through experiment, the verdict may be for a trimodal distribution according to stability coefficients. For the score on the phasic trait change factors will change from time to time, but in an orderly growth fashion that will give stabilities well above those of fluctuant states.

This procedure of examining stability coefficients of R-technique-estimated factor scores over varying time intervals and conditions certainly deserves to be followed. But, partly because of the degree of error in score estimations, a more convincing and illuminating procedure for separating states, traits, and trait change entities is to contrast the results of R-technique with the results of dR- and P-techniques. The invention of P- and dR-techniques was in fact designed to deliver such state factors in clean separation from traits.

The psychologist should perhaps be reminded that in dR-technique one measures n variables on N people, and then remeasures them on the same set of variables after environmental and internal changes have produced changes of mood. Since the difference scores between the first and second occasion by definition knock out what is trait, with the outcome as shown in Equation (3) below, factoring such differences should tell us the number and nature of the dimensions of mood change.

$$(a_{ijk_2} - a_{ijk_1}) = \sum_{x=1}^{x=t} b_{jkx} T_{u \cdot xi(k_2 - k_1)} + \sum_{y=1}^{y=u} b_{jky} T_{p \cdot yi(k_2 - k_1)} + \sum_{z=1}^{z=v} b_{jkz} S_{zi(k_2 - k_1)} \quad (3)$$

The notation in (3) is as in (1), except that every k subscript to a b should here have a subscript (2–1), at present omitted to avoid a cluttered formula.

Correspondingly, in P-technique we take measures of n variables on one person on N occasions. The P-technique equation, as shown in (4), is the same as the dR, except that it has only a_{jk} (a deviation from the individual's mean instead of a difference of two occasions) on the left. The k subscript becomes in P-technique a particular instant in time (an "occasion") which has sometimes been written o (Cattell, 1966a).

$$a_{jk} = \sum_{x=1}^{x=t} b_{jkx} T_{u \cdot xk} + \sum_{y=1}^{y=u} b_{jky} T_{pyk} + \sum_{z=1}^{z=v} b_{jkz} S_{zk} \quad (4)$$

Here i is omitted, as we have the same individual all the time, so that it is "understood."

The only difference between any single dR and any single P-technique outcome when the n variables are the same should be that the former might contain some expression peculiar to the one time interval, and the latter anything idiosyncratic to the one person. The general sense of the already appreciable volume of experiment with variables common to dR and P-techniques is that there is very little idiosyncrasy either way, as far as the response patterns are concerned, though the relative variance magnitudes of the factor influences in various P- and dR-studies may show appreciable quantitative differences.

Present conclusions must rest at the position that as far as patterns of expression (the V_{fp} columns) are concerned, (1) there is about as much variation among dR studies on different environmental occasions, and among P-technique studies on different people as one would expect from chance, (2) the goodness of internal agreement in each on any given factor pattern is such as would justify averaging to get a single central tendency, as a "typical" pattern, and, (3) when this is done the central tendency for dR-technique agrees well with the central tendency in P-techniques as to pattern. (Regarding absolute factor variance magnitudes, there are, of course noticeable differences. Indeed, as we shall see below, the absolute variance in dR studies is systematically bigger than in P-technique.) However, it would not be surprising if more refined experiment and statistical analysis should eventually show that some significant individual differences in P-technique or occasion differences in dR-technique patterns exist.

Since the first search for state factors by P-technique (Cattell *et al.,* 1947), at least a dozen studies (H. V. Williams, 1954; Cattell & Luborsky, 1950; Haverland, 1954; Cattell & Cross, 1952; Karvonen & Kunnas, 1953; Shotwell, Hurley, & Cattell, 1961; Mefferd, 1966; Cattell & Scheier, 1961; Williams, 1959; Moran & Mefferd, 1959; Curran, 1968; Van Egeren, 1963), covering about thirty individuals, have yielded about fifteen tolerably replicated and seven well replicated patterns in the general state area, as well as some nine or ten in the strictly motivational area (specific ergic tension patterns).

The number of adequately interlocking dR-technique studies yet achieved is less than those by P-technique (Cattell & Scheier, 1961; Nesselroade, 1965; Bartlett, 1968; Cattell & Kawash, in press; Cattell & Krug, in press). A brief survey of both is shown in Table 4.2. As pointed out below this deficiency is an unfortunate concession to the effort demanded; due to the greater cost in organization of testing many individuals on objective (T-data) tests at the same time. These studies yield a reasonably clear P-technique outline of the anxiety state pattern, but the dR results are as yet too scanty. The definition one reaches of anxiety as a state here is of a response in which, at a behavioral or conscious level, such variables as raised irritability, lack of self-confidence, reduction of fluency, a sense of guilt, and a sense of high drive tension covary in combination. Physiologically, there is a rise in blood pressure (both systolic and diastolic), pulse rate, metabolic rate, respiration, and secretion of saliva (note contrast with the dry mouth of fear). The rise in cholinesterase may be explained as an adaptive rise in the esterase in the serum necessary to reduce the acetylcholine

TABLE 4.2

Similarity of P- and dR-Patterns for Anxiety as a State: Objective Test and Q-Data[a]

Variable title	Studies employing dR-technique			Studies employing P-technique				
	Cattell & Bartlett, 1971	Cattell & Scheier, 1958	Cattell & Scheier, 1961	Grinker *et al.*, 1961[c]	Mefferd & Moran, 1961[c]	Trunnel & Damarin, 1961[c]	Van Egeren, 1963	Williams, 1950, 1954
High systolic pulse pressure[b]		+30		(+08)	(+08)		+37	+71
Faster heart rate[b]				+30	+20	+15	+51	(−04)
More plasma 17-OH (ketosteroids)[b]				+43	+22	+23		+10
Faster respiration rate[b]				+45		+21		
Lower absolute level of galvanic skin resistancy[b]		−26						−25
Lower pH saliva (acid)		(−04)						−42
Lower urea concentration				−06	−32			
Greater volume of saliva secreted		27						(−01)
Lower cholinesterase in serum								−78
Higher m-OH-Phenyl hydracrylic					+74			
Higher m-OH-hippuric					+74			
Higher basal metabolic rate								+59
Higher histidine (in urine)					+52			
Lower pH urine (acid)								−32
Fewer staff Neutrophils								−30

Small R wave, EKG							−30	
Less confidence in assuming skills in untried performances[b]		+35		+22				
Total U.I. 24 Anxiety, from all markers				+72				
More common frailties admitted[b]	+18			+58				
Susceptibility to annoyance				+46				
Low verbal fluency, story writing							−42	
Small ataxic sway							−39	
Short length of previous night's sleep							−39	
Low ratio emotional/non-emotional recall								−37
Less long circuited (predominance in short-term goals)		−32						
Questionnaire Measures (Q-Data):								
Ego weakness (C−)[b]	−77	−29	−53					
Guilt proneness (O)[b]	+57		+20					
Self-sentiment (Q_3) low[b]	−62		−51					
Ergic tension (Q_4) high[b]	+50	+40	+44					
Low IPAT anxiety scale[b]	+92						−33	

[a] Except where parentheses are added, there is no inconsistency in sign or through pressure of nonsignificant loading on repetition. The blanks simply mean that the variable in question was not used in the research indicated. The most recent statements of the objectively-measured anxiety-state pattern, in relation to stress and arousal, are in Barton, Cattell, & Conner, 1972, and Cattell & Bartlett, 1971.

[b] Variables that show loadings in two or more researches.

[c] Unpublished data reported in Cattell & Scheier, 1961.

rise in the central nervous system. The reduction in the EKG wave, R, is probably part of a heart constriction pattern not yet sufficiently explored. With this go signs, in the amino acid changes in the urine, of an upset of anabolic processes probably largely accounted for as an effect of the sharp increase in 17 OH ketosteroids.

Contrasted with the trait pattern, as now given in Table 4.3, the above state pattern is seen to emphasize (in Q-data) the sense of inability to cope (C–, Q_3 –), while showing less of the characterological habits of protension (L) (projection of tension), and guilt (O), and the temperamental tendency to threctia (H–) (threat susceptibility). All the physiological signs are more prevalent. This last change of emphasis may be responsible for some psychologists mistakenly concluding that the state response is all physiological and that the questionnaire and behavioral signs do not go with it. Our conclusion from the extensive studies in Tables 4.1, 4.2 and 4.3, and others not included, is that the physiological changes are reduced and modified in the trait, by the dictatorship of homeostasis, and that, conversely, the Q- and T-data behaviors are reduced in the state–notably by the weight shifting to C, Q_3, and Q_4 factors (with some O). But except for extremely short term provocations of anxiety the state, like the trait, is centrally marked by irritability and loss of confidence, by reduction of fluency, upset of memory (notably in reduced memory for emotional meaning), and loss of attention and interest (especially for general long term goals). The reduction of ataxia is also characteristic of the state and may be partly due to greater muscle rigidity in the upper spinal region (Cattell & Scheier, 1961) and partly to the improved circulation in the cerebellum with raised blood pressure.

As will be seen from Table 3.3, the checking of the factor pattern of anxiety as a trait, in both T-data and Q-data, is at present far more extensive (17 researches) than for the state pattern. Incidentally, perhaps a majority of the individual measures found to load and define the anxiety pattern U.I., 24 have been confirmed by bivariate researches (as far as any bivariate study can logically be said to do so). For example, Sarason (1966) has shown that in a half hour fluency test, the high anxious show more self-depreciation (readiness to evaluate own performances as failures, as in U.I. 24 above). Sarason (1966) also found that high anxious subjects tended to "imitate" performers more when admitted to a preview of other subjects tackling the problems they would be exposed to. This has the same meaning as "Tendency to agree" in U.I. 24, betokening the same "imitative" lack of self-confidence. Although Lazarus' conclusion that raised "vigilance for dangers" is not experimental in basis, it can be supported, though at a low level, by the U.I. 24 loadings on "perceived dangerous objects in unstructured pictures." (The greater part of the variance on this belongs, however, to a different pattern from anxiety, namely, to U.I 17, *General Inhibition* (Hundleby, Pawlik, & Cattell, 1965).

Strategically designed research demands such essential features as the carrying over of a sufficiency of identical marker variables from study to study; the inclusion of representative "hyperplane stuff" to permit rotation to a unique position; and, especially, quantitative indices of matching to pick out from R-technique factorings those patterns also indubitably found in dR and P-technique, so that trait and state patterns can be separated. Even though the above researches are among the minority observing the first two requirements, they have not yet met thoroughly the last. However, let us ask how further experiment may best design itself to separate not only state and trait, but also trait change factors.

In fact, with this brief illustration of results from R, dR, and P-techniques with respect to anxiety, let us now systematically attack the general problem of separating trait, trait change, and state factors. For an adequate solution it needs to be attacked both by (1) regard for the choice in variables in terms of those which gradually become known as largely trait or state indicators, and (2) the deliberate and crucial comparisons of patterns turned out by R-, dR-, and P-technique experiments (Cattell, 1966). As regards the first—the choice of variables—let us note that any set of variables designed to measure trait change patterns will necessarily measure, in R-technique, traits too. (The converse will not hold in dR- and P-techniques, where trait change patterns alone will appear. And measuring traits alone is possible, of course, only if we can choose variables for traits that we already know exhibit no trait change effects.) Recognizing these exceptions we find there are, exhaustively, just eight kinds of data (sets of variables and their potential structural content) with which one can enter any experiment, as shown along the top of Table 4.4. (Actually ${}^4C_4 + {}^4C_3 + {}^4C_2 + {}^4C_1 = 18$ mathematical combinations are possible, but most are not viable for reasons just mentioned.)

Thus Table 4.4 sets out along the top these eight possible choices of data, in terms of the "intentions to measure what." That is to say, it states what kind of data the experimenter, guided by existing indications, is taking into his experiment, as indicated by the kinds of factor he is looking for, in the three rows underneath, it then proceeds to show what types of trait or state patterns the different experimental designs—R-, dR-, and P-technique experiments, respectively—can expect to extract from each of these kinds of available experimental data.

By contrasting the outcomes from the three experimental techniques, on the same and different data, one obtains a more positive and final verdict than anything obtainable merely by manipulating the choice of variables (the column letters) which can never be absolutely certain as to their content and will always offer little more than a somewhat different emphasis on elements within the general mixture of state and trait variables inevitable in any state investigation.

The choice of experimental design and analyses is more positive than choice

TABLE 4.3

Seventeen Multivariate Researches Defining the Pattern of Anxiety as a Trait: Indexed as U.I. 24

Master index number	Variable title[a]	Research study (see key)																
		C5[b]	C6	Ros	R1	R2	R3	R10	HI	R4	C7	R12	R15	R14	CS	DC	N1	N2
219	More common frailties admitted	42	19	38	37	33	11	09	43	59	34	21	(−01)	19	51		25	42
152	More tendency to agree	24	63	26	17	07	11	66	13	29	39			24				
211a	More overall susceptibility to annoyance	52	39	49	15					48	08	81	82	20		47	48	44
108	Less confident assumption of skill in untried performance	−11	−03		−27	−21	−35	−52		−19	−23			−04				
116a, b	Higher critical severity (hard-headed cynicism)	28		33	11	18	04	15		15	37							
205	More emotionality of comment	35	13							27	05	11			35			
464[c]	Lower average handwriting pressure				−05	−26	−30											
473	Lower total number of friends recalled on fluency test				−27			−15										
	Higher anxiety: Taylor manifest anxiety scale			85														
	IPAT Anxiety Scale	94		(See also the two columns of Q-data in Table 3.1)														

	Investigation	Sample size	Age of subject	Factor number in study
C5	Cattell (1955)	500	Adult	(1+)
C6	Cattell (1955)	250	Adult	(9−)
Ros	Rosenthal (1955)	70	Adult	(1+)
R1	Scheier & Cattell (1958)	86	Adult	(1+)
R2	Cattell & Scheier (1959)	86	Adult	(12+)
R3	Cattell & Scheier (1958)	86	Adult	(12+)
	Cattell & Scheier (1960)	86	Adult	(12+)
R10	Cattel & Damarin (1962)	168	Adult	(9+)
HI	Horn (1961)	137	Adult	(9+)
R4	Cattell & Scheier (1961)	187	Adult	—
C7	Cattell & Gruen (1955)	184	9–12	(12+)
R12	Cattell & Peterson (1959)	80	4–5	(5+)
R15	Cattell & Howarth (1964)	197	7–10	(9+)
R14	Cattell & Hundleby (1968)	129	3–7	(7+)
CS	Cattell & Scheier (1961)			
DC	Damarin & Cattell (1968)	128	4–7	
N1, N2	Nesselroade (1965)	94	Adult	(2)

[a] Additional variables which, though not factored, are known to correlate with these are listed in a ten-year review of the literature by Cattell & Scheier (1957).

[b] The early factor of Brogden (1940) is not included here, though the variables were used and came out as hypothesized, in C5. The rationale for considering this pattern the same as the clinician's definition of anxiety is given in Cattell (1964). Precise description of the objective tests listed in this and other tables may be obtained in Cattell & Warburton (1968). See also Yrinker (1966).

[c] This agrees with the findings of Wells (1958) on physical fitness and anxiety.

TABLE 4.4

Structural Entities Obtainable from Three Techniques of Experiment Applied to Eight Planned Choices of Variables[a]

Experimental design and analysis	Choice of data in terms of potential coverage of structures							
	1	2	3	4	5	6	7	8
	T Tu Tp S	*T Tp S*	*T Tu S*	*T Tp*	*T Tu*	*T S*	*T*	*S*
R-technique	*T, Tp, S*	*T, Tp, S*	*T, S*	*T, Tp*	*T*	*T, S*	*T*	*S*
dR-technique	*Tu, Tp, S*	*Tp, S*	*Tu, S*	*Tp*	*Tu*	*S*	None	*S*
P-technique	*Tu, Tp, S*	*Tp, S*	*Tu, S*	*Tp*	*Tu*	*S*	None	*S*

[a] *T*, Trait; *Tu*, Uniform Trait Change Factor; *Tp*, Phased Trait Change Factor, *S*, State. Entries in the table are types of structure that are potentially discoverable.

of content, because in no circumstances can a trait be obtained from dR- or P-technique, and whatever appears in dR- should check by also appearing in P-technique. The only difficult case, needing discussion, is that of the uniform type of trait change factor, T_u, which, by definition, has the same loading pattern as the trait. This, like the phased trait change pattern represents some increment (or decrement) in the trait which the individual incurred since the trait was first formed and which is still in progress at the time of measurement. However, in the case of the T_u (uniform trait change), the change is part of a trait change which, even if not temporally continuous and without pauses, is always uniform in pattern with the trait. Consequently this pattern will not separate from the trait factor pattern in R-technique.[4] With T_p factors, on the other hand, provided there is, over and above the generic resemblance of T_p and T, some real distinctness of pattern between them, even R-technique will yield T_p as well as T. This raises the question of the scale origin from which such a T_p is measured, and the answer is surely that it is scored from the zero level existing at that point in time at which T_u began as a separate growth from T.

In connection with T_p and T concepts, we must recognize that in the broadest theoretical context and the most general case, T is nothing but the summation of a series of T_p growths—T_{p1}, T_{p2}, etc.—and that if a trait development had highly distinct phases, the T would resolve itself into separate members in a series of T_p patterns, only the last of which would, however, still

[4] The usual test for number of factors will not help, because an endowment of an amount a in T and b in Tu is equivalent to an endowment of $(a + b)$ in T. In snort, T and Tu will be run together as a single T factor in R-technique. The Tu part will nevertheless be separated in dR- and P-techniques.

be in process of growth. Thus, in fact, any T would be a series of T_p's (completed T_p developments), plus the last, still developing, T_p. That this is not a purely academic case in factor analysis is shown by the recent work on fluid and crystallized general intelligence, where factors appear at a given cross-sectional analysis (R-technique), some of which are present developments and some the residual monuments from past historical growth (Cattell, 1971).

This issue cannot be pursued further here. Its importance to us is primarily in clarifying the border country around states, and saving us from false identifications. But a more inescapable issue is the question of what conceptual difference remains between T_u and T_p patterns and S patterns. This becomes still more subtle if we should be compelled to accept the model discussed below that states (S's) themselves have a different real mean for each individual. In that case both T_u's and S's would be characterized by having a fixed value from which they depart (in episodic fluctuations or in steady trends), and in which the factor pattern of the departures would be exactly the same as the individual difference factor pattern for the differences in the means.

The model espoused here is that a difference would still remain between T_u and S concepts in that the variance of the steady mean in the T_u (the corresponding "trait" value, T) across individuals would be large and the trait change variance small, whereas in states, the opposite would be the case. This, of course, involves hypothetical definitions which should, and readily can, be put to the verdict of experiment. However, the positive verdict would still not have practical utility and validity unless it met the criterion of any true type distinction, namely, a discrete, bimodal distribution in the index constituted by the ratio of variance over occasions to variance over means (over people). That is to say, a mere arbitrary cut in a normal distribution of such ratios would be conceptually pointless. (Incidentally, we are speaking of what is a more refined examination of modes in the stability coefficient distribution discussed earlier).

The most common situation in research will be that shown in column 1 of Table 3.4, where variables covering, as far as one knows, every type of structural pattern are present in the study. Then the T patterns can be separated by their appearing in R-technique but not dR and P. The T_u patterns will have exactly the opposite occurrence. Only the S and T_p patterns will appear through all three modes of analyses. The separation of S and T_p must therefore rest on the same kind of variance ratio distribution as just discussed. In addition, however, their separation, and that of all other structured patterns, can be further aided by attention to relative variance magnitudes across the various techniques, that is, invoking quantitative evidence, beyond absolute presence or absence. Examination by quantitative evidence is continued on p. 145, below because earlier sections must intervene to handle concepts involved in the definition of the variance needing to be measured.

Further Characteristics Needing Definition in the State Model: Measurement Origins, Frequency, and Speed of Oscillation

Before the issue of comparative variances of T, T_u, T_p, and S factors across R, dR and P experiments can be handled with precision, it is desirable that some definition be given to other aspects of the state concept as it commonly enters experimental and clinical discussion. The core of the definition, as given on p. 128 above, and in the exact expression of the definition in factor patterns, has been one of a simultaneous change in several responses (or simultaneous modification of preexisting responses to focal stimuli). Around this core, however, various additions and elaborations have occurred in the literature (Spielberger, 1966). Some of these speculated associations seem probable, some improbable, but regardless of whether a shrewd bet would include them in the model, it is vital that they be made far more explicit and operationally clear than it has been their fate to be in the literature so far.

The chief further characteristics needing evaluation are:

1. The conceived measurement origin. Do states oscillate about a common zero for all people, or a characteristic level for each?

2. The conceived sigma. Do all persons oscillate over the same range?

3. The relation to stimuli. Is the magnitude of the number of the stimuli reacted to a part of the "level of anxiety" concept and measurement?

4. Is the individual with higher mean anxiety (Assumption 1b) assumed to be also possessed of a higher sigma of fluctuation?

5. What correlations are, in general, conceived to be nonzero among the above? For example, where there is a trait and a state of the same generic nature are their levels hypothesized to be positively correlated?

6. How do we conceive the sheer speed of onset of response to be related to the extremity of response?

7. Is the pattern during the rise of a state the same as that of the coordinated manifestations during its homeostatic decline? And do ceiling or floors effects modify the pattern?

8. What higher order relations are supposed among state dimensions? Particularly, what are the relations between general states (arousal, anxiety, effort stress, depression) and dynamic states (ergic tension levels on hunger, assertion, sex, etc.)?

These are only the beginning questions, that can and need to be answered to make current experiment meaningful; but there are many others that can only appear once this degree of structuration is achieved.

The beginnings of adequate treatment of these features of a precise model have been carried farther in factor analytic than in other approaches (see, for example, Cattell, 1957a; Cattell & Scheier, 1961). Indeed, unambiguous statements about these parameters and structural relations is scarcely possible except on a prior foundation of factorial identification of the measures to which such statements are to be applied. The above list could present many derivative combinations, but since these can be made by the reader according to his choice, and since it would take too long to go over all, it is proposed to define and discuss here only the particular combination which constitutes my own preferred theoretical model.

That model should surely not make the assumption, in relation to issue (1) above, that all people take off in their oscillations from a common central mean value. Instead we shall suppose the most comprehensive model: that there is a significant deviation of a person's state mean from the grand state mean, and a difference of his deviation from his own mean from those of others from their means. Then if the facts in a given case require it, this more general model can be reduced to a more specific, simplified case by setting the former to zero, and the latter to equality. However, in regard to the latter issue, it is surely contrary to all preliminary findings that the variability (sigma) of one person's measurements about this mean should be exactly equal to those of another. There are equable people and emotionally extreme people.

Regarding the relation of frequency of reaction to intensity (sigma), common learning experience in a common culture is likely to lead to persons of equal intelligence, experience, and memory storage encountering about the same number of realistically dangerous or depressing stimuli. Endler, Hunt, and Rosenstein (1962) seem to the present writer to have mistaken an easily made conceptual difference for a functional difference when they assert that one person may be intensely anxious about a few things and another less anxious but about a much greater number. This can happen, of course, but minor individual differences in experience are balanced out and the only systematic difference in the number of stimuli provocative of anxiety would spring from a fundamental individual difference in proneness to anxiety (the factors of intelligence, experience, and memory being duly factored out from the anxiety factor). Then the individual who, by count, exceeds a given minimum anxiety reaction to many things (this can be defined as "breadth of susceptibility") will also tend to be more intensely anxious (this can be defined as the mean over several occasions) about any given stimulus. This relation can be most quickly appreciated from Figure 4.1, when it will be seen that breadth, intensity and speed would almost certainly tend to be highly correlated, across individuals.

As to question (4) above, we have answered it in Figure 4.1, as in our main model below, by saying it is most likely that the person with a large sigma across occasions (variability) will also have a high mean. There can be no linear correlation, of course (by the same algebra as dictates the analysis of variance rule), between an individual's deviation on one occasion from his mean, and the magnitude of his mean. There can and is, however, a correlation across individuals between the magnitudes of their sigmas (taken over occasions) and

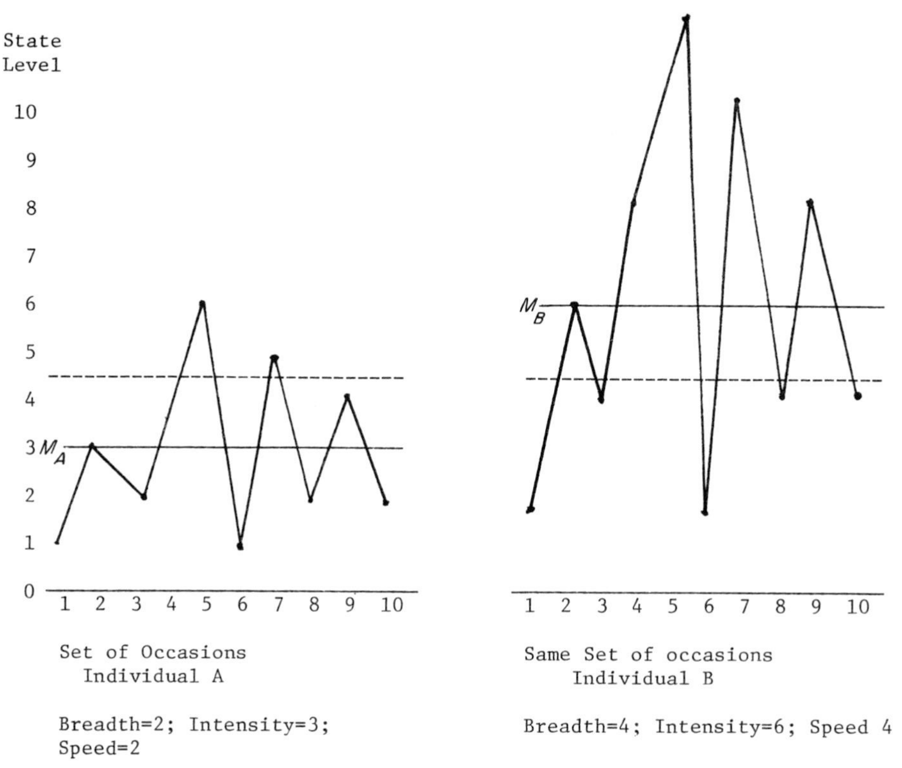

Figure 4.1. *Correlations expected from model among breadth (frequency), intensity, and speed of onset of states. Dashed line represents the threshold of noticeable raction; solid line represents the mean intensity for the given individual. Speed taken only between 1 and 2, as rise per occasion.*

their means, as instanced above, but this would appear as a curvilinear correlation between individual deviations on one occasion and individual's means. It would also appear as a linear correlation between absolute (no sign) state score on any one occasion, and mean score.

The question of correlation between the mean state level and the trait level on the trait deemed generically like it ("anxiety as a state, and anxiety as a trait") is a matter for purely empirical study. By present definition this trait is not the average of the state values; it is a distinct but similiar pattern. Nor is it as yet hypothesized to be related to the sigma of the state. The special theory developments in the following section, going beyond the main model, raise possibilities of such trait–state correlation for investigation.

Questions (6) and (7) have to do with the possible differences in the speed and pattern in the rise and fall of states. Let us set aside, as likely to be different, the phenomenon of high changeability in terms of shift from one kind of mood to another, such as is associated, for example, with low ego strength (Factor C in the personality domain). Here, as in Figure 3.1, we are speaking instead of change in level on one kind of emotional state as the individual encounters a standard series of stimuli in a given time. Obviously, as indicated at the foot of Figure 4.1, the individual with greater intensity (and therefore breadth) is going to show steeper rises and declines over time. Actually, there is a well known instance of this, in that the rate of rise of pulse rate in the cold pressor test is highly correlated with scores on the anxiety factor (U.I. 24) representing the general intensity of the individual's anxiety.

Elsewhere (Cattell, 1957a, Chapter 14; Cattell, 1963a, Chapter 10) the whole question of possible change of form of the state loading pattern (the rate of change of level on variables with the level of the state) with upward and downward movement, with homeostatic influences, and with scale changes close to ceiling and floor, has been discussed with greater precision, as far as existing experiment makes it profitable. Although all variables that deviate in an emotional state have eventually to return to a central value, they may return at different rates and thus cause a P-technique definition of a state to go through phases, discernible by factoring over separate intervals.

Finally, we come to the particular questions about the most probable model raised under (8) above. The second order relations among general states are initially matters for empirical investigation, and Figure 4.4 below (p. 174) shows that, so far, two broad factors are recognizable. This analysis begets the theory that approach toward and grappling with a problem tends to involve one set of primaries (effort stress, adrenergic response, etc.) while another dimension (anxiety, pathemia) tends to be associated with retreat. The important new principle to keep in mind here is that the second order factors, at least some of them, are no longer likely to represent a unity of innate response pattern, but may represent typically groupings of provocations in the environment. Alternatively, they may represent the correlations produced in cross section by rising and declining primaries as determined by some typical process sequence (see discussion on process on p. 165 below).

The related issue of interrelations at the higher order between general states (arousal, anxiety, effort stress, etc.) and dynamic states (ergic tension levels on gregariousness, hunger, sex, etc.) is a more speculative extension of the model best discussed later (p. 165).

The Integration of State Research with the Concepts of State Liability and Modulation

It has been suggested above (Figure 4.1) that the simplest functional model—that which makes a person's mean on a state proportional to his variability (sigma)–is also best in accord with initial experimental data on state behavior. Actually, this model would fit very well into one introduced on wider grounds (including the need to handle roles) into the new factor specification equation, known as the modulation model, which we will now discuss.

As far as states are concerned, this development requires the notion that any ambient situation, k, characteristically raises any person's state level on state z by a multiplier which is represented by the index, s_{kz}. This latter is called the modulating index. The remaining part of the theory is the conception that with respect to any given emotion, z, every person has his own specific sensitivity to excitement, or proneness to the emotion. This proneness we shall characteristically refer to as a liability to emotional state z and represent it by L_z.

It is now possible to take any state S_{zi} in the general equation (1) above, on a given ambient stimulus occasion k, and substitute for it $s_{kz}L_{zi}$, that is, the liability (proneness) of individual i to state z multiplied by the general emotion evoking character (for emotion z) of the situation s_{kz} for all people in situation k. Thus, for the whole complex of primary state dimensions on a given occasion k we may write:

$$\sum_{z=1}^{z=v} b_{jkz}S_{zki} = \sum_{z=1}^{z=v} b_{jkz}s_{kz}L_{zi} \tag{5}$$

We may leave the reader to produce his new total specification equation by substituting the right for the left part of Equation (5) in Equation (1).

As mentioned above, the modulation principle has applicability simultaneously to several problems in this area. In addition to covering role phenomena (see Cattell, 1963b), it has the broader value of bringing bivariate manipulative experiment into the same framework as multivariate manipulative experiment. Normally the former is concerned with what happens only to the average person, for example, it plots a general learning curve, whereas the latter asks only how each individual differs from the average. (Thus, for the latter, the scores in Equation 1, both for variables and factors, are in standard deviations from the mean.) The application of s_k, however, to each individual's liability, will both shift the mean, for all people together, and change the deviation of individuals from the mean. Thus, as a statistical matter, we should note that the value a_{ijk} on the left of Equation (1) will require a metric which expresses both the shift of the mean and the shift of each individual relative to the mean (Cattell, 1971a) as in real base factor analysis (Cattell, 1972).

However, our concern here is more with psychological meaning than with psychometry, and the reader must pursue elsewhere (Cattell, 1971b) both the scaling issue and the ways of calculating s_k and b_{jk} from experimental data. It should be noted that whereas previously we could not use Equation (1) for prediction in the sense of foretelling, that is, calculating before the event, because we could not know the individual's state score until the moment itself, now we can predict his state level (as an estimate) from his known proneness– a storable trait characteristic–and from the equally storable index–the known provocativeness (the s_{kz}) of a particular ambient situation for a particular state. Whereas the behavioral index, b_{jm}, in factor analysis previously showed us only how much a given focal stimulus, *j*, and its associated response uses the particular trait, *m*, in accomplishing the response, the new modulator index, s_k, tells us how the situation (the ambient part of it, *k*) first alters the individual–provokes a state level in him. Thus s_k brings about a given state level (through the individual's liability, L_z, a trait) and b_{jz} says how useful it then is in bringing about the given behavior.

The implication of this use of s_k is that all individuals are considered to start from the same zero level on any state scale (not the same mean). An alternative model is possible in which this supposition is not made, but it is a simplifying assumption and not unreasonable. It would not fit observation so well to suppose that all persons experience their deviations from the same mean (and our assumption of the same zero does not imply equality of means, but in fact denies it). But if we suppose that all states require some energy for their maintenance, it is consistent to suppose that all persons will tend to return to an absolute zero of expression of anxiety, anger, etc., when provocative situations are removed. And in passing it should be noted that although there are psychometric difficulties with absolute zero scales in regard to traits, some of these difficulties vanish in regard to states.

The main implications of modulators *S*'s and liability traits *L*'s can be seen at a glance in Figure 4.2, in which the vertical axis represent the level on a particular state *x*, all persons being measured on the same and taken from an absolute zero common to all. The horizontal axis represents a series of ambient situations to which people can be exposed, arranged in increasing magnitude of their modulating effect upon the given liability.

The main points to note from Figure 3.2 are four, as follows:

1. Individual differences in liability scores are represented by differences in the slope of the lines. Lines for only three people–a high, a low and an average–are shown. The value L_{xi} is the tangent of the line.

2. A person's mean score on a state over a standard set of occasions is directly proportional to his L_{xi}. It is L_{xMi} where S_{skM} is the mean intensity of the modulator situations sampled for state *x*.

3. A person's deviation from the mean score of the group on any occasion k_p will be proportional (by a function of L_{xi}) to the deviation of the group mean from zero on occasion k_p.

4. As any group of persons is exposed to a series of situations, its sigma of state scores will be simply proportional to the mean of its state scores (on the absolute scale) on the given occasion, as a function of the nature of the given

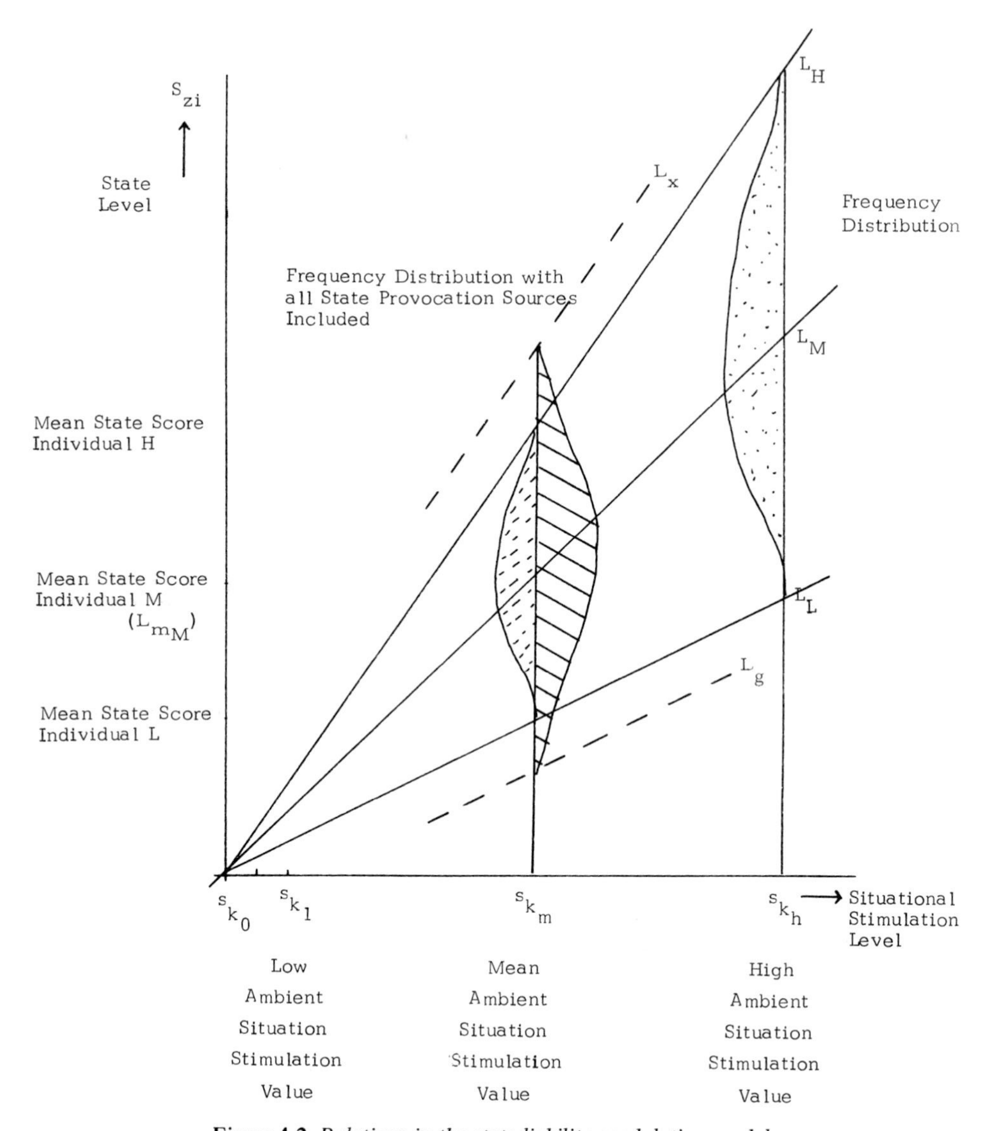

Figure 4.2. *Relations in the state liability modulation model.*

state liability. The mean is itself proportional to the intensity of the ambient situation.

Additional definition needs to be given, however, particularly in regard to (3) and (4), according to what assumption is made about the extent to which people can be experimentally exposed in controlled fashion exclusively to a single ambient situation. When a set of subjects is manipulatively exposed to a particular anxiety-provoking ambient situation, k_1, we are bound to recognize (a) that they permit themselves, perceptually, to be exposed to it in varying degrees, and (b) each is simultaneously exposed, in different degrees from others, to a variety of additional private anxiety-provoking stimuli, $k_{i2}, k_{i3}, k_{i4} \ldots$, etc.

Accordingly, it would seem that in any actual experimental or natural situation it is necessary to handle the varying relevance of situations of known ambient intensities by means of an additional term, which we may call the "proximity" or "pressingness" of any given ambient situation. Thus the intensity of anxiety provocation, s_{kti}, to which an individual i is exposed may be conceived as the sum of the standard provokingness of each of a total series of possible common situations, each qualified by a value p which is its proximity (relevance, pressingness) to him at the moment, thus:

$$s_{kti} = p_{1i}s_{k_1} + p_{2i}s_{k_2} + \ldots p_{ni}s_{k_n} \tag{6}$$

When, in an experiment, all are exposed to s_{kj}, the value p_j will be high for all, but other values will also enter into $s_{k_{ai}}$. The result is that in any actual experiment all subjects will not stand exactly at the same level of stimulation as depicted in Figure 4.1, but will scatter over a stimulation range. The ensuing anxiety state variance will be the sum of that from two sources, and will be greater than that expected from the common main manipulated stimulus, as shown by the bounding, interrupted lines L_x and L_y in Figure 4.2. Neither the mean nor the sigma of anxiety will fall to zero (converge on the origin in Figure 4.2) when the main manipulated ambient situation reaches zero intensity. However, what is depicted in Figure 4.2 will be correct if we speak of the ideal condition in which all ambient stimulation can be simultaneously reduced to zero, and the horizontal axis represents the total of all of them as a combined intensity. What is being discussed here is, of course, a special case of the familiar manipulative experiment in which there is "error variance," because not every independent variable can be controlled or measured. It is important to recognize it before proceeding, however, because, despite the fully understood interaction of L_{zi} and S_{kz} (according to the model) we still cannot fully predict S_{zki}, using common terms, but must admit an "error" term in each individual measurement.

The State and Trait Variances to be Expected under R-, dR-, and P-Designs

The assertion has been made above that the distinction and recognition of the classes of concept we call traits, trait change factors, and states (S's, T_u's, T_p's and S's) can be most positively made by strategic comparison of R-, dR-, and

P-technique experimental outcomes in terms of presence or absence of various factor patterns. But it was added that the taxonomic separation could be further aided by comparing the relative variances of the factors (not merely total presence or absence), which could be settled more definitely after attending to the nature of the model in the last section above.

Meaningful comparisons of factor variances can be made only if we rest our experiments on definable samples, preferably stratified, or populations both of tests and people. Elsewhere (1957a, 1968) I have suggested solutions to the problem of getting a fair sample of behavior variables for a given culture and I shall assume we are now operating with such a sample. I shall also assume we have a fair, stratified sample of state-provoking situations (which have here consistently been called ambient or background situations, to distinguish them from the focal stimulus to which a specific response is made and measured).

Now the estimation of the variance for states (that for traits is routine and requires no comment) can be made according to either of two models—the simple and the interactive. Although as Figure 4.2 and Equation (5) indicate, we have here adopted the interactive model of liability endowments and ambient stimulus intensities on psychological grounds, yet the possible preference of some readers for the simple model, as well as its value as an introduction, suggest that we encompass the simpler approach en route. In both models the important features are retained that individuals may differ on their mean state levels as well as the sigmas of their state fluctuation over occasions, but in the first we take the simplest analysis of variance situation without interaction, while in the second we hypothesize interaction and, indeed, interaction of the special (product) kind demanded in the modulation theory.

In making these comparisons, a comprehensive treatment permitting all necessary comparisons is possible only if we start our thinking within the framework of the complete "data box." By the data box or basic data relation matrix is meant the complete set of scores (and implied possible relations) for a sample of people across a sample of tests across a sample of occasions, as discussed in the *Handbook of Multivariate Experimental Psychology* (Cattell, 1966a). However, since a factor score, with which we begin, is a weighted composite of test scores (and since we need not get involved in issues of estimation here) discussion can immediately be cut down to consideration of a single facet of the data box, by taking a single test variable as giving us directly a state factor score. That is to say, we are no longer concerned with covariance of variables since we can make our factor a single variable (a factor battery score) and can operate then in the person-condition (treatment) facet matrix only. Thus our concern is with the data from measuring N people on a single good state measure, j across v occasions. From such a rectangular facet of the data box—an $N \times v$ score matrix as illustrated in Table 3.5—any value (a raw score) for a person i on occasion l can be broken down as follows:

$$A_{il} = M_g + m_i + m_l + p_{il}$$
$$(\text{or } = M_i + M_l + p_{il} - M_g) \qquad (7)$$

Here M_g is the grand mean across people and occasions, m_i the deviation of a given person, that is, of his own mean, across all occasions, from the grand mean, and m_l the deviation of a given occasion across all people, from the grand mean. That mean may be written M_l across all people for that occasion, l just as the individual's mean over all occasions may be written M_{il}, p_{il} is then an individual's deviation from the typical person–occasion cell value. Statistically this is just "error" and could have any source, but by our model (and assuming instrument error to be zero) it is conceived as that effect on a given occasion for a given person which is not due to the common "public" effect upon his anxiety of the occasion which all persons share, but to private personal concerns which cannot be experimentally controlled. The mean, M_i, for a person across all occasions is, as just indicated, an estimate of his trait level and/or his mean state level if, as above, our model supposes this mean state level to differ from zero. Parenthetically, if we were concerned with sampling inference here, which we are not, we should recognize that M_i is an estimate of his trait, relative to a whole population of occasions; but this aspect can be set aside as another question. The student will recognize Table 4.5 as in the generic class of analysis of variance, at the limiting case of one case per cell, and where interaction and significance consequently cannot be considered.

Our aim here is to compare the variances for states (and in two cases, R-technique and G-technique, see below, for traits too) resulting from covariance factoring. (This means factoring products of raw score deviations. In this kind of analysis, that factor, for example, anxiety, will not have unit variance, but will have a value which is a function of the raw scores.) The variance of any factor (as a raw score function) will now differ in its various appearances, for example, in R-technique, P-technique, etc. *The object is now to use the expected change in variance from technique to technique as an additional basis of evidence for recognizing given states and for distinguishing them from trait factors.* Let us first consider the simple case, with no interaction, as in Table 4.5.

In R-technique, the deviation, $a_{i(l)}$ of any person's score from the sample mean on one occasion, l, will be, from Equation (7):

$$a_{i(l)} = m_i + p_{il}$$

and the variance (dropping the label for identity of variable a will be:

$$\sigma^2_{i(l)} = \frac{\sum_{i=1}^{i=N} m_i^2}{N} + \frac{\sum_{i=1}^{i=N} p_{il}^2}{N} \qquad (8)$$

Since $\sum_{i}^{N} m_i \, p_{il} = 0$, there is no product term.

TABLE 4.5

Facet of Data Box Showing Score Matrix of Persons Over Occasions, and the Result (Block Design) Analysis into Variance Components

Cells with raw scores A_{il}:

		ν Occasions					
		1 Home	"1" "1"	$(\nu-1)$ Play	ν Work	M_i	m_i
	1. Adams	1	5	1	2	2.25	−1.15
	2. Brown	3	6	4	5	4.50	1.10
N	"i"	2	4	1	4	2.75	−.65
People	$(N-1)$ Yost	4	3	2	3	3.00	−.40
	N. Zubin	4	5	3	6	4.50	1.10
	M_l	2.80	4.60	2.20	4.0	M_g =	3.40
	m_l	−.60	1.20	−1.20	.60		

$$A_{il} = M_g + m_i + m_l + p_{il} = M_i + M_l - M_g + p_{il}$$

Cells with deviation scores by person and occasion: $a_{i(l)}$ and $a_{l(i)}$

		1 Home	"1" "1"	$(\nu-1)$ Play	ν Work
1. Adams	upper right	−1.25	2.75	−1.25	−.25
	lower left	−1.80	.40	−1.20	−2.00
2. Brown	upper right	−1.50	1.50	−.50	.50
	lower left	.20	1.40	1.80	1.00
"i"	upper right	−.75	1.25	−1.75	1.25
	lower left	−.80	−.60	−1.20	0
$(N-1)$ Yost	upper right	1.00	0	−1.00	0
	lower left	1.20	−1.60	−.20	−1.00
N. Zubin	upper right	−.50	.50	−1.50	1.50
	lower left	1.20	.40	.80	2.00

$a_{i(l)}$ is lower left. Different persons; same occasion

$a_{l(i)}$ is upper right. Different occasion; same person

Table 4.5–(*Cont.*)

Cells with "error" or personal concern scores: p_{il}

	1 Home	"1"	$(v-1)$ Play	Work
1. Adams	−.65	1.55	−.05	−.85
2. Brown	−.90	.30	.70	−.10
"*i*"	−.15	.05		
$(N-1)$ Yost	1.60	−1.20		
N. Zubin	.10	−.70		

$p_{il} = A_{il} - (M_g + m_i + m_l)$

In P-technique, where we take a column instead of a row, the argument leads symmetrically to:

$$\sigma^2_{l(i)} = \frac{\sum_{l=1}^{l=v} m_l^2}{V} + \frac{\sum_{l=1}^{l=v} p_{il}^2}{V} \tag{9}$$

Thus R- and P-technique lead to the same size factors if the variance over people is the same as that over occasions, for the average person and the average occasion.

In dR-technique, there are extra steps which for clarity must be set out. The difference scores, for each of N people, with which this technique operates, derive from (7) thus:

$$(A_{im} - A_{il}) = (m_m - m_l) + (p_{im} - p_{il})$$

where l and m are the two occasions.

Changing the above to a deviation from the mean of difference scores we have:

$$\text{The mean difference} = M_{(m-l)} = (m_m - m_l) + \frac{\sum^{N} p_{im}}{N} - \frac{\sum^{N} p_{il}}{N}$$

$$\text{Whence,} \qquad a_{i(m-l)} = \left(p_{im} - \frac{\sum^{N} p_{im}}{N}\right) - \left(p_{il} - \frac{\sum^{N} p_{il}}{N}\right)$$

$$= p_{im} - p_{il} \quad (\text{since } \sum p_{im} \text{ and } \sum p_{il} = 0)$$

$$\sigma^2_{(m-l)} = \frac{\sum^{N} p_{im}^2}{N} + \frac{\sum^{N} p_{il}^2}{N}$$

if we have no reason to expect any correlation of the p's on the first and second occasion. If, as also seems assumable, the p variance is the same on the two occasions, this becomes:

$$\sigma^2_{(m-l)} = 2\sigma^2_p \tag{10}$$

In G-technique (G for "grid analysis," Cattell, 1966a) the factoring is across both variables and occasions, and any single factor has the total variance in the matrix in Table 4.5. It can be shown, taking an M_g from (7), that the variance is:

$$\sigma^2_{il} = \sigma^2_{mi} + \sigma^2_{ml} + \sigma^2_p \tag{11}$$

For none of the three product combinations should represent any significant correlation, and the products can be taken (in the population) as zero.

Equations (8) through (11) are put together as a summary of the simple case in Table 4.6. Since we believe the interaction model, that is, that with a modulation effect, is strongly indicated by general state research to be a better fit, Table 4.6 may be taken as an introductory step to the somewhat more complex statistics we must now derive and set out. Instead of equation (7) the basic equation is now:

$$A_{il} = M_g + m_i + m_l + km_i m_l + p_{il} \tag{12}$$

TABLE 4.6

Magnitudes of Variances in State and Trait Factors Obtained from R–, dR–, P– and Grid Techniques: A, Model Without Interaction[a]

R-technique:

$$\sigma^2_{i(l)} = \sigma^2_{mi} + \sigma^2_{pil}$$

P-technique:

$$\sigma^2_{l(i)} = \sigma^2_{ml} + \sigma^2_{pil}$$

dR-technique:

$$\sigma^2_{(m-l)} = \sigma^2_{pil} + \sigma^2_{pim}$$

$$= 2\sigma^2_{pil} \quad \text{(with equality assumption)}$$

Total Grid Analysis (G-technique):

$$\sigma^2_{il} = \sigma^2_{mi} + \sigma^2_{ml} + \sigma^2_{pil}$$

[a] In R-technique the two terms are, respectively, the trait (trait and state mean) and the state (true state and phase trait change) variances In P- and dR-technique, they are wholly state (true state and trait change variance). In T-technique the first is trait (trait and state mean) and the second state (state and trait change). The factoring of covariances here should be compared with Nesselroade's (1967) interesting approach of factoring cross-products.

where k is a constant–essentially the signia of this liability index, L, in the given population for the given trait, as shown in the angle L_H, O, L_L in Fig. 4.2 (p. 144), which is characteristic of the trait.

It would be equally acceptable on general grounds to write it, parallel to the second form of equation (7) as:

$$A_{il} = M_i + M_l - M_g + kM_iM_l + M_ip_{il}$$

but in this introductory treatment we wish to avoid the complications of the grand mean entering into the variance. It is a fact that the grand mean does enter the variance, according to the modulation model (Figure 4.2), but we can restrict the comparisons here to a fixed grand mean, assumed taken for a typical population of persons and occasions. Another reason for ignoring the grand mean is that with most psychological scales lacking a true zero it is an artificial concept.

The product term km_im_l simply recognizes the modulation effect whereby the deviation of an individual from the expected row–column sum is a function of state Sx the occasion, m_l. What needs a little more discussion is the term M_ip_{il}. The argument is that in a person of high liability, and therefore high M_l, the nonpublic stimuli for anxiety will also have a greater than average effect. Thus if we regard p_{il} as summing to zero by rows and columns, as before, yet a high M_i person will have greater variance on this term than a low person. However, in this introductory analysis we shall stand by the simpler assumption that the p deviations are unrelated to the individual's liability index and to the magnitude of the main modulation effect.

Thus in R-technique the deviation will be an expression of the occasion as follows:

$$a_{i(l)} = m_i + km_im_l + p_{il}$$

Squared, summed and divided by N this becomes:

$$\sigma^2_{(l)} = \sigma^2_{mi} + k\sigma^2_{ml}\sigma^2_{mi} + \sigma^2_{pil} \quad (13)$$

(For $\sum m_ip_{il}$ and $m_l\sum m_ip_{il}$ can be assumed zero, m_i and p_{il} being uncorrelated. In as much as the product of two variances is the variance of their product, the second term can alternatively be written or calculated $k\sigma^2_{m_im_l}$.)

In P-technique:

$$a_{l(i)} = m_l + km_im_l + p_{il}$$

whence:

$$\sigma^2_{(i)} = \sigma^2_{m_l} + k\sigma^2_{ml}\sigma^2_{mi} + \sigma^2_{pil} \quad (14)$$

In dR-technique, as before, the steps need setting out:

$$(A_{im} - A_{il}) = (m_m - m_l) + km_i(m_m - m_l) + (p_{im} - p_{il})$$

$$M_{(m-l)} = (m_m - m_l) + k\frac{\sum^N m_i}{n}(m_m - m_l) + \frac{\sum^N}{n}(p_{im} - p_{il})$$

Subtracting $M_{(m-l)}$ from $(A_{im} - A_{il})$

$$a_{i(m-l)} = km_i(m_m - m_l) + (p_{im} - p_{il})$$

$$\sigma^2_{(m-l)} = k^2\sigma^2_{mi}\sigma^2_{mm} + k^2\sigma^2_{mi}\sigma^2_{ml} + \sigma^2_{pim} + \sigma^2_{pil} \tag{15}$$

In G-technique:

$$a_{il} = m_i + m_l + km_im_l + p_{il}$$

$$\sigma^2_{il} = \sigma^2_{mi} + \sigma^2_{ml} + k^2\sigma^2_{mi}\sigma^2_{ml} + \sigma^2_{pil} \tag{16}$$

These results for the modulation model—equations (13) through (16)—are set out in Table 4.7. A comparison of Tables 4.6 and 4.7 will show that the chief systematic difference is a product of person and state variances in the latter, and that the effect is particularly large in dR-technique. In both there will be a tendency for the variance of a state to be about equal in R- and P-techniques, and to be larger in dR- and G-techniques. The conclusions cannot be more succinctly put into words than they are given in the equations, which can be

TABLE 4.7

Magnitudes of Variances of a State Measure (When Individuals Differ on State Mean as Well as the Occasion) Compared Over the Main Experimental Techniques: B, Model with Interaction from Modulation

1. R-technique:

$$\sigma^2_{(l)} = \sigma^2_{mi} + k\sigma^2_{ml}\sigma^2_{mi} + \sigma^2_{pil}$$

2. P-technique:

$$\sigma^2_{(i)} = \sigma^2_{ml} + k\sigma^2_{ml}\sigma^2_{mi} + \sigma^2_{pil}$$

3. dR-technique:

$$\sigma^2_{(m-l)} = k^2\sigma^2_{mi}\sigma^2_{mm} + k^2\sigma^2_{mi}\sigma^2_{ml} + \sigma^2_{pim} + \sigma^2_{pil}$$

4. Total grid analysis (G-technique):

$$\sigma^2_{il} = \sigma^2_{mi} + \sigma^2_{ml} + k^2\sigma^2_{mi}\sigma^2_{ml} + \sigma^2_{pil}$$

used to check assumptions about (a) which factors are states and which traits, in R-technique, and (b) the relation of state intraindividual to state mean (interindividual) differences. In fact the equations of Tables 4.6 and 4.7 provide the means of solving for the variances of states, state means, traits, and so on, from empirically determinable variances, and thus answer various theoretical questions concerning any given state often raised in current discussions.

It must be kept in mind that these formulae apply to raw score variances. Where the total variance of a measure which is affected both by states and traits is set at unity, as in ordinary factor analysis, the above analyses tell us about the fraction of that variance due to a particular state or trait. In that case, in R-technique, the loading of a state is likely to be much smaller than in P- or dR-technique. With the above fundamental sorting of states from traits we can now proceed to their distinction from one another.

Conditions Required for Defining Anxiety, in Relation to Effort Stress, Arousal, Depression, and Fear

The meaning of a state response connotes three definers: the nature of the response itself, the nature of its usual causes, and its usual consequences. Certain writers are evidently satisfied to discuss only one of these, usually the second. Mandler would define anxiety as due to helplessness, and Lazarus as due to interruption and "appraisal." But others see these same situations as causes of depression and despair, or of anger and aggression, rather than anxiety. At the stage of research now reached above neither this degree of confusion nor the methods which lead to it, need be tolerated by serious investigators.

If anxiety, stress, arousal, etc., can be uniquely, differentially, factorially defined and measured then the question of what specifically provokes each can be positively answered by comparatively straightforward experimental designs (for example, bivariate). In fact, at the outset it was pointed out that although different ambient stimuli may be effective in provoking some one state, due to differences of learning experience, etc., yet if we proceed by first identifying the pattern there is every hope that some orderliness will be found in the mechanisms of what Lazarus calls "appraisal" and others "general perception of the situation," that is, the triggers for the states. One may hope to find innately prescribed prepotent situations, like frustration, suspense, threat, and helplessness, as well as prepotence with regard to the form of the common cultural dress in which such situations and response patterns appear in any experimentally effective state provocation.

Even if one prefers to concentrate his theories on the processes which lead up to and follow an anxiety (or other definitive) state response, leaving to others the technical task of uniquely defining the state pattern to which one seeks to relate the processes, he still needs to do a better job of defining the process per se than the above *verbal* presentations of the perceptual and expression process are capable of doing. There exist models and statistical analyses for recognizing processes (Cattell, 1966a; Fleishman, 1954; Tucker, 1966) almost as effective as those for recognizing and defining cross-sectional patterns, but not one of the discussants in this symposium has discussed them. The verbal circularities offered do not come to grips with the level of research at which we should and can now operate. For example, they do not begin to offer operational distinction between the processes involving experience of an interrupted plan on the one hand, and, say, helplessness, or reappraisal of a situation on the other, any more than they offer experimentally meaningful detection and identification of the various state patterns themselves.

Before attacking the question of recognizing the sequential process in the temporal development of any states (and the associated theoretical explanations) in the next section below, it is methodologically and logically desirable to dwell on the unique characters of the states themselves. This was initially done in the present writer's contribution in Spielberger (1966) five years ago, but should be broached again for the unhappy reason that the knowledge and the gains in practical measurement offered in these patterns are not being used as powerfully as they could be, and for the happy reason, on the other hand, that further progress in the definitions now exists to be reported.

As to the first, it is indeed an unhappy state in any area of science when communication breaks down to the point where technical advances fifteen years old are not being used—especially when current investigations are nullified for lack of those techniques and their associated measuring instruments. If the findings on anxiety, stress, etc., measurement are incorrect they should be experimentally challenged; if they are correct many "theories" still being discussed are already defunct or irrelevant, and more powerfully predictive theories could now become the focus of discussion.

To be explicit about what some of the resulting problems are, it must be said that a problem of experimental comparability of results arises when, outside the relatively small group of well trained multivariate experimentalists, a much larger group of writers in this field have been making up their anxiety and arousal measures essentially by fiat. One can confidently predict, before we go any further, that Smith's measure of, say, arousal, thus put together, will correlate no more than about 0.5 to 0 with Brown's and, what is worse, correlate better with Jones' measure of anxiety or elation than with Brown's measure of arousal. Thirty years of watching the parade of this kind of "experiment" has unfortunately revealed to me that logic of the kind which says that to define a straight line we need two points, a plane, three, and a factor, decidedly more, is lost on a majority of those trained as psychologists have been. To mention the possibility of a unique objective determination of intelligence (Spearman, 1904), anxiety or anything else is to be accused of "a habit of believing his measures are better than other people's." It is little wonder that students, bewildered by a history of psychology which fits Oscar Wilde's definition of history as "an account of things that should never have happened," are unhappy with their teachers. Although not illustrating the utter naïveté over scientific debate and procedure just instanced, the discrepancies of conclusion between the Eysenck and the Manifest Anxiety Scale do witness that we are by no means past the stage where serious attention to locating the unique pattern of anxiety is still needed. Meanwhile multiple state scales are apt to rest on a priori definitions, e.g., in Clyde's Mood Scale, 1963.

When Scheier and the present writer built the IPAT Anxiety scale in 1960, based on repeated unique determination of the factor in several samples (see Tables 4.1 and 4.3, p. 140 and p. 166) we finished by putting all three scales for anxiety proposed at that time–the IPAT, the MAS and the Eysenck–into a common analysis. We found that the Taylor Scale, as was to be expected from items taken from clinical data, diverged from the factor axis in the direction of including neuroticism, for example, Factors I and C– in the 16 P.F., while the Eysenck scale (checked in its recent form), diverged in another direction from the same factor axis. Part of the information in this statement of factor axis relations can be given in simple correlation terms by saying that these two scales correlated better with the IPAT scale than with each other. But now to make a masterpiece of confusion for students, Eysenck has insisted on calling his anxiety scale a neuroticism (N) scale. So that we have on the one hand something explicitly called an "anxiety scale," which proves to have marked neurotic intrusions, and something called a neuroticism scale which measures anxiety more than it measures anything else. Furthermore, if we check this by going into the objective test, T-data realm, Eysenck's neuroticism scale correlates with the O–A anxiety factor (Cattell & Scheier, 1961; Hundleby *et al.*, 1965) which we have long indexed as U.I. 24 and which has aligned with all criteria of anxiety tried. But by our findings and those of others the various Q-data anxiety scales–including the N-scale–correlate scarcely at all with the U.I. 23 T-data factor, Regression, which Eysenck has called the Neuroticism factor.

Among several recent studies in which the differences between anxiety measurements are not adequately analyzed, is a research of a more constructive nature by Hundal, Sudhakar, and Sidhu (1970) who entered with a sufficient diversity of variables to obtain simple structure and whose results are shown in Table 4.8.

The pattern of loadings on the 16 P.F. primaries here (though in Indian translation and on an Indian sample) is very similar to that repeatedly found for the anxiety factor, and there is little doubt that Factor 1 (with intelligence, age, height, education, achievement, etc., defining its hyperplane) is a well determined identification of the anxiety factor. By this definition of the criterion, the validities of the commonly used scales show such a wide range as

TABLE 4.8
The Concept (Construct) Validities of Some Important Anxiety Scales

Scale or other variable	Factor			
	Anxiety	g_c^a	Physical size	Neuroticism[b]
1. The IPAT Anxiety Scale	98	01	02	−03
2. The Maudsley (MPI) N-Scale	62	00	07	−26
3. Taylor Manifest Anxiety Scale	69	03	−08	−41
4. Sinha Anxiety Scale	53	−01	01	−64
5. Low self sentiment (Q_3− in 16 P.F.)	39	−17	−01	14
6. Low ego strength (*C*− in 16 P.F.)	63	−01	03	−19
7. High protension (*L* in 16 P.F.)	51	23	−19	−01
8. Guilt proneness (*O* in 16 P.F.)	74	−00	11	−03
9. Ergic tension (Q_4 in 16 P.F.)	82	05	00	−03
10. IPAT Culture Fair Intelligence Scale	−09	57	00	17
11. Maudsley (MPI) Extraversion Scale	−24	−06	−01	15
12. Achieve't score in college entrance (matric)	05	84	−06	−08
13. Achieve't score in B.A. degree exam	11	76	06	01
14. Age	−10	04	41	−31
15. Height	03	03	67	00
16. Weight	02	01	79	00

[a] Because of the greater loading on achievement than fluid intelligence (g_f: the culture fair score) this is deemed to be crystallized intelligence.

[b] This interpretation, in the absence of any high loadings, is speculative. Since the tendency all along in anxiety scale constructions (other than by factor validity) has been to include pathological (mostly neurotic) items, the probability is that this represents the personality factors other than anxiety (see Cattell & Scheier, 1961) that enter into defining the neurotic.

This data has especial interest because it represents a cross validation in a different language and culture—that of India—and is thus free of some local language effects of the original. The data is from the original study of Hundal *et al.* (1970), since republished with the improved simple structure (used here) of an oblique rotation. The correlations of the four factors are:

	1	2	3	4
1. Anxiety	100			
2. Intelligence	−23	100		
3. Physique	−04	06	100	
4. Neuroticism	00	−05	17	100

The stability of factor patterns for anxiety and arousal found across cultures and individuals contrasts with the assertions of Lacey (1967) that considerable uniqueness exists.

would invalidate many conclusions that one might attempt to carry from one to the other. (The percentage of anxiety factor variance accounted for, as shown by the corresponding correlations in Table 4.8, varies from about 96% for the IPAT scale to 48% for the MAS, 38% the MPI, and 28% for the Sinha scale. Furthermore, it is evident from column 4 that the last three tend to compound anxiety with neuroticism or, at least, some essentially distinct factor. Since the strictly neurotic primaries are not included, one cannot definitely say how much clinical neuroticism is involved, but there is certainly much outside anxiety in the total variance of the MPI N-scale and the MAS.

The main advances in the last five years have resided in (1) an increasing definition of the known state factors in the questionnaire medium, where previously they had been stably replicated only in T-data, (2) some clarification, in one or two dimensions, of the difference between the state and the trait factor, and (3) a slight augmentation of evidence on the relation of the response pattern to process events.

A problem in all state work concerns the length of time that is optimum for experiments designed to locate and define patterns of change. Between a startle reaction, or a flush of shame, appearing in a matter of seconds, to a manic-depressive swing taking days, weeks, or more, there are all degrees of speed of state and mood onset. If the actual measurement time for the necessary battery of measures is short enough to be considered "cross-sectional," that is, simultaneous, it does not matter how long the retest interval is. History repeats itself, and on any state that changes in a few hours we can get just as good dR pattern results by retesting after a month, as on the next day. The only limitation is in regard to such states as fear or startle, where all the necessary battery cannot be given at just the same phase of the process. Spielberger has argued that the questionnaire is good in this respect, while the present writer has urged the value of physiological measures, many of which can be quickly taken.[5]

Actually it is questionable whether an adequate questionnaire is so much quicker that other drawbacks should be forgotten. About 40 items are the least that will give a 0.8–0.9 reliability, and this means 10 minutes. The objective battery of Scheier for anxiety, or that of Nesselroade and Cattell (1962) for each of seven states, requires only about 20 minutes, so that time consumption is at

[5] The argument for utility of physiological measures must not be mistaken for any defense of the confident habit of taking a mere one or two measures, as Epstein takes a measure of pulse rate and dubs it a measure of arousal and/or anxiety. The excuse often given for this bivariate research is that it takes too much time, trouble, or apparatus to measure the total true pattern. Yet heart rate, for instance, is a measure of just about every state from arousal, effort stress, elation, anxiety, and so on, to indigestion and a momentary allergy or the onset of a fever, so that maybe 5% of its variance belongs to each. The only result that can come from an experiment claiming to find relations between "something" and anxiety, when anxiety is measured only as pulse rate, is a storing of the reader's mind with misleading generalizations.

least of the same order. It is not our purpose here to go into minor matters of technique in Q-data research, but in the IPAT Q-data state batteries we have favored a four choice answer (so that the respondent is compelled to avoid a noncommittal average), and a graphic scale, so that a specific word will not be remembered in a short interval retest. The instruction to "Respond as you feel now" is, of course, desirable. Yet it can be shown that it is not essential, because clear cut, consistent state patterns can be found, as shown in Table 4.1, when persons respond to a questionnaire unaware that they are being asked "now" That is to say, the momentary mood effectively projects itself into the subject's perception of what usually happens to him.

True dR or P-technique analyses of mood questionnaire responses are extremely rare. For example, they were not carried out on the Clyde Mood Scale, the Spielberger Anxiety State Scale, Beck's depression scale, or Knowlis's alleged "state" factorings (which were R-technique). The presently existing researches are a P-technique by Curran on six housewives over a total of 100 days, a P-technique by Connor on one woman over 70 days, a dR study on anxiety in adults by Nesselroade and Cattell, and a dR study by Shrader, Cattell, and Barton on high school children. The outcomes are consistent in showing (a) an exvia–invia state pattern, as before (Table 4.1), (b) a single state anxiety factor, also as before, (c) three depression factors (at the second order to seven primaries, as in the, assumedly, trait realm, (d) an effort stress state, also as before, (e) an arousal-versus-fatigue factor not previously located in Q-data, and (f) indications that about three more state dimensions exist which cannot, at present, be closely pursued. Items salient on some of these are shown for illustration in Table 4.9.

Although Q-data researches are usually simpler than those with objective tests, it is relevant to report that many technical difficulties need attention if one is to get consistent results in this area. Some have been dealt with elsewhere (Cattell, 1963a). Working with items it turns out that one first gets primaries, in state work just as in trait work, at the level of (and largely corresponding to) the 16 P.F. factors. From these, one has to go to a second order analysis to locate anxiety, exvia, cortertia, etc. Second, in order to rotate at this second order level one has to carry primaries for second orders outside the content of the particular second order, for example, anxiety, with which one is concerned. This means a fairly large (100–200) total of items (most already known to be salients), and consequently calls for a large person N to be retested.

A puzzle in this area is the failure of two successive and carefully planned researches to separate (high) arousal and (low) fatigue, which in T-data are believed represented by distinct state factors (Cattell, 1957a). The factor so far appearing is one which has arousal-excitement items at the positive pole and fatigue statements at the negative. Do we have a "permissive" factor relation here (Coombs & Kao, 1955) in which stimulation is simply incapable of producing high arousal when fatigue happens to be high? The riddle is only likely to be solved when the Q- and T-data patterns have been systematically brought into the same experiments. And that can happen only when the Q-data state factors are as clearly defined as the T-data. But that time is fast approaching.[6]

The Nature and Theoretical Distinction of Anxiety, Effort Stress, Arousal, Depression, and Fear

With the degree of definition of Q-data and T-data state, and Q-data and T-data trait patterns now visible—though still with some major scotomas—in carefully set out tables available in the literature, it is timely to proceed to more interpretation and theoretical development than was possible five years ago. In this section we shall confine discussion of meaning to anxiety, arousal, effort stress, fear, and depression, still sketching in the last four mainly as a background for heightening the meaning of the first.

Although sound observations are the beginning of viable theory, in the theoretical development coming from the typical inductive-hypothetico-deductive process (see discussion Cattell, 1966a), they are also not the end of it. From this point on we propose to stand on the above precise evidence and take off into the realm of theory development, particularly as it concerns deductions for further research. This will have two parts: (1) theories of the nature of the states themselves, beginning with their identified patterns, in the present section, and (2) theories of the processes which generate states, in the next section. Under (1) we shall consider only anxiety, effort stress, arousal, and depression, as follows.

Anxiety is centrally a suspension of behavioral expression paradoxically combined with a heightening of dynamic readiness. That this state should ensue is natural when we consider the process leading to it in the Adjustment Process Analysis Chart shown in Figure 4.3 (p. 166). Since it connotes an inability to cope, that is, to produce a solution, it is not surprising that, when prolonged, it engenders the discovered associates: lack of confidence, irritability, complaisance (seeking security by a tendency to agree), reduction of self-sentiment (Q_3-), and guilt (0). [See also the "disorganization" responses in Izard and Tomkins (1966).] We would still expect these expressions, though substantially correlated, to be secondary and derivative and, as the state-trait comparison shows (p. 166), to become more prominent as the condition continues. Incidentally, the need to distinguish between the intensity and

[6] It does not suffice to say that because rather inadequate correlations are obtained between Q- and T-measures of anxiety we are justified in concluding that they are not the same thing. In the instances quoted, only single and impure measures were used. With a dozen variables per factor, and therefore adequate factor estimation, the conclusion could be entirely different. The problem is one of eliminating instrument factors, but not in the manner of Edwards' Social Desirability Factor (1957) which is practically anxiety-invented.

environmental frequency of anxiety responses claimed by Endler & Hunt (1966) seems to this writer not to be established.

The heightening of need for dynamic discharge is seen mainly in the numerous physiological changes listed earlier (p. 130) which do not take the form of any one emotion. This associate of anxiety we shall call "general ergic tension" defined as in the MAT (Motivational Analysis Test) research (Cattell, Horn, Radcliffe & Sweney, 1964) and definitely not to be identified with the arousal pattern below. The response patterns of anger, effort and even fear are also distinct from this (Cattell & Bartlett, 1971). One should also note the distinctness of the adrenergic pattern (Cattell & Luborsky, 1950; Cattell, 1957b). Physiologically, the anxiety pattern is peculiarly its own, probably a composite of ACTH and the general ketosteroid output, plus high acetylcholine generation in the central nervous system due to high cognitive action in connection with the conflict and suspense situation.

Effort Stress is distinguished from anxiety by having much less conscious content, for example, it does not project itself into the general 16 P.F. questionnaire domain very much, and certainly not with any such sense of inability to cope, lack of confidence, shame, etc., as characterizes anxiety. It does, however, show several "tension" introspections that happen to be almost identically loaded by anxiety, thus causing Q-data confusion with anxiety in scales which do not balance such items. On the other hand, it differs from anxiety by showing low susceptibility to embarrassment, and manifesting calmness and stability, self sufficiency and confident adventurousness–but also such high aspiration that the individual does not feel he is coping as well as he really might. Behaviorally, it differs also in loading: good memorizing, effective calculation, low suggestibility, high performance, for example, on the Cursive Miniature Situation test, and steady control and small myokinesis. Since several of the last (memory, calculation) are precisely opposite in sign to anxiety, that is, anxiety reduces them, there is no excuse for confounding the stress and anxiety responses. However, in the physiological area there is marked common loading, namely of pulse rate, 17-OH ketosteroid output and serum cholinesterase (though the last has lower loading than on anxiety).

This overlap of anxiety and stress in the physiological area, and in awareness of pressure and tension, is accounted for in our theory as due to stress being associated with strong dynamic action, but not with any internal conflict and suspension which colors the ergic tension in anxiety. From some of our data it is evident even that a person can be stressing himself most when he is calm, concentrated, and successfully working hard. Recent data (Cattell & Nesselroade, in press) shows the stress pattern occurring with raised super ego and self-sentiment, and to some extent raised ego-strength conditions–again opposite to anxiety.

The stress pattern probably also differs from anxiety by appearing in most factor analyses at the first rather than the second order, that is, it is more

TABLE 4.9
Q-Data Markers for Stress, Arousal, Anxiety, and Depression

P.U.I. 1 Arousal	Direction of scoring	Technique	Loading
1. I feel sluggish and my limbs feel too heavy to move	No	dR	.47
2. My liking for work is up to its usual level	Yes	dR	.49
3. These days I feel full of pep and vigor	Yes	dR	.67
P.U.I. 9 Anxiety			
1. Even if something upsets me badly, I calm down quickly	No	dR	.25
2. Recently I did something that made me very ashamed	Yes	dR	.31
3. Lately I've been thinking a lot about death	Yes	dR	.24
P.U.I. 4 Stress			
1. I feel as if I am very tense	Yes	P	.22
2. Right now there is a great deal of pressure on me	Yes	P	.20
3. These days I have the feeling that I am not doing as well as I really can	Yes	P	.24
P.U.I. 2 Depression			
1. Lately I don't seem to care what becomes of me	Yes	dR	.34
2. Lately I feel happy most of the time	No	dR	.39
3. I am in a mood in which I feel worthless and of no use to anybody	Yes	dR	.46

ancillary to larger mood conditions, more specific to a limited situation, and probably more momentary (limited in period of rise and fall). Items representative in Q-data are shown in Table 4.9. Objective test and physiological associations for P.U.I. 4 are given elsewhere (Cattell, 1957a, p. 651; Cattell & Scheier, 1961, pp. 164–170).

Depression, as indicated above, occurs in Q-data in seven distinct primaries and three distinct second stratum factors. Space forbids entering on their natures here, but the second orders (one seems close to the Beck *et al.*, 1961, scale) apparently stand at the same level as the anxiety factor, and this is supported also by the tentative matching of the three depressions with objective test factors U.I. 21(–), U.I. 23(–), and U.I. 33. States tend to parallel trait factors, as stated earlier, but much remains to be cleared up, as only one P-technique state factor for depression, in T-data has been indubitably found, namely, P.U.I. 2. The three second order factors appear to be agitated depression, depression with fatigue or low energy, and simple depression, and it is the first that is frequently confused with anxiety. One well known anxiety scale is in fact more heavily loaded on the agitated depression factor (Cattell & Nesselroade, 1970) than on anxiety.

The confounding of other states with anxiety—to the confusion of experimental conclusions as shown in various surveys—nowhere reaches such proportions as with arousal. Indeed, the confusion ranges from being unaware of the need to distinguish them, through conceptual separations with no accompanying operational separation, depending on operational distinctions made by fiat, and which consequently do not agree. For example, Dr. Epstein's treatment falls in one of the two first, it is not clear which.

In Q-data, as stated elsewhere, an arousal pattern clearly separates itself from anxiety, etc., (see Table 4.9), but so far it has not been possible in dR- or P-technique to show that high arousal and low fatigue are different. In objective test data the first proof of a virtual linear relation between galvanic skin conductance and degree of "awakeness" (versus torpor) in thousands of introspective protocols, was given (as far as can be found) by the present writer (1928). But it quickly became evident as factor analytic methods were applied to further variables that this resistance measure is only one part of a whole pattern of arousal, P.U.I.1, marked by high conductance, high blood glucose, small upward drift of skin resistance when relaxed, much interruption of EEG rhythm (Pawlik & Cattell, 1964), small ataxic sway suggestibility, high cholinesterase in blood, and small size (%) G.S.R. deflections. These have mostly been used one at a time in most "classical" experiments (animal and physiological) to mark arousal. Indeed, most writers in the bivariate field have completely failed to avail themselves of the precision of conception which the factor pattern provides (Duffy, 1962; Bandura & Rosenthal, 1966; Haywood & Hunt, 1963; Venables & Warwick-Evans, 1967; Ward & Carlson, 1964). Moreover, experimental results are inconsistent or uninterpretable when only two variables—say skin conductance and pulse or EEG—have been used as the operational markers in "arousal" experiments, because these are also appreciably loaded on anxiety and exvia states. If the neurological phenomena in "arousal" can indeed be shown to be restricted largely to P.U.I.1, then arousal can be distinguished from anxiety primarily in terms of arousal, P.U.I.1, being a state of the central nervous system—indeed, largely of the cortex—while anxiety involves primarily excitation of the autonomic system. As hypothesized in the next section, ergic tension, that is, strictly dynamic need level, is something different again (measured operationally by, for example, total score on the MAT objective motivation measures) though it should significantly correlate with both—with arousal as the precondition of motivation level and anxiety as a degenerate product.

The first indication that anxiety might be considered a general autonomic activity factor—distinct from a parasympathetic or a sympathetic response

TABLE 4.10
Three Major Factors in the Expression of Autonomic System Activity[a]

I. General Autonomic Activity
High metabolic rate
High pulse rate
High blood pressure
High ratio pupil to iris diameter
High ratings on "vigorous," "active"
High ratio emotional to nonemotional word recall
High body temperature
High G.S.R. deflection size
Brief duration of after-images
II. Sympathetic–Autonomic (Adrenergic) Pattern
High pulse rate
High respiration rate
High ratio of G.S.R. response to systolic B.P.
Low skin resistance
High pH (alkalinity) of saliva
High blood glucose
Large performance upset by noise
High lymphocyte count
III. Parasympathetic-vs-Arousal
High skin resistance
Rating relaxed, torpid
Low cholinesterase
Large G.S.R. response magnitude
Slow pulse rate
Low blood glucose

[a] These three patterns are a composite from matching factors in Herrington (1942), Darrow and Heath (1932), and from a refactoring of Wenger's Air Force data (1958), together with indications in Freeman and Katzoff (1942) and Cattell and Luborsky (1950) –all before the systematic P– and dR-technique work reported in these pages. Now we would identify "General autonomic" with anxiety, U.I. 24; Adrenergic with P.U.I. 5, and "Parasympathetic" with the inverse of Arousal, P.U.I. 1. The three patterns were first reported, as a refactoring, in Cattell (1950).

pattern–came from the present writer's factor analysis of Wenger's (1958) very carefully gathered multivariate data, on a sufficient sample, which gave three factors as shown in Table 4.10, where data from several major autonomic studies has been combined.

Previously, most discussion simply conceived two "opposed," sympathetic and parasympathetic, response patterns. This analysis supported that neurologically-inferred distinction as behaviorally correct, but added a massive factor of general autonomic action, which raises either form of expression and seems to support the notion of conflict or suspension of any particular expression as central to the definition of anxiety. The agreement with the P-technique pattern, P.U.I.9 (Cattell, 1957a), points to this general autonomic arousal as being the essential physiological aspect of expression of anxiety.

If this is correct one may still speculate, as the present writer did earlier (1957), that the arousal pattern (not anxiety) could be the obverse of the parasympathetic pattern (which has low conductance, low cholinesterase, large G.S.R. deflection, and some loading on low blood sugar and low pulse–just like P.U.I.1). Neurological experiment has so far said nothing about this, but the similarities of the behavioral expression pattern demand that high arousal and low parasympathetic tone be seriously considered as either identical or, for some functional reason, highly related.

An adequate interpretation of arousal (P.U.I.1) as a state is not possible without noting, as we did in the case of anxiety, the relation of the state pattern to a corresponding trait pattern, which is similar but distinct. This latter, U.I. 22 (see 18 replications thereof in Hundleby *et al.,* 1965, p. 207) has been called "Cortertia"–indicating a high level of cortical alertness–and loads fast reaction time, fast ideomotor performance, rapid alternating perspective, etc. It has striking resemblance to the neurological descriptions of arousal phenomena, and has such significant criterion relations as to positive air pilot performance and low liability to neurosis. However, as Nesselroade has clearly shown (1967), it does not fluctuate and retains a highly characteristic level for each subject in his waking life. Nevertheless, under special temporary conditions of stimulation the individual certainly experiences changes on the related pattern of arousal, that is, in P.U.I.1. These findings do warn us, nevertheless, that in actual measures of alertness we are in danger of confusing state and trait arousal. Neither, however, need be confused with anxiety. Although arousal (P.U.I.1) does have low loadings on pulse rate and blood glucose these are of a lower order than the extensive general autonomic upset and overfunction seen in anxiety, and are only outlying reverberations of that central nervous system alertness which is arousal.

Finally, in regard to fear, though Freud considered it the main expression needing separation from anxiety, it is in fact far less likely to be confounded in the measurement field than are arousal, stress, and even one of the depressions. It is a reaction to a definite external stimulus, with a sudden and usually short duration entirely different from anxiety. However, introspectively (and this is Freud's angle), it has the same generic quality, and granted (1) uncertainty in the stimulus, and (2) very prolonged duration, it could, as argued in the next session, theoretically, generate a "variety" of fear which becomes identical. At present, the reason for not considering that all anxiety comes from fear is the simple experimental fact that the factor of ergic tension for the fear erg in the MAT (Cattell *et al.,* 1964) does not correlate to more than a minor extent with the factor measures of anxiety (U.I. 24 or IPAT Anxiety scale). Moreover, as a state, in dR-technique, Bartlett (Cattell & Bartlett, 1971) has obtained clear indications that the fear measures factor out separately from the anxiety measures.

Anxiety and Other States Defined in a Theory of Dynamic Process

A state achieves its full definition and explanation by being understood as part of a temporal process, but the recognition of the response pattern cross sectionally as in the previous 8 sections, must come first, since otherwise it would be uncertain which of the states one is following up in its process manifestations.

Our next purpose will be to consider the rise of anxiety as a dynamic process. However, we must first make a clear distinction between the description of a process, as a kinetic phenomenon, that is, one involving velocities and sequences, which belongs to the necessities of a good taxonomy, and the interpretation of such sequencies causally, by dynamic (energy) or other concepts. Psychologists as yet have provided virtually no firm science of process, as kinetic description, though there are beginnings in learning theory (Hull, 1943; Skinner, 1953) and in the unfolding of states (Cattell, 1963a; 1966b).

Without such descriptive foundations, and general familiarity of psychologists with the concepts involved, we must nevertheless attempt to set out theories of the dynamics of the anxiety development process. Any description of a psychological process—which is achieved by a matrix whose columns are moments in time—must contain an account both of the sequence of stimulus situations and of the sequence of responses. A first model with psychological concepts for analyzing the typical sequence of encounter of an animal or human being, impelled by a drive, and a typical external environmental situation was worked out by Cattell and Scheier (1961) and developed further (Cattell, 1964b) under the title of Adjustment Process Analysis, which can be summarized by a chart as in Figure 4.3.

The APA chart consists of an inevitable series of choice points, dynamic cross-roads, or, most briefly, chiasms, in any attempted adjustment process (food seeking, career, marriage, adjustment to peers). The first three cross-roads apply to all animals, the last three only to man or such animals as can learn to inhibit in relation to internalized standards (super ego, *G,* and self sentiment, Q_3, in man).

The initial arousal of any drive is hypothesized to consist of a general cortical excitation, or arousal, *E,* and a specific ergic tension level, E_s, for example,

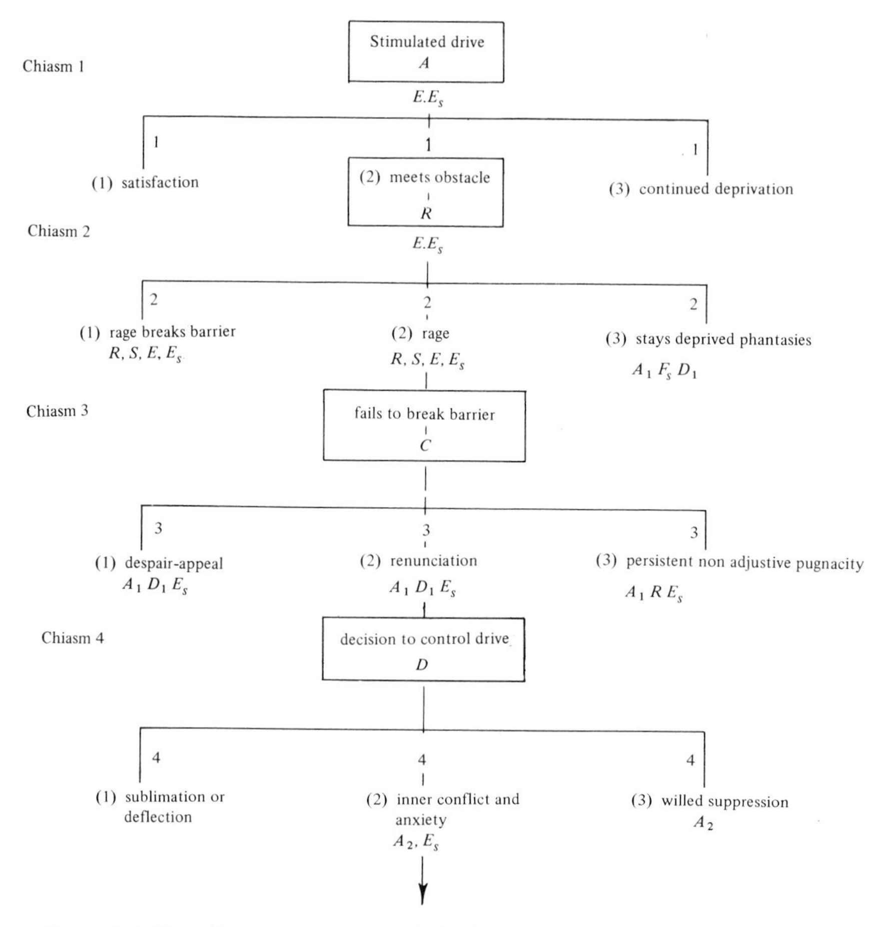

Figure 4.3. *The adjustment process analysis chart and the principal stimuli of states.*

hunger, sex. (As set out below, the preliminary evidence is that these are distinct, though positively correlated.) Descriptively, the drive E_s is either satisfied [1(1)], in which case both E and E_s are reduced virtually to zero, or continues without satisfaction but no further stimulation [1(3)]. In the latter case we may suppose either that E disappears, or persists and encounters a new focally perceived obstacle [1(2)].[7]

At this second chiasm anger, R, may develop which will be accompanied by effort stress, S, continuing high arousal, E, and unchanged ergic tension, E_s. This

[7] If we consider the total, nonsituational ergic tension, characteristic of the individual at the time, to be that which is involved in any given calculation, then E becomes the personality term Q_4, general ergic tension.

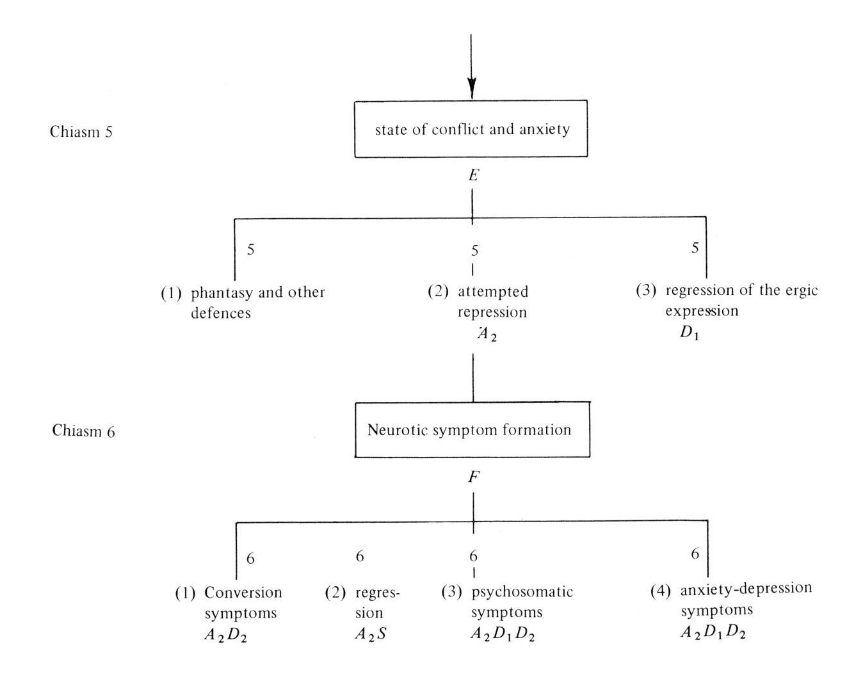

A_1 = anxiety, regarding external situation, P.U.I. 9
A_2 = anxiety regarding internal control situation, P.U.I. 9
D_1 = depression of failure, P.U.I.2
D_2 = depression of exhaustion (U.I. 23-), P.U.I. 8
E = arousal, excitement at the cortical level, P.U.I. 1
E_s = ergic tension (appetive and stimulated) in a specific erg or ergs
R = rage anger, P.U.I. 5(?)
S = effort stress response, P.U.I. 4

combination may either solve the problem by breaking the barrier [2(1)], or fail to break or circumvent it [2(2)]. Alternatively, however, the possibility exists that anger may not develop, the obstacle being perceived as insuperable. Here, [2(3)], while E_s stays high and E declines, the anxiety, A, develops—through uncertainty and lack of confidence about ability to cope with the external situation—and some depression, D, can for the first time enter the state mixture. With this introduction to the symbolism the remaining part of the APA chart may be left to speak for itself.

The APA Chart, which yields an operationally translatable account of the rise of anxiety and other states, is thus more precise and more clear in determining hypothetico-deductive consequences for testing, than many "theories of anxiety stimulation" that have preceded and followed it. Freud spoke of anxiety as a product of over-stimulation (in its external origins) and of threat to ego control (in its internal situation). As to the first the APA formulation says stimulation (of a particular kind) without comparable possibilities of expression is a cause of anxiety, and as to the second, discussed below, it is also in full accord. Pavlov's "incongruity" is a special perceptual case of stimulation without a solving response, and Lazarus' "response unavailability," expresses the same idea. Mandler's "absence of, or interruption of, a specific plan" or a previously "well organized sequence of behavior," is also obviously a special aspect of the formula, though it adds a condition which is ambiguous. It suggests there must be a specific conscious plan, whereas the generic APA formula in Figure 3.3, above, includes both unconscious, inborn ergic plans and conscious, learned plans.

So much for general agreement, but there is also disagreement—if one can hope to compare verbal notions with the operational sequence and P.U.I. states in Figure 3.3. For example, Mandler defines "helplessness" as the trigger for anxiety, but the APA Chart makes uncertainty in the external signals, [2(3)], and in the inner control of a renounced drive, "suspense" [4(2)], [4(3)], etc., the main precursors of anxiety, whereas helplessness is primarily the condition of depression or despair [3(1)]. Incidentally, the notion "inability to cope" is too wide for anxiety, covering, as it does, depression, anxiety and persistent nonadaptive pugnacity [3(3)].

In the APA chart, by the symbols A_1 and A_2 we have preserved the possibility that the anxiety from external uncertainty and that from internal suspense and difficulties of control might be qualitatively different, corresponding to differences of origin. This deserves being pointed out for future more refined factor analytic research, but, from P.U.I. 1 to P.U.I. 12, no pattern has been found which yet strongly suggests such a second form of anxiety. Accordingly, in analysis from now on we shall use only one symbol, A, for anxiety, but in the process of generation of A we shall clearly distinguish the kind of uncertainty in the external world which first generates anxiety, and which we may best term the suspense situation, from that in the internal, symbolic control domain, which we shall call the threat-to-control situation.

Regarding the suspense situation, there seems no need so far to amend the formulation in my earlier Chapter (Spielberger, 1966). This stated that the difference between fear and anxiety resides in the cognitive situation, in the latter being ill-defined, notably as to if, when and how much reward or punishment may occur. It also assumed that all fear can be subsumed under fear of deprivation, which covers punishment as lack of reward (deprivation), of (1) the need to escape pain, etc., and (2) the deprivation contemplated in any other erg whatsoever. Experiment can readily be arranged concerning the effect of uncertainty of cognitive expectation ("subjective probability") and in this

Epstein has made an excellent beginning (except for the anachronisms in anxiety measurement itself, mentioned above). A conceptual point which requires clarification concerning suspense anxiety is whether an obstacle, producing continued deprivation (as in chiasm 2 of the APA chart) is essential to its production, or whether mere incongruity of reward signals will suffice. The answer would seem to be that incongruity is a special case of an obstacle, that is, cognitive obscurity; in fact it postpones satisfaction and produces suspense.

Regarding what we have called the inner control source of anxiety, experimental attack is going to require precise trait and state concepts and more sophisticated designs. The original insight here is Freud's view that undischarged drive is a threat to the ego, experienced as anxiety, proportional to the tension of the thwarted drive (the "transference neuroses"). High anxiety calls for the individual eventually to take stock of the reinforcements and resources of the self (which in structured personality theory are the ego, as measured in strength by C factor, and the self-sentiment, as measured in development by Q_3, assessable in ratings or in the 16 P.F. test, the HSPQ, etc.). This may account for the crises of identity ("losing my mind"), the free floating anxiety, etc., in the anxiety neurotic and the rise of Q_3 in phases of schizophrenia (Cattell, Tatro, & Komlos, 1964). Incidentally, one need not adopt a merely historically defined psychoanalytic position, but can move within the better checked realm of structured personality theory in interpreting the notion of "threat to the ego". It suffices in the latter that, in early childhood, loss of control has been consistently punished, either by parents or the discipline of natural consequences, so that a generalization takes place to generate anxiety about any loss of control. The suspense, now directed to inner cues, concerns "How long can I maintain inhibition of this dangerous impulse?"

The unfinished development of the above general theoretical position was formulated in my earlier chapter by:

$$A = A_x + A_y = f(E)(V_e)(V_o/H) + f(1/H)(E/R) \tag{17}$$

$$\text{Since } A_x = f(E)(V_e)(V_o/H) \quad \text{and} \quad A_y = f(1/H)(E/R)$$

where V_o is the variability (uncertainty in general terms) of the environment, V_e is the variability of ergic tension (internal uncertainty of control) as here defined, E is the ergic tension now needing discharge, and $1/H$ is the individual's general proneness to fear. (It is so written because H in the 16 P.F. is insusceptibility to threat, and we wished to relate the formula to actual available factorially-defined measures.) Thus, the first expression on the right, which represents one component in anxiety, A_x, is simply the magnitude of the undischarged drive, multiplied by the objective and subjective uncertainty, and multiplied again by the subject's general proneness to fear of anything. The second increment to anxiety, A_y, takes into account not the uncertainty of reward, as in A_x, but the regular degree of deprivation that may ("unfortunately") be confidently anticipated by the organism from previous experience. Here R is the reward (ergic tension reduction regularly encountered), and E the demand. The $1/H$ is again the multiplier for the individuals general reactivity to threat of any kind. Several participators in this symposium have doubted whether unquestioned future deprivation excites anxiety, for example, the human mortality we all face, and I would agree that this term might vanish; but initially, to provoke experiment, it is best retained.

From certain advances in this area since the original formulation (16), above, it seems appropriate to develop it to a model in which there are three components in the final anxiety level instead of two. These, written a_e, a_c and a_p, will be defined below. Meanwhile, however, let us recognize that the main model, though perhaps oversimplified, has shown a good enough fit to have its essentials retained. For example, in support of carrying a term V_e, for inner variability of desires, we showed that anxiety is inversely proportional to ego strength (r of about $-.5$ with C factor); in support of the importance of the present ergic tension term, E, we showed a high (about 0.8) correlation with Q_4 (in 16 P.F., HSPQ, etc.). Threctia ($H-$, or $1/H$) behaved as expected. We have not investigated V_e and R, but Epstein's work, and particularly that on the parachute jump, supports V_e, and possibly R, if we interpret the lower anxiety of experienced jumpers as "knowledge" of higher reward and less punishment than a beginner anticipates.

Apart from our not knowing whether to use linear or nonlinear relations, differences, or ratios, the chief deficiency of the above formula is (1) omitting the strength of control (notably of the self-sentiment, Q_3) from the expression for effect of inner uncertainty—"doubt about control" V_e—since Q_3 control reduces this uncertainty about the self (2) omitting also the superego, and guilt proneness, which empirical correlations show to be actually involved in anxiety level, and (3) leaving the external uncertainty—"suspense," V_o—insufficiently expressed in actual measures of probability, time intervals, etc.

In the space that remains available in this presentation for a more up-to-date refinement of the dynamic process concepts presented earlier (Spielberger, 1966), a systematic examination of all promising alternatives is not possible; only the most likely theory among several closely related can be developed. It will already be clear that any and all of these developments reject the notion that anxiety, arousal, elation–depression, effort stress, etc., are primary dynamic forces. These kinds of pattern, which, descriptively, as factor analytic discoveries, have been called general states, to distinguish them from the similarly discovered but experimentally different ergic states (ergic tensions of sex, fear, gregariousness, etc., with their particular emotional, dynamic qualities), are here considered as by-products of a dynamic process, itself recognizable in ergic tension states. These general states will admittedly have some of the effects of dynamic states; but their total properties justify and require our considering them as a different species. Anxiety may in some ways motivate, but it does so with several limiting conditions not present in the primary motivators which are the specific ergic tensions. This theory stands in direct contrast to that of Spence (1956) and the consideration of anxiety as a simple motivating force in Spence & Spence (1966).

To remedy the shortcomings mentioned in the paragraph before last, the first development necessary in a more refined statement is a redefinition of "uncertainty." it becomes reasonably certain that two terms should enter where in (17) we used only V_o to express the uncertainty of the environment. Besides environmental uncertainty, we shall now introduce a new term, U_t, for the uncertainty regarding the length of time that the individual has reason to expect the inhibition has to be maintained; while the environmental term V_o will become U_g for uncertainty of gratification (reward). (The symbol change from V_o to U_g is not trivial but represents a conceptual change made because the operational definition of uncertainty simply as actually experienced variability is too gross. The operational meaning of U has to be developed. The total formulation now requires an anticipated deprivation–punishment term as in A_y in (17) (though this is more powerful in its effect on depression than on anxiety), and a splitting of the first term A_x into more completely independent external, cognitive, and internal dynamic uncertainties.

Furthermore, it would assist clarity of experimental operation designs here if the ergic tension were split, as in the dynamic calculus (Cattell, 1958, 1959), into the inner need strength—the present appetitive, physiological need strength, defined in detail as $N = [C + H + (P - aG) - bG]$ (Cattell, 1965a, p. 202)—and the ambient stimulation, s, which converts this into drive strength. Ambient stimulation is written $(s + k)$ in the standard formula, where k defines the "resting level" of the need to prevent the term going to a limit of zero, signaling the expected satisfaction (here better written $E - G$ rather than E/G). If we call these (1) external cognitive evaluation, (2) subjective control, and (3) future punishment–deprivation components, writing them respectively, a_e, a_c, and a_p, then:

$$a_p = F(E - G) = (E - G)/H \tag{18}$$

Here E is existing ergic tension level, G [formerly R in (17)], is the cognitively expected gratification reward—tension reduction—from whatever experience the individual possesses to guide his estimation of the usual gratification, and F is the normal score of the individual on the fear erg (e.g., in the MAT), which we may perhaps equate to $H(-)$—susceptibility to threat—(e.g., on the 16 P.F., HSPQ, etc., personality measures). It is a complication, though a necessary one, to recognize that the current ergic tension level, E, is the result partly of an appetitive need component, N, and partly of a stimulation effect, s. The stimulation, s, in most real life situations will already be adjusted to the accustomed reward, that is, s is the cue for G. Thus $E = (s + k)N$ where s is itself a function of G. Consequently, a more fully spelt out (18) formulation becomes:

$$a_p = F(kN + cGN - G) \quad (19)$$

where c is an experimentally determined constant.

Thus (19) states that the anxiety from the anticipated relation of present need to the future gratification–punishment ratio is a function of the individual's fearfulness in general (F or $1/H$), his present appetitive tension, kN, and his gratification expectation. This ergic tension is taken as a firm known quantity, and the uncertainty is expressed in the other two terms, which follow. The external situation cognitive uncertainty hypothesis is thus comparatively simple:

$$a_e = E(U_g + U_t)(Fc - d) \quad (20)$$

Again F is added, since temperamental susceptibility to threat should affect this too, though the constant, c, will probably turn out to give it a small role. As before $1/H$ can be substituted for F if one uses the personality measure for Threctia instead of the MAT measure for fear tension, F.

It is the third term–for "self control" anxiety, that is, fear of threat to self control–which presents most complication. Here one must undoubtedly include more personality determiners, notably, (1) ego weakness ($C-$), (2) threctia ($H-$ or F) as in (20), (3) guilt proneness (O) (inasmuch as failure is an affront to the superego), and (4) the strength of development of the self sentiment (Q_3), (inasmuch as any threat from a strong impulse that might imply that control will be overthrown is reduced by a high development of self sentiment). All four of these terms can be incorporated in the hypotheses with considerable confidence, since, as several of the above tables show, they have repeatedly been found significantly correlated with individual anxiety level, in the directions indicated.

It is the incorporation of the situational terms that involves more assumption. Our hypothesis regarding the internal situation is that high ergic tension, relative to the individual's C and Q_3 resources, is a first determiner, for this is the magnitude of threat of loss of control. Second, the length of time that inhibition is perceived as probably needing to be maintained is another. There is no need to use the old term V_e for ergic variability as an inner uncertainty, since in so far as this is characteristic of the individual it is already in $C(-)$, and in so far as it derives from the situation the chances of a threateningly high variation from the present level are proportional to the length of time the suspense situation has to be endured. Thus we reach:

$$a_c = E(T + U_t)(F - d) + \frac{O + H}{f(C + Q_3) - E} \quad (21)$$

Here the first term (in which $1/H$ may be substituted for F) expresses the internal situational aspect of anxiety due to the time, uncertainty, and strength of impulse to be controlled. The second term expresses the personality component in the internal control anxiety. A Freudian might ask where the superego term, G, appears. The accumulated evidence from "structured personality" research is that the expressed superego, G, is significantly *negatively* correlated with anxiety (Horn, 1961; Gorsuch, 1965) as Mowrer's theory would require. But O, guilt proneness, which was never located in psychoanalytic observations (and is, if one wishes, in psychoanalytic views, a second superego concept) is substantially positively correlated with anxiety.

The reader may be left to put these detailed terms for a_e, a_c and a_p above, together, in:

$$A = a_e + a_c + a_p \tag{22}$$

(where A is total anxiety) in what is now offered as an adequate theoretical model for anxiety. There is no objection to handling this formulation alternatively with differences where we have used quotients (or vice versa), and, of course, various constants could be applied relative to scaling, etc., to virtually all terms. It may appear complex, and it is certainly multivariate. Yet, in fact, it takes the simplest linear relations to begin with, and it claims that the number of concepts required E, G, U_g, T, U_t and N in the dynamic inner and outer situations, and C, H (or $F-$), O, and Q_3 in individual differences is minimal. Moreover, it has the attractive quality to the experimentalist that it is composed of concepts which largely are now already uniquely factor analytically defined and measurable.

The culminating formulation just given is for anxiety, but corresponding special developments could be made for the other types of mood response appearing in the APA chart, now factor analytically recognizable, such as arousal, depression, etc. Indeed, our next concern must be with what the implications of the APA process are for the correlations to be expected among such states. In the APA chart it will be seen that there are no fewer than 19 possible different paths (more if we consider all clinical alternatives at chiasm 6). There is a corresponding number of "endings for the story" that begins with "stimulation of a drive." It cannot be our purpose here to follow these in specific situations, and we have no basis for calculating their relative frequencies in life situations, but the central fact can be noted that all sequences of experience that reach and pass through chiasm 5, and finish on the threshold of "starting neurotic defenses," will have followed a common path with the same, typical succession:

1(2). E . E_s. General arousal (P.U.I.1), and arousal of a specific erg

2(2). Rage,[8] effort stress, and continued E and E_s

[8] Incidentally, no presently known P.U.I. pattern has been assigned to anger, because introspective ties are few. But P.U.I. 5, adrenergic response, seems probable. Actually, introspected responses of anger have been recorded along with the Effort Stress response (Cattell & Scheier, 1961); but it seems likely that this is due to the usual high contiguity [2(2) above] of anger and stress; at least anger brings a stress response though stress does not necessarily have anger.

3(2). Depression, anxiety, and continued E and E_s
4(2). Sheer anxiety

Now inasmuch as APA phases overlap and are subject to reverberating circuit lags, the sequence above might be expected to show itself in correlations among states measured at any given moment. The only data in existence on the correlations and the second orders that appear among state primaries is that in Figure 4.4.

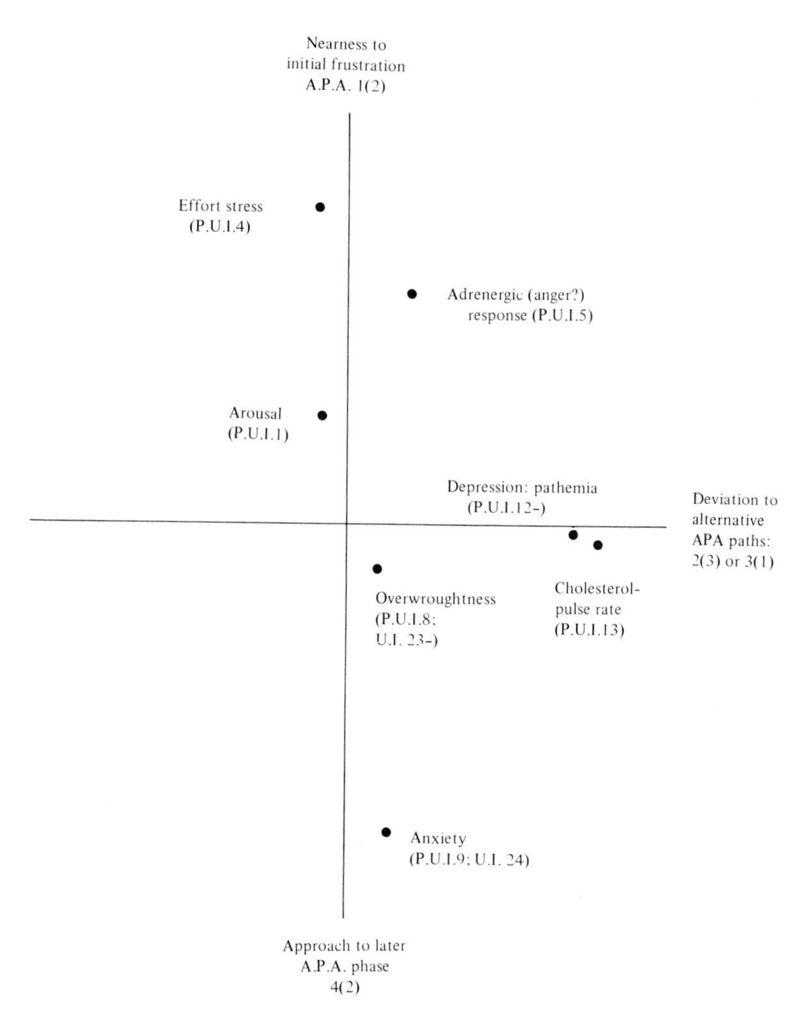

Figure 4.4. *Second order relations among primary response states.*

At best this is one glimpsė, where systematic sections at different phases would be desirable, but it does show effort stress, adrenergic response and arousal positively related, as one might expect at this early phase of the APA path, while anxiety stands toward the opposite pole, presumably belonging to the distinct later phases of the sequence. That pathemia and depression are orthogonal to the anxiety-versus-effort stress polarity, would be in keeping with their lying along a total different alternative path [2(3)] in the adjustment process analysis chart.

Although Figure 4.4 is a primitive beginning, not in fact primarily planned experimentally as process evidence, it is time to recognize that the illumination of cross-sectional by sequential evidence, which was indicated at the outset of this chapter to be the ideal methodology, is beginning to come within our experimental grasp. The question of whether "suspense," or "helplessness," or "an appraisal of inability to cope," or "interruption of a plan" is the true generic trigger for anxiety (and what the generic stimuli are for other, different, general states) is capable of being decided now that we have (a) valid measures for the unique states, and (b) the beginnings of a methodology for recognizing standard, modal sequences, in processes. The latter–in the work of Tucker, Fleishman, and the present writer–(chapters in the *Handbook of Multivariate Experimental Psychology*, Cattell, Ed., 1966a) presents P-technique, T-technique and repeated R-technique methods for analyzing both the modal features of a repeating process, and the learning changes in a process. By incorporating measures of strength of stimulus situations with response measures it should be possible to put generalizations about the origins of anxiety, arousal, depression, etc., on something better than the journalistic type of psychology which often continues as the mode of discussion on these process issues.[9]

[9] The almost invariable defense against undertaking the complexity of a multivariate analysis is a misunderstanding expressed by saying that a multivariate approach involves "slapping together some variables to see what happens." This is a travesty–deliberate or ignorant–of factor analytic and other multivariate designs. Methods are not responsible for the poor designs of those that use them, and in both multivariate and bivariate research, the choice of variables for theory development is often sad. The process description in APA is at present purely clinical-descriptive, but in suggesting that it be tested by multivariate P- and T-technique designs, etc., we are not abandoning the use of existing insights as far as they will carry us. What the defensive evasion of multivariate experiment overlooks is that–even if one went on only a representative design as far as variables are concerned–he would yet have a far more delicately perceived set of relations than in bivariate work from which to develop the next round of insights. The discussion (and, alas, teaching) of a travesty of multivariate research design is all the more uncalled for because–at least in the state field–there are already 25 years of strategic research showing how, in fact, new theoretical concepts have been repeatedly defined by factor analysis, culminating in clarifications not obtained by bivariate methods. The list of "theories of anxiety" in a neighboring chapter, shows at what degree of vagueness the latter methods leave the field.

One major aspect of the theoretical position taken here—first from the cross-sectional definition of the response pattern of anxiety as distinct from other factors; in formulae 19, 20 and 21; and second in the hypothesized outcome of process analysis in APA—is that motivation is something distinct from anxiety, though anxiety is a degenerate form of motivation. It is degenerate in that it is no longer fully available for motivation;[10] in that it has consequences in metabolism and fatigue production which are different from those of strong motivation alone, and in that it has lost some specificity of goal. Nevertheless, this implies that anxiety is only to be understood in a context of dynamic structure. For example, as Sarason points out, a child highly anxious about a dental visit, may lose anxiety if a quite different dynamic system, for example, one connected with school ambition, is stimulated. It is the product of a dynamic system, but in part escapes from any utility therein.

In challenging again here the equating of anxiety with simple ergic tension (as I did in the earlier chapter, Spielberger, 1966), at the very least on the grounds that the theory that all motive is anxiety is a dreary *fin de siècle* illusion) the issues can be stated in somewhat more developed form. The view is frequently uncritically repeated that the individual strives for reduction of arousal and for reduction of anxiety, and that since the same can truly be said of ergic tension, that is, of basic motivation in general, this justifies a monism of interpretation. The distinction here between general arousal (excitement, P.U.I.1), and ergic tension (as measured in the MAT or any objective motivation component measures), permits us to recognize that the demand is always for reduction of ergic tension, but that in bored, torpid, or sensorily deprived states individuals will welcome increase in arousal.

Anxiety is in this respect more like motivation, in that reduction is always desired, though the ergic expression channels for doing so have become unavailable. Furthernore, it must be freely admitted that personality learning, as distinct from simple cognitive or motor learning, proceeds more rapidly with higher anxiety. (The learning distinction here is that between integration learning, in which goal readjustments are made among drives, and simple operant

[10] The finding by Cattell & Scheier (1961) and by Spence (1956) and others that conditioning proceeds more quickly with higher anxiety must be regarded as a special case, misleading if one has no positive operational concepts of motivation per se. That autonomic conditioning should occur more rapidly with general autonomic excitation (P.U.I.9) should surprise no one. More discriminative cognitive learning is mainly negatively correlated with anxiety. The factoral evidence (Cattell & Scheier, 1961) is likewise that capacity to memorize, to calculate without error, and to perceive accurately, are reduced by anxiety states. There is no convincing evidence that this disorganizing effect of anxiety is definitely associated with the level of intensity of the anxiety. The experiments suggesting this can be better interpreted as showing effects of true motivation, as measured in objective devices valid against the two main motivation components (Cattell *et al.,* 1964), with which anxiety happens to be obliquely associated, as in equation 18 above.

conditioning, means–end learning, in which new skills are directed to still accepted goals.) The finding both by Pierson (Pierson, Barton, & Hay, 1964) and by Sarason (1966)—though with slightly different conditions—that more anxious delinquents acquire new, more socially appropriate behavior more rapidly than do low anxious delinquents—illustrates this. The same conclusion may be supported across wider ranges of personality learning. This finding would be expected from equation (21) above, and from other findings (summarized in Cattell, 1950a) that the personality (not the situational) component in anxiety is identical with poor general dynamic integration. The person who is highly anxious (when the contribution from any particular situation is partialled out) has much integration to learn and can reduce anxiety directly by such integration learning. This theory does, therefore, if one wishes so to express it, recognize anxiety as motivation of "a special kind."

The recognition that anxiety can have its meaning and its relation to other states understood only in the total dynamic context in which it has developed, calls in question not the usefulness but the interpretation of studies such as those of Schacter (1966) or Cannon & Rosenblueth (1937) which attempt to study anxiety by creating it through "artificial" physiological conditions. The results turn out be in fact (as Lazarus has said) in some respects anomalous,[11] which is not surprising in view of (1) the impossibility by any simple biochemical injection of coming at all close to the complex pattern of physiological change (Cattell & Scheier, 1961, p. 208) which defines the total somatic anxiety response. In other words there is no justification for identifying the "injection pattern" as anxiety rather than as, say, P.U.I.4, stress, P.U.I.5, adrenergic response, or P.U.I.13, "cholinersterase and pulse rate change;" (2) The fact that the persisting elements from the earlier part of the usual dynamic sequence are not present. In the ordinary environmental manipulative experiment (without getting under the skin) sufficient possibilities now exist, through cleaner measurement of the components in composite responses, and in the greater precision of sequential analysis, for elucidating the origins, nature, and effects of anxiety.

In concluding with this reminder of the possibilities of more careful attention to valid measurement of anxiety, in manipulative or nonmanipulative experiment, and for measuring and partialling out the influence of such quite

[11] In other experiments, too, rather suddenly induced changes in anxiety sometimes fail to produce change in the whole pattern. Thus in Bartlett's (1968) work, there are indications that the physiological changes may occur without the full accompaniment of attitude changes. In the various injection studies, on the other hand, the conclusion is sometimes stressed that the individual believes situations to be threatening when he has no systematic cognitive–dynamic background that would justify his seeing them as dangerous. Sarason has said that danger creates anxiety, and anxiety creates increased vigilance and sensitivity to danger. Yet somewhere there must be a fallacy in this position, for such a simple positive feedback would quickly carry anxiety to infinity.

different emotional responses as effort stress, depression, arousal, etc., we must meet one more question from the alert student. "If anxiety is a unitary factor only at the second order, and resolves into $C-$, $H-$, O, Q_3-, and Q_4 at the first order, should not the above argument be carried to the logical conclusion that these primaries also need to be separately measured in any truly analytical experiment?" The reply is, first, that the vexed question of whether these primaries are (a) distinct domains in which the effects of the second stratum unitary anxiety influence shows itself, or (b) circularly interacting sources of anxiety (see discussion Cattell & Scheier, 1961) is still unanswered. Until we know whether we are dealing with different modes of expression of anxiety or different sources of contribution, firm conclusions as to where their separate measurement is vital and where irrelevant cannot be reached.

However, since this additional information is obtainable, at least in Q-data measures, for example, the 16 P.F. or HSPQ, with relatively little effort, it might as well be gathered wherever possible; for only by exploring new relations can the answer to the above causal questions be obtained. Indeed, already there are numerous findings that have proved easier to understand (e.g., the changing pattern of anxiety with age; its differences with sex and culture; the difference of state and trait; the relation to the total dynamic situation) when the anxiety score is visible in terms of the primaries, rather than as a single composite score.

In summary, it will be seen that this chapter is partly a proposal for investigating the relation of anxiety and other states to the dynamic process by a precise theoretical model; partly a demonstration of the gains that are possible through integrating anxiety phenomena with such aids as are present in more advanced psychometry, in the concepts in the dynamic calculus, and in the analysis of the total personality; and partly a plea to give up anachronisms in anxiety measurement. Regarding the last, it is not suggested that all problems are solved in the aim to reach valid and practicable measurements targeted against the several distinctive factors for anxiety, stress, arousal, etc. On the contrary, the loading patterns that must determine the construction of valid batteries urgently need to be pursued in regard to their stability across wider changes of population—in age, sex, education, clinical selection, etc.—than has yet been possible for the unnecessarily small group engaged in these multivariate experiments.

References

Bandura, A., & Rosenthal, I. Classical Conditioning as a Function of Arousal Level, *Journal of Personality and Social Psychology,* 1966, **3.**

Bartlett, H. W. The separation of state and trait anxiety, stress and fear. Unpublished master's thesis, University of Illinois, 1968.

Barton, K., Cattell, R. B., & Conner, D. V. The identification of "state" factors through P-technique factor analysis. *Journal of Clinical Psychology,* 1972, In press.

Basowitz, H., Persky, H., Korchin, S. J., & Grinker, R. R. *Anxiety and stress: an interdisciplinary study of a life situation.* New York: McGraw-Hill, 1955.

Beck, A. T., Ward, C. H., Mendelson, M., Mock, J., & Erbaugh, J. An inventory for measuring depression. *Archives of General Psychiatry,* 1961, **4,** 561–571.

Brodgen, H. E. A factor analysis of forty character tests. *Psychological Monographs,* 1940, **234,** 35–55.

Cannon, W. B., & Rosenblueth, A. *Autonomic neuro effector systems.* New York: Macmillan, 1937.

Cattell, R. B. The significance of the actual resistances in psycho-galvanic experiments. *British Journal of Psychology,* 1928, **19,** 34–43.

Cattell, R. B. *Personality, a systematic theoretical and factual study.* New York: McGraw–Hill, 1950. (a)

Cattell, R. B. The discovery of ergic structure in man in terms of common attitudes. *Journal of Abnormal and Social Psychology,* 1950, **45,** 598–618. (b)

Cattell, R. B. Psychiatric screening of flying personnel: Personality structure in objective tests–a study of 1,000 Air Force students in basic pilot training. Report No. 9, Project No. 21-0202-007. Randolph Field, Texas: U.S.A.F. School of Aviation Medicine, 1955.

Cattell, R. B. *Personality and motivation structure and measurement.* New York: World Book, 1957. (a)

Cattell, R. B. The conceptual and test distinction of neuroticism and anxiety. *Journal of Clinical Psychology,* 1957, **13,** 221–233. (b)

Cattell, R. B. The dynamic calculus: a system of concepts derived from objective motivation measurement. In G. Lindzey (Ed.), *Assessment of Human Motives.* New York: Rinehart, 1958. Pp. 197–238.

Cattell, R. B. The dynamic calculus: concepts and crucial experiments. In M. R. Jones (Ed.), *The Nebraska Symposium on Motivation.* Lincoln, Nebraska: University of Nebraska Press, 1959. Pp. 84–134.

Cattell, R. B. The structuring of change by P-technique and incremental R-technique. In C. W. Harris (Ed.), *Problems in Measuring Change.* Madison, Wisconsin: The University of Wisconsin Press, 1963. Pp. 167–198. (a)

Cattell, R. B. Personality, role, mood, and situation-perception: a unifying theory of modulators. *Psychological Review,* 1963, **70,** 1–18. (b)

Cattell, R. B. The definition(s) of anxiety. *Journal of the American Medical Association,* 1964, **190,** 859. (a)

Cattell, R. B. Psychological definition and measurement of anxiety. *Journal of Neuropsychiatry,* 1964, **5,** 396–402. (b)

Cattell, R. B. *The scientific analysis of personality.* London: Penguin Books, 1965. (a)

Cattell, R. B. A cross-cultural check on second stratum personality factor structure–notably of anxiety and exvia. *Australian Journal of Psychology,* 1965, **17,** 22–23. (b)

Cattell, R. B. (Ed.) *Handbook of multivariate experimental psychology.* Chicago, Illinois: Rand McNally, 1966. (a)

Cattell, R. B. Anxiety and motivation: theory and crucial experiments. In C. D. Spielberger (Ed.), *Anxiety and behavior.* New York: Academic Press, 1966. Pp. 23–62. (b)

Cattell, R. B. Trait-view theory of perturbations in ratings and self ratings (L(BR) and Q-data): Its application to obtaining pure trait score estimates in questionnaires. *Psychological Review,* 1968, **75,** 96–113.

Cattell, R. B. (Guest Ed.) Progress in clinical psychology through multivariate experimental designs. *Multivariate Behavioral Research,* 1968, Special Issue.

Cattell, R. B. Estimating modulator indices and state liabilities. *Multivariate Behavioral Research,* 1971b, **6,** 7–33.

Cattell, R. B. *Real base, true zero factor analysis.* 1972. Multivariate Behavioral Research Monograph, **72(1),** 1972.

Cattell, R. B., & Bartlett, H. W. An R–dR-technique operational distinction of the states of anxiety, stress, fear, etc. *Australian Journal of Psychology,* 1971, **23,** 105–123.

Cattell, R. B., Cattell, A. K. S., & Rhymer, R. M. P-technique demonstrated in determining psycho-physiological source traits in a normal individual. *Psychometrika,* 1947, **12,** 267–288.

Cattell, R. B., & Cross, K. Comparison of the ergic and self-sentiment structures found in dynamic traits by R- and P-techniques. *Journal of Personality,* 1952, **21,** 250–271.

Cattell, R. B.,& Damarin. F. *A factor analysis of the anxiety pattern in 168 adult subjects.* Champaign, Illinois: Laboratory of Personality and Group Analysis Publication No. 7, 1962

Cattell, R. B., & Gruen, W. The primary personality factors in eleven year old children, by objective tests. *Journal of Personality,* 1955, **23,** 460–478.

Cattell, R. B., Horn, J. R., Radcliffe, J., & Sweney, A. B. *The motivation analysis test.* Champaign, Illinois: Institute for Personality and Ability Testing, 1964.

Cattell, R. B., & Howarth, E. Verification of objective test personality factor patterns in middle childhood. *Journal of Genetic Psychology,* 1964, **104,** 331–349.

Cattell, R. B., Kawash, G. F., & De Young, G. E. Test of a theory of ergs and sentiments as dynamic states: by a dR analysis of ninety objective motivation measures In preparation.

Cattell, R. B., & Luborsky, L. B. P-technique demonstrated as a new clinical method for determining personality and symptom structure. *Journal of General Psychology,* 1950, **42,** 3–24.

Cattell, R. B., & Nesselroade, J. R. The discovery of the anxiety state pattern in Q-data, and its distinction, in the LM modal, from depression, effort, stress and fatigue. *Multivariate Behavioral Research,* 1972 (in press).

Cattell, R. B., & Peterson, D. R. Personality structure in four and five year olds in terms of objective tests. *Journal of Clinical Psychology,* 1959, **15,** 355–369.

Cattell, R. B., & Scheier, I. H. Discovery and development of measurement scales for the dimensions of anxiety. Report on Department of the Army Contract No. DA-49-007-MD-620. Dayton, Ohio: Armed Services Technical Information Agency, 1957.

Cattell, R. B., & Scheier, I. H. Factors in personality change: a dimension of the condition-response incremental design and application to 69 personality response measures and three stimulus conditions. Urbana, Illinois: Laboratory of Personality Assessment and Group Behavior. Advance Publication No. 9, 1958.

Cattell, R. B., & Scheier, I. H. Extension of meaning of objective test personality factors, especially into anxiety, neuroticism, questionnaire and physical factors. *Journal of General Psychology,* 1959, **61,** 287–315.

Cattell, R. B., & Scheier, I. H. Stimuli related to stress, neuroticism, excitation, and anxiety response patterns: Illustrating a new multivariate experimental design. *Journal of Abnormal and Social Psychology,* 1960, **60,** 195–204.

Cattell, R. B., & Scheier, I. H. *The meaning and measurement of neuroticism and anxiety.* New York: Ronald Press, 1961.

Cattell, R. B., Tatro, D., & Komlos, E. The diagnosis and inferred structure of paranoid and non-paranoid schizophrenia, from the 16 P.F. profile. *Indian Psychological Review,* 1964, **1,** 52–61.

Cattell, R. B., & Warburton, F. W. *Objective personality and motivation tests.* Champaign, Ill.: University of Illinois Press, 1968.

Clyde, D. J. *Manual for the clyde mood scale.* Coral Gables, Florida: University of Miami Biometric Laboratory, 1963.

Coombs, C. H., & Kao, R. C. Nonmetric factor analysis. *Bulletin of Department of Engineering Research. No. 38.* Ann Arbor, Michigan: University of Michigan, 1955.

Curran, J. The dimensions of state change, in Q-data and chain P-technique, on twenty women. Unpublished M.A. Thesis, University of Illinois, 1968.

Damarin, F., & Cattell R. B. Personality factors in early childhood and their relation to intelligence. *Monograph of the Society for Research in Child Development,* 1968, No. 122.

Darrow, C. W., & Heath, L. H. Reaction tendencies relating to personality. In K. S. Lashley, *Studies in the dynamics of behavior.* Chicago, Illinois: University of Chicago Press, 1932.

Duffy, E. *Activation and behavior.* New York: Wiley, 1962.

Edwards, A. L. *The social desirability variable in personality assessment and research.* New York: Dryden, 1957.

Endler, N. S., & Hunt, J. McV. Sources of behavioral variance as measured by the S–R Inventory of anxiousness. *Psychological Bulletin,* 1966, **65(6),** 336–346.

Endler, N. S., Hunt, J. McV., & Rosenstein, A. J. An S–R inventory of anxiousness. *Psychological Monographs,* 1962, **76** (Whole No. 536).

Epstein, S. Toward a unified theory of anxiety. In B. A. Maher (Ed.), *Progress in experimental personality research.* Vol. 4. New York: Academic Press, 1967. Pp. 1–89.

Fleishman, E. A. Dimensional analysis of psychomotor abilities. *Journal of Experimental Psychology,* 1954, **54,** 437–454.

Freeman, G. L., & Katzoff, E. T. Individual differences in physiological reactions to stimulation and their relation to other measures of emotionality. *Journal of Experimental Psychology,* 1942. **31,** 527–537.

Gorsuch, R. L. The clarification of some superego factors. Unpublished doctoral dissertation, University of Illinois, *Dissertation Abstracts,* 1965, **26,** 477–478.

Grinker, R. R. The psychosomatic aspects of anxiety. In C. D. Spielberger (Ed.), *Anxiety and behavior.* New York: Academic Press, 1966. Pp. 129–142.

Grinker, R. R., & Spiegel, J. P. *Men under stress.* Philadelphia, Pennsylvania: Blakiston, 1945.

Haverland, E. M. An experimental analysis by P-technique of some functionally unitary varieties of fatigue. Unpublished doctoral dissertation, University of Illinois, 1954.

Haywood, H. Carl, & Hunt, J. McV. Effects of epinephrine upon novelty preference and arousal. *Journal of Abnormal and Social Psychology,* 1963, **67.**

Herrington, L. P. The relation of physiological and social indices of activity level. In Q. McNemar and M. A. Merrill (Eds.), *Studies in personality.* New York: McGraw–Hill, 1942. Pp. 125–146.

Horn, J. L. Structure in measures of self-sentiment, ego, and super-ego concepts. Unpublished masters thesis, University of Illinois, 1961.

Horn, J. L. Organization of abilities and the development of intelligence. *Psychological Review,* 1968, **75,** 242–259.

Hull, C. L. *Principles of behavior.* New York: Appleton, 1943.

Hundal, P. S., Sudhakar, Y. P., & Sidhu, K. Factor analytic study of measures of anxiety, intelligence and academic achievement, 1970. In press.

Hundleby, J. D., & Cattell, R. B. Personality structure in middle childhood and the prediction of school achievement and adjustment. *Monographs of the Society for Research in Child Development,* 1968, **33,** 1–61.

Hundleby, J. D., Pawlik, K., & Cattell, R. B. *Personality factors in objective test devices.* San Diego, California: Knapp, 1965.

Izard, C. E. The emotions and emotion concepts in personality and culture research. In R. M. Droger & R. B. Cattell (Eds.), *Handbook of modern personality theory.* Chapter 21. In preparation.

Izard, C. E., & Tomkins, S. S. Affect and behavior: Anxiety as a negative affect. In C. D. Spielberger (Ed.), *Anxiety and behavior.* New York: Academic Press, 1966. Pp. 81–125.

Karvonen, M. J., & Kunnas, M. Factor analysis of haematological changes in heavy, manual work. *Acta Psychologica Scandinavia,* 1953, **29,** 220–231.

Krug, S. A demonstration of the functional unitariness of dynamic structure factors. *Journal of Personality.* In press.

Lacey, J. I. Somatic response patterning and stress: Some revisions of activation theory. In M. H. Appley & R. Trumbull (Eds.), *Psychological stress: issues in research.* New York: Appleton–Century–Crofts, 1967. Pp. 14–37.

Lacey, J. I., & Lacey, B. C. Verification and extension of the principle of autonomic response-stereotypy. *American Journal of Psychology,* 1958, **71,** 50–73.

McDougall, W. *Energies of Man,* London: Mittmen, 1932.

Mefferd, R. B., Jr. Structuring physiological correlates of mental processes and states: The study of biological correlates of mental processes. In R. B. Cattell (Ed.), *Handbook of multivariate and experimental psychology,* Chicago, Illinois: Rand McNally, 1966. Pp. 684.

Moran, L. J., & Mefferd, R. B., Jr. Repetitive psychometric measures. *Psychological Reports,* 1959, **5,** 269–275.

Nesselroade, J. R. An empirical examination of factor invariance with different rotational methods and indices of matching. Unpublished M.A. thesis, University of Illinois, 1965.

Nesselroade, J. R. Factoring cross products of difference scores as a method for factoring change. Unpublished Ph.D. thesis, University of Illinois, 1967.

Nesselroade, J. R. The definition and the measurement of psychological states. In: R. B. Cattell (Ed.), *Handbook of modern personality theory.* Chicago, Illinois: Aldine Press, 1971.

Nesselroade, J. R., & Cattell, R. B. The IPAT Seven State Battery. IPAT, Champaign, Illinois, 1962.

Pawlik, K., & Cattell, R. B. Third-order factors in objective personality tests. *British Journal of Psychology,* 1964, **55,** 1–18.

Pierson, G. R., Barton, K., & Hay, G. SMAT motivation factors as predictors of academic achievement in delinquent boys. *Journal of Psychology,* 1964, **57,** 243–249.

Rosenthal, I. A factor analysis of anxiety variables. Unpublished doctoral dissertation, University of Illinois, 1955.

Sarason, S. B. The measurement of anxiety in children: some questions and problems. In C. D. Spielberger (Ed.), *Anxiety and behavior.* New York: Academic Press. 1966.

Schacter, S. The interaction of cognitive and physiological determinants of emotional state. In C. D. Spielberger (Ed.), *Anxiety and behavior.* New York: Academic Press, 1966.

Scheier, I. H., & Cattell, R. B. Confirmation of objective test factors and assessment of their relation to questionnaire factors: a factor analysis of 113 rating, questionnaire and objective test measurements of personality. *Journal of Mental Science,* 1958, **104,** 608–624.

Shotwell, A., Hurley, J., & Cattell, R. B. Motivational structure of an hospitalized mental defective. *Journal of Abnormal and Social Psychology,* 1961, **62,** 422–426.

Skinner, B. F. *Science and human behavior.* New York: Macmillan, 1953.

Spearman, C. General intelligence, objectively determined and measured. *American Journal of Psychology,* 1904, **15**, 201–293.

Spence, J. T., & Spence, K. W. The motivational components of manifest anxiety: Drive and drive stimuli. In C. D. Spielberger (Ed.), *Anxiety and behavior.* New York: Academic Press, 1966. Pp. 291–326.

Spence, K. W. *Behavior theory and conditioning.* New Haven, Connecticut: Yale University Press, 1956.

Spielberger, C. D. *Anxiety and behavior.* New York: Academic Press, Inc., 1966.

Tucker, L. R. Learning theory and multivariate experiment: illustration by determination of generalized learning curves. In R. B. Cattell (Ed.), *Handbook of multivariate experimental psychology.* Chapter 16. Chicago, Illinois: Rand McNally, 1966.

Van Egeren, L. F. Experimental determination by P-technique of functional unities of depression. Unpublished master's thesis, University of Illinois, 1963.

Venables, P. H., & Warwick-Evans, L. A. Cortical arousal and the two-flash threshold. *Psychonomic Science,* 1967, **8.**

Ward, W. D., & Carlson, W. A. Cognitive dissonance, opinion change, and physiological arousal. *The Journal of General Psychology,* 1964, **71.**

Wells, H. P. Relationships between physical fitness and psychological variables. Unpublished doctoral dissertation, University of Illinois, 1958.

Wenger, M. A. Studies of autonomic balance in Army Air Force personnel. *Comparative Psychology Monographs,* 1958, **19**, 1–111.

Williams, H. V. A P-technique study of personality factors in the psychosomatic forces. *Microfilm Abstracts,* 1950, **9**, 177–178.

Williams, H. V. A determination of psychosomatic functional unities by P-technique. *Journal of Social Psychology,* 1954, **39**, 25–45.

Williams, J. R. A test of the validity of the P-technique in the measurement of internal conflict. *Journal of Personality,* 1959, **27**, 418–437.

COMMENTS ON DR. CATTELL'S PAPER

Seymour Epstein

What I find most attractive about Professor Cattell's research approach is his use of repeated measures in order to examine patterns of variation within individuals over time. Using traditional R-technique, he was able to establish traits, although, as he points out in his paper, such traits are confounded with states, as an individual tested at a moment in time must be in a particular state. Using P-technique and dR-technique, Cattell has been able to measure states, while holding traits constant. As a result, there is the bonus that he can determine what in R-technique is unique to traits by a subtractive process. Since personality refers to characteristics of individuals, it is heartening to see someone doing intensive, objective studies of individuals, and not relying exclusively on the questionable assumption that group data adequately describe processes within the individuals comprising the groups, which many psychologists appear to be content with.

The strengths and weaknesses of Cattell's approach are necessarily the strengths and weaknesses of factor analysis and therefore of correlational data.

As every freshman knows, a correlation indicates how closely two measures vary together, but provides no information about causality. If *A* and *B* are correlated, *A* may cause *B*, *B* may cause *A*, both may exert an effect upon each other, or both may be caused by a third variable. Correlational data, when restricted to response processes, which unfortunately is usually the case, pose a problem for deriving a theory in which causal relationships are considered. While factor analytic studies have been weak on the stimulus side, it should be acknowledged that they have been strong on the response side. With the aid of high-speed computers, it has been possible to intercorrelate very large numbers of responses and to derive a limited number of relatively independent factors.

The correlational method as applied to measures derived from people in natural circumstances can be contrasted with the experimental method, in which there is manipulation of one or a few independent variables, and effects observed on a relatively small number of dependent variables. In a typical factor analytic study by Cattell, a great many measures are taken on a group of individuals tested once (R-technique), on one individual tested many times over an extended time period (P-technique), or on a group of individuals tested twice (dR-technique), in which case the differences between the two sessions provide the data to be correlated. Such measures are usually taken over nonselected, hopefully random, samples of everyday behavior, and Cattell speaks of the desirability of obtaining adequate representative samples of individuals and occasions. In a typical anxiety experiment, a relatively small number of individuals is divided into groups receiving different artificial treatments. For example, in the type of studies I reported, one group may be threatened with a mild shock, another with a moderate shock, and a third with an intense shock. A few dependent variables are then chosen, such as heart rate, skin conductance, and ratings of intensity, because of their interest to the investigator and, based on previous information, their appropriateness for the experimental paradigm. The effect of the experimental manipulation upon each of the dependent variables is then statistically analyzed, and the differences in results among the measures is considered to be as of much importance as their correspondence. In such experiments, we have generally found that while there is some correspondence among the measures, each has a considerable unique contribution, so that combining them into an overall score would introduce serious distortion. Moreover, until a measure is carefully studied within a particular context, one is apt not to know how to combine it appropriately with other measures.

Using the correlational method, the investigator can obtain information about a great number of responses, and use factor analysis to reduce correlations to a manageable number of clusters or patterns, which can then be arranged according to "deeper" levels presumed to be more basic or general in significance. The difficulty enters in rationalizing the factors, and developing theories which consider sequential influence. For example, Cattell finds that guilt has a loading on the anxiety state factor. What does this mean? One might expect guilt to appear in a depression factor, but why in anxiety? Does this mean that guilt produces anxiety, or that anxiety produces guilt, neither, or both? Does another variable produce both? The parachutists Fenz and I studied became manifestly anxious whenever there was a minor mishap, and this occurred whether or not they had any responsibility for it. Thus, there was frequently no reason for guilt, and in such circumstances they gave no evidence of feeling guilt. I suspect if such populations were studied, for whom anxiety is tied to dangerous events (and I am not talking about fear, although this also is involved, but can be distinguished according to criteria laid down in my paper), guilt would not be found to load on the anxiety factor. If this is true, then the relationship found by Cattell depends upon the vicissitudes of guilt and anxiety during ordinary situations in everyday life. This suggests to me that people feel guilty in everyday life because of experiences that threaten their self images as decent, likeable people, and that they experience anxiety, at the same time, because a threat to the integrity of the self-concept automatically induces anxiety, as I suggested in my paper in this volume. If this is true, then guilt and anxiety are associated in everyday living in our culture because of certain transient experiences which threaten self-concepts. Cattell explains the relationship by assuming that anxiety is produced by a blocked drive, which implies an inability to cope, and that the reaction to an inability to cope is to feel guilt. Who is right? Perhaps neither of us is, or both are. This can only be settled by experiments that manipulate the critical variables.

Now, there is no reason for correlational studies not to include stimulus variation, and for experimental studies not to include a large number of responses. When this is done, the two approaches begin to merge. Putting it otherwise, the experimental approach, naturalistic observation, and self-report differ with respect to data gathering, but do not have to differ on the method of analysis. As it happens, it is a rare factor-analytic study that includes experimental manipulation, and it is to Cattell's credit that he has made a beginning in this direction, and has indicated the need for expanding this approach. He will still have the problem of coping with interactions, for which analysis of variance is well suited, but given his factor-analytic ingenuity, it will not be surprising if he comes up with a solution. To date, however, Cattell's program consists almost exclusively of response–response correlation, and it is in this light that his findings must be evaluated. We shall proceed with a critique of a few of his basic assumptions which we believe are in particular need of being challenged.

Assumption 1: It is desirable to measure as many possibly relevant responses as possible, since only by factor-analyzing all relevant responses can a concept be adequately defined. This assumption is the basis of Cattell's most severe criticism of the work of others, including mine. Using my own work as an example, he notes that by employing a few physiological measures, such as heart rate and skin conductance, I am in no position to come to conclusions about concepts such as anxiety, as both of these measures load on other factors, such as effort-stress, as well as on anxiety. What Cattell fails to realize is that manipulating a particular stimulus, while controlling others, provides a highly effective means of eliminating alternative explanations. That, of course, is what the experimental method is all about! It would be a poor experiment that would not allow me to differentiate the effects of active problem solving or exertion from those produced by threat, per se. When threat is manipulated in a count-up to an unavoidable noxious stimulus, there is no problem to solve and no effort to exert. If heart rate and skin conductance are found to rise in anticipation of the forthcoming shock, and the rise is proportionate to the intensity of the threat, while all other conditions remain the same, it is not unreasonable to assume that the threat produced the rise, and that heart rate and skin conductance serve as indexes of threat. It is of no matter that heart rate can also rise from doing push-ups or from other incidental sources, such as being ill. My subjects are not doing push-ups, and it would be strange, indeed, if they were selectively ill in a manner exactly corresponding to my assignment of them to experimental treatments, particularly as the assignments were random. It could be argued, of course, that I have learned something about reactions to threat, but not anxiety. The answer is that it depends upon how one defines anxiety. In any event, the information gained about threat is meaningful and interpretable, and it should be recognized that definitions are but useful tools. Moreover, the argument is irrelevant to the point, which is that because an index is responsive to several dimensions does not mean that it cannot be interpreted to reflect variations along one of the dimensions. With appropriate controls, interpretation can be straightforward and uncomplicated, which is obviously not true of factor-analytic definitions of concepts that are based only on response–response correlations.

Granted that a single measure, under appropriately controlled circumstances, can produce meaningful information, is it not true that a combination of many responses for measuring a concept is superior to the use of one or a few? The argument for combining multiple measures rests upon the assumption that each measure contains a true source of variance and an error source, and that the proportion of true variance can be increased by the combination. While this may be a good assumption for intelligence testing, it is a poor one for physiological measures, as each physiological system has its own local controls independent of the concept in question and its own time constants, in a manner such that indiscriminate pooling is apt to result in a cancelling-out process or serious distortion (cf. Taylor & Epstein, 1967). The solution lies not in pooling, but in establishing the stimulus parameters of each measure through experimental study. Only then can it be determined how, if at all, certain measures can be appropriately combined. As an example, it has been well established that heart rate exhibits a unique property of decelerating before the onset of an anticipated stimulus. In awaiting a threatening stimulus, heart rate normally accelerates until shortly before anticipated impact, and then exhibits a sharp deceleration. Following impact there is a sharp acceleration, followed by a rebound deceleration, which is usually followed by a rebound acceleration. Skin conductance shows neither the anticipatory deceleration nor the rebounds. It would thus be foolish to combine skin conductance and heart rate into an overall measure of some concept such as anxiety in such an experiment. During the early anticipatory period, the two measures would rise together, but shortly before impact, as heart-rate would decelerate and skin conductance accelerate, they would tend to cancel each other out, and, during recovery, the two would again be completely out of phase. If one factor-analyzed such data over the total count-up, and was unaware of the unique properties of each measure because the appropriate experiments had not been done, one would have factor-analytic chaos. This is not to say that Cattell's factors which include physiological reactions are necessarily invalid. He may be fortunate, and the problems that I am describing in my experimental situation, which involves a very brief time span, may not apply to his situations. The point, however, is, that until one knows one's measures intimately by having studied them individually and intensively, one is in a poor position to know when and how to obtain scores that can profitably be subjected to factor analysis. That Cattell may not be fortunate is suggested by inspection of the loadings on state anxiety for different studies, as presented in his Table 4.2. He informs us that state anxiety includes rises in systolic blood pressure and in heart rate. In one of the studies, the loading for systolic blood pressure is +.71, and in two others +.08. Heart rate loads +.51 on anxiety in one study and −.04 in another. Cattell assures us that his theory is based upon a firm foundation of objective factor-analytic procedures in which concepts are empirically defined rather than defined by fiat, as other are prone to do. If so, the lack of consistency from study to study suggests that the firm foundation is undermined by resting upon unstable sands of data-gathering and reduction.

There is a second difficulty in using large numbers of physiological measures which Cattell appears to be unaware of when he suggests that because the measures that constitute his factors are widely applicable, and can be obtained in a short time, the only reason they are not used extensively by others is because of laziness. For some kinds of experiments, such as in the ones reported in my paper, many of Cattell's measures take too long, and others would interfere with the experimental situation. We have learned through bitter experience that by trying to get a great deal of data, we can change the experimental situation. In a recent doctoral dissertation, blood pressure, heart rate, muscle action potential, skin conductance, and ratings were taken continuously. For blood pressure an arm cuff was mechanically inflated and deflated repeatedly, producing no small distraction. We hoped to demonstrate differences between hypertensives and normotensives in their physiological reactivity to aggression and the threat of retaliation. However, the recording and rating procedures were in themselves so stressful, that our experimental manipulations exerted little further effect. We learned that human beings are not machines from which an unlimited amount of information can be extracted without the measuring process itself affecting the results. What may possibly work in Cattell's situations may not be applicable to other situations.

Assumption 2: It is necessary to factorially define a variable before it can be used in an experiment. As noted above, it is apt to be the other way around. One often cannot know how to appropriately measure a response until one learns its essential features through experimental investigation of its stimulus parameters. If this is not done, factors may be misleading and inconsistent.

I cannot resist the temptation of asking the reader to consider the contribution of a noted physiologist who had the presumption to believe he could discover basic laws of conditioning by using a single response, salivation. It is tempting to speculate about whether his contribution would have been greater or lesser had he attempted to comprehensively factor the learning domain before conducting his first experiment. Parenthetically, it might be noted that the secretion of saliva can indicate not only learning, but eating, and anxiety, and, therefore, according to Cattell, should be worthless as a single measure.

Assumption 3: Physiological variables, anxiety, and related concepts produce linear relationships. I cannot imagine a worse assumption, since there is overwhelming evidence, from Pavlov to current investigators, that many relationships involving motivation, stimulus intensity, performance, and physiological arousal tend to be inverted U-shaped. This was recognized by Pavlov with respect to simple conditioned autonomic responses in his concept of paradoxical phases, appears as a broad generalization with regard to performance and motivation in the Yerkes–Dodson Law, and is recognized in Wilder's Law of Initial Value as applicable to physiological reactivity as a function of increasing base levels. The only apparent reason for the assumption is that it is necessary in order to obtain Pearson-product-moment correlations. It is interesting, in this respect, that Cattell finds that his arousal factor is associated with good performance and his anxiety factor with poor performance. Experimental evidence has repeatedly shown that performance is curvilinearly related to both. Given an assumption of linearity where there is curvilinearity, a single dimension could appear as two factors, one associated with performance increment and one with performance decrement. To what extent such confusion is involved in Cattell's findings is difficult to say in the absence of careful investigation over the possible range of his variables.

Again, let me turn to research findings in my own laboratory, this time to illustrate how failure to recognize that relationships which, among physiological variables and mounting stress, are not linear could have produced a serious misinterpretation. In a study of novice and experienced parachutists, Fenz and Epstein (1967) obtained intraindividual correlations over 14 points in time for a number of physiological variables recorded before, during, and after the flight from which a parachute jump was made. We were astonished to discover that the distribution of correlations was not significantly different from zero for the novices, while for the experienced parachutists the correlations were uniformly positive and substantial. Our first thought was that different integrative processes might be associated with different levels of mastery. It then occurred to us that the strength of relationships among the physiological measures might vary with the level of stress, which could be assumed to be greater for the novices. This turned out to be correct. When both groups were restricted to measures that did not include those taken very shortly before a jump, when levels of reactivity became inordinately high for the novices, both groups produced similar positive correlations. Imagine factor-analyzing the original correlations without separating subjects by experience or recognizing that synchrony at low levels of stress gives way to asynchrony at higher levels of stress. Or imagine the contradictions that would be reported if one factor analyst investigated novices and another experienced parachutists. It is true, of course, that, as Cattell notes, the criticism that one can get out only what one puts in applies to all techniques, not only factor analysis. However, it should be recognized that techniques, like theories, tend to serve as blinders, and variables that are noted in one approach are apt to be overlooked in another. One can only hope that by pointing out biases and questionable assumptions, investigators will test the assumptions in their own data.

In view of the above arguments, it can be concluded that factor analysis provides no royal road to truth, nor even a uniquely sound empirical basis for theory construction. Like other techniques, it has its own advantages and limitations. Science proceeds by successive approximation and by integrating clues that are less than perfect. Cattell's approach has produced some interesting and suggestive relationships among responses. It has told us little, as yet, about the reasons for the relationships. As we learn more about stimulus conditions through experimentation, it will influence what and how we will measure, and factor complexes will, in all likelihood, exhibit changes, perhaps drastic ones. On the other hand as we learn more about response complexes, through factor analytic studies, it will affect the course of our experimentation, and our attention may be directed to new stimulus situations, and to the necessity for obtaining more or different responses. If there is a Berlin wall, as Cattell claims, between the two approaches, it should be recognized that a wall blocks vision in both directions. There is a distinction between such a wall and a one-way mirror which, I suspect, we all feel we are on the side of that permits vision. And, so, we come full cycle to the six blind men mentioned in my paper, which is apparently the story of everyman, including distinguished scientists. Given such a consideration, it is particularly heartening when different procedures produce some convergence. Despite our basic procedural and conceptual differences, it should be noted that Professor Cattell and I are in agreement that fear is an avoidance motive (or erg), that anxiety refers to a state of unresolved tension in which uncertainty often plays an important role, that arousal should be distinguished from anxiety, and, if physiologically defined, can most reasonably be related to the cerebral cortex, and that specific motive states differ from anxiety and general arousal in that they are more focussed, and the arousal associated with them less distressing.

References

Fenz, W. D., & Epstein, S. Gradients of physiological arousal in parachutists as a function of an approaching jump. *Psychosomatic Medicine,* 1967, **29,** 33–51.

Taylor, S., & Epstein, S. The measurement of autonomic arousal: Some basic issues illustrated by the covariation of heart rate and skin conductance. *Psychosomatic Medicine,* 1967, **29,** 514–525.

PART III

Neurophysiological and Biochemical Aspects of Anxiety

Chapter 5

ANXIETY AND IMPULSIVENESS: TOWARD A NEUROPSYCHOLOGICAL MODEL[1]

Ernest S. Barratt

This paper will present the case history of a research project aimed at defining two personality traits (behavioral predispositions): impulsiveness and anxiety. I will summarize the over-all design and rationale of the research project, some selected results obtained to date, and briefly describe research in progress and projected research. I will also present some thoughts about a neuropsychological model; the model is tentative and continues to evolve as new data are obtained.

Overview of Research Project and Rationale

One of the general goals of this research project is to study the brain-behavior correlates of personality using an interdisciplinary approach. We feel that this is

[1] This research has been primarily supported by the Physiological Psychology Branch, Office of Naval Research, Contract 1598-06. Collaborators in this research project include: Glenn Russell, Ph.D., Dept. of Anatomy; Robert White, M.D., Dept. of Psychiatry; Daniel Creson, M.D., Dept. of Psychiatry; and Harold Goolishian, Ph.D., Division of Psychology. Parts of this paper have been summarized in ONR Progress Reports.

a valid goal in its own right. Among the behavioral sciences and especially within psychology, the traditional choices for understanding and predicting behavior have often appeared incongruent. One appeared to have only a choice among the horns of several dilemmas including: a social view of man versus a physiological or somatic view; the study of lower animal behavior versus the study of human behavior; the use of psychological tests versus the experimental laboratory approach. This list can easily be extended. The important point for this discussion is that there are both positive and negative values within each approach from the standpoint of predicting behavior.

The general research design for our research (Figure 5.1) involves interrelating four classes of data using both human and infrahuman subjects, and a wide range of techniques. The four classes of data collected among human subjects include: (1) everyday life experiences, for example, peer ratings, punctuality in keeping appointments, hobbies, family relationships, school achievement; (2) psychometric reports or psychiatric rating scales, for example, Overall and Gorham's (1962) Brief Psychiatric Rating Scale, the Guilford–Zimmerman (1949) Temperament Schedule, The IPAT Anxiety Scale (Cattell, 1957); (3) laboratory behavioral tasks, for example, two dimensional tracking, classical eye-blink conditioning, critical flicker frequency; (4) psychophysiological measurements, for example, cortical evoked potentials, GSR, heart rate. The four classes of data are the same for the research with infrahuman subjects. Examples of data within each class obtained from infrahuman subjects include: (1) everyday life experiences, for example, eating habits, activity level in home cage; (2) rating scales, for example, mood changes, dominance behavior; (3) laboratory behavioral tasks, for example, reaction time as part of a chained operant task or

Four Classes of Data (with Typical Examples)

	Everyday life experiences	Psychometric and psychiatric interviews	Laboratory behavioral measures	Psychophyological or neuro-physiological
Human subjects	School achievement family life hobbies	IPAT Anxiety Scale Overal Brief Psychiatric Rating Scale Guilford-Zimmerman Temperament Scale	Reaction time tracking off classical eyeblink conditioning	Heart rate visual evoked potentials EEG
Infrahuman	Eating habits percentage of sleep time activity level	Rating mood changes	Chained operant tasks Avoidance conditioning	Acute: cortical evoked potentials from subcortical stimulation Chronic: cortical and subcortical EEGs

Figure 5.1. *Overall design for impulsiveness-anxiety research with typical examples.*

avoidance conditioning; (4) physiological measures, for example, threshold for producing seizures by subcortical brain stimulation or evoked cortical potentials resulting from stimulating subcortical nuclei. The experiments with lower animals are designed to gather information which cannot be meaningfully obtained from human subjects; the behavioral tasks are designed to be as similar as possible to tasks being used with humans.

This project design, then, allows for the interdisciplinary study of a particular variable(s) (hypothetical constructs) using a wide range of techniques in both longitudinal and cross sectional studies. The experiments to be discussed here are held together by the common goal of trying to understand better the interaction of impulsiveness and anxiety. In one experiment, the dependent variable may be an "everyday life" measurement with the independent variable being performance on a laboratory task; in another experiment, this dependent variable may become the independent variable. The results of these concantenated experiments have more meaning in the context of the overall design than they would have individually because they can readily be related to several classes of data.

Parenthetically, there are several drawbacks to explicitly following the overall design. First, the research progresses slowly, especially in the beginning phases, because the experiments are concantenated and following one lead may take several series of experiments. Second, communication among disciplines is difficult (even within subspecialities of one discipline such as psychology). Because research is interdisciplinary, it is not "automatically" better than an intradisciplinary approach. It takes time for a team to learn to communicate and for each member to learn his appropriate role on the research project.

In the human level research, we distinguish between process and population research. Population research involves obtaining measurements on all of the members of a circumscribed social unit, for example, the anxiety scores for all of the male students in a particular high school. The extent to which the results of this research can be generalized depends on how typical the social unit being studied is relative to other comparable social units. One can, of course, sample across social units.

Process research involves selecting samples of subjects from a social unit on the basis of an objectively measured personality trait, a behavioral measure, or psychophysiological measure. One has to be cautious in generalizing from process research to populations not only because of the smaller *N* usually involved but also because of the biases introduced into the data from using subjects who are often at the extremes of a measuring scale; if the units of measurement for the selection device are nonhomogeneous at all, the chances are good that they will be nontypical at the extremes. However, process research is valuable for several reasons: first, it allows more complex data to be gathered on individual subjects for exploratory purposes; second, it allows for a more in-depth analysis of the data to search for the basis of observed interrelationships.

Most of our population research has involved either everyday life measures or psychometric measures, usually including factor analyses or item analyses of the data. Our construct research has involved selecting samples from the larger populations on the basis of various combinations of anxiety and impulsiveness scores and then studying these subjects within one or more of the other three classes of data. One could start the process research to explore for the interrelationships among the classes of data by selecting subjects using data from any of the four classes. The choice of what class of data to use to first select subjects represents essentially a value judgement. We start with psychometric measures of impulsiveness and anxiety because: (1) we can reliably measure these traits (high test–retest reliability) with relative ease in large samples over fairly long time periods; (2) the psychometric measures of impulsiveness and anxiety have consistently been orthogonally related to each other over a wide variety of subjects; (3) the behavior and feelings described by the respective sets of items for each trait appear to make psychological and psychophysiological sense on an a priori basis.

Our goal in the process research is to determine where the most significant interrelationships will occur among the four classes of data and, subsequently, to study these particular relationships in a population research design. For example, using process research, we have been studying the effects of anxiety and impulsiveness on subjects' performance on a broad spectrum of perceptual-motor tasks for the past several years. On the basis of the results from the process research, we are now gathering data on several large social units; in this population research we will include psychometric questionnaires, perceptual-motor tasks, and psychophysiological measurements (e.g., visual evoked potentials). We have made predictions about the number of factors we will obtain and which performance tasks will have high loadings on the impulsiveness and anxiety factors. This combined use of process and population research represents our interpretation of multivariate experimental psychology. Royce (1950) has proposed a somewhat similar approach.

I will now present a brief summary of some of our results obtained to date starting with the human research and considering the four classes of data separately.

Psychometric Research (Human)

In numerous factor analyses of personality questionnaires involving male subjects (16–50 years) from a wide range of social units, inpulsiveness and anxiety have appeared as orthogonal factors (Table 5.1). The correlations between questionnaires which have the highest loadings on each of these factors are usually not significantly different from zero (Table 5.2). The scores for these questionnaires are also symmetrically distributed. The Barratt Impulsiveness Scale (BIS; Barratt, 1959) has been used most often as a marker variable for impulsiveness in the factor analyses. The Taylor Manifest Anxiety Scale (TMAS; Taylor, 1953) and the IPAT Anxiety Scale (Cattell, 1957) have been used most often as anxiety marker variables.

There are a number of scales that correlate significantly with the BIS and TMAS or IPAT Anxiety Scale (Table 5.2). In general, the anxiety scales have low correlations with the impulsiveness scales. Also, some scales correlate significantly with either the impulsiveness or anxiety scales, but also relate to other factor measures. For example, Eysenck's (Eysenck and Eysenck, 1964) extraversion (E) scale correlates significantly with the BIS and has a high loading on the impulsiveness factor; however, it also loads on other factors. Eysenck (1967, pp. 36–37) has suggested that impulsiveness is part of his extraversion dimension and one would expect this finding.

We regularly do item analyses of both the impulsiveness and anxiety scales as part of our ongoing research. Our goal is to arrive at two sets of items that are independent of each other, but which have high correlations among the items within each set. Ideally we would like to be able to rank the items within each set using scaling techniques. The item analyses of the impulsiveness items have indicated six subsets which we have combined into a single questionnaire (BIS-6); we also score the original BIS items (BIS-5) as a seventh score (Table 5.3). The six subsets with examples of typical items are: (1) motor control, for example, I usually act before I think or I answer questions quickly; (2) intraindividual variability, for example, I change my plans often or I like new situations; (3) impulsive interests, for example, I like work that has lots of excitement or I don't like detailed work;; (4) risk taking, for example, I like to take a chance just for the excitement; (5) impulsive interpersonal relationships, for example, I let myself "go" at a party or I would rather talk than listen; (6) cognitive impulse control, for example, I make up my mind quickly or my mind wanders.[2] These six subsets are all highly correlated with the total BIS-6 score; the BIS-5 also correlates highly with the BIS-6 total score (Table 5.3). These subsets of impulsiveness items correspond fairly well with impulsiveness factors reported by Twain (1957). We are now using the subset scores as well as the total BIS-6 scores in selecting subjects for our process research experiments.

We have not found response set (true versus false items) to be related to impulsiveness. Also, differences in the number of favorable versus unfavorable items checked on the Gough–Heilbrun Adjective Check List (Gough–Heilbrun,

[2] These examples as presented here have been worded for a "yes" to indicate impulsiveness; within the BIS, the items are counterbalanced to control for response bias.

TABLE 5.1
Orthogonal Rotated Varimax Solution[a, b]

Number	Battery	Variable	Factor						h^2
			I	II	III	IV	V	VI	
1		Taylor Manifest Anxiety Scale	−11	−78	−17	08	−06	−17	69
2		Barratt Impulsiveness Scale 5	77	−12	09	03	27	−04	70
3	IPAT Anxiety Scale	Cattell Anxiety Covert (A)	15	−75	−14	00	09	06	61
4		Cattell Anxiety Overt (B)	02	−78	−34	05	03	−16	75
5		Otis Intelligence Scale	−10	17	03	01	04	52	32
6	Barratt Impulsiveness	Lack of persistence	51	−22	−13	−06	16	−11	37
7	Scale 4	Social optimism	74	07	28	02	08	−19	67
8		Lack of motor inhibition	53	−51	11	00	−03	−02	55
9		Aggression–autonomy	34	−32	37	−30	−04	17	47
10		Action oriented	67	−01	33	−10	23	−08	63
11	Guilford–Zimmerman	General activity	24	18	33	−15	64	−06	64
12	Temperament Schedule	Restraint	−86	04	−11	02	03	01	75
13		Ascendance	14	27	70	−07	21	06	64

14		Emotional stability	–09	84	04	00	15	06	74
15		Objectivity	–11	77	–06	–01	11	07	62
16	Cattell 16 P.F.	A. Warm–Aloof	17	03	18	48	03	–10	31
17		B. Bright–Dull	–04	07	08	–04	–03	52	28
18		C. Calm–Emotional	04	56	–02	–29	06	01	40
19		E. Aggressive–Mild	27	10	60	–12	22	19	54
20		F. Enthusiastic–Glum	69	05	37	06	12	–12	65
21		G. Conscientious–Casual	–51	15	05	–05	05	–26	36
22		H. Adventurous–Shy	19	31	67	24	16	–01	66
23		I. Sensitive–Tough	–02	–15	–06	59	–02	04	38
24		O. Timid–Confident	12	–65	–20	23	05	–10	55
25		Q_3. Controlled–Uncontrolled	–38	40	13	–08	–12	–10	35
26		Q_4. Excitable–Composed	04	–83	–08	–03	07	03	70
27	Thurstone Temperament	Active	31	–01	26	–01	59	08	52
28	Schedule	Vigorous	21	21	18	–59	19	–03	50
29		Impulsive	57	30	24	–10	38	–25	69
30		Stable	02	72	04	–03	19	09	56

[a] From Barratt (1965, p. 552).
[b] All entries to two decimal places.

TABLE 5.2
Intercorrelations among BIS-5, IPAT Anxiety Scale, TMAS, and other Selected Scales[a]

	BIS-5	IPAT Anxiety scale	TMAS
BIS-5		17	01
IPAT Anxiety Scale	17		68
TMAS	01	68	
Eysenck's "E" Scale	60		−11
Eysenck's "N" Scale	−09		78
Guilford–Zimmerman Temp. S. "E"	−16	−63	−68
Guilford–Zimmerman Temp. S. "R"	−66	−09	09
IPAT 16 P.F. "F" Scale	63	−09	−12
Thurstone Temp. Schedule "Impulsive"	56	−18	−34
Thurstone Temp. Schedule "Stable"	−02	−54	−62
Jacksons Personality Form "Impulsive"	51	14	08
Omnibus Personality Inv. "Impulsive"	49	24	
Omnibus Personality Inv. "Anx. Level"	05	−76	
Spielberger, *et al.*, 1970, STAI–State Anx.	04	62	
Spielberger, *et al.*, 1970. STAI–Triat Anx.	−08	74	
IPAT 16 P.F. Calm–Emotional	00	−41	−49
IPAT 16 P.F. Q_1-Excitable–Composed	14	62	64
Otis Intelligence Test	−02		−08
Gough–Heilbrun Adj. Checklist–Self Control	−34	−34	
Gough–Heilbrun Adj. Checklist–Lability	26	−02	
Gough–Heilbrun Adj. Checklist–Favorable Items	06	−26	
Gough–Heilbrun Adj. Checklist–Unfavorable Items	17	43	
Barron Ego Strength Scale	−02	−52	
Penny Stimulus Variability Seeking Sc.	−10		05
Penny Lie Scale	09		00

[a] *N* for each correlation is between 140 and 160.

1965) was not related to impulsiveness (Table 5.2). Since we had found intraindividual variability of performance and ANS measures to be related to impulsiveness, we predicted that the Penney Stimulus Variability Seeking Scale (Penney & Reinehr, 1966) would relate significantly to the BIS, but it did not (Table 5.2).

The item analyses of the anxiety items have indicated two major subsets: (1) awareness of somatic changes, for example, I blush often or I am often aware of my heart beating; (2) conscious awareness of unpleasant feelings about self or external stimuli, for example, I frequently find myself worrying about something or I have many fears or I am tense. Beyond these two large clusters of items, there are usually about fifteen subsets of items that cluster together but which are not significantly independent of each other. Our psychometric data, then, clearly indicate that the two large sets of items labeled impulsiveness and

TABLE 5.3
Intercorrelations among Total and "Subset" Scores for BIS-6 and BIS-5[a]

		1	2	3	4	5	6	7	8
1	BIS-6 Total score	–							
2	BIS-6 Motor control	60	–						
3	BIS-6 Interindividual variability	51	16	–					
4	BIS-6 Impulsive interests	74	23	19	–				
5	BIS-6 Risk taking	60	21	13	40	–			
6	BIS-6 Interpersonal relationships	67	30	25	48	30	–		
7	BIS-6 Impulse control	62	28	36	42	08	28	–	
8	BIS-5 (tot. sc.)	82	46	39	73	45	57	44	–

[a] $N = 149$; subjects were male freshmen medical students.

anxiety are orthogonal, but the subsets of items within each set are not clear at this time.

We have also administered the anxiety and impulsiveness scales to male subjects in the age range 12 to 15 years. (Barratt and Fruchter, 1967). The factor analyses of these data do not indicate a clear distinction between the two factors similar to that obtained with subjects from age 16 upward. There is some suggestion that impulsiveness and anxiety start diverging as one approaches age 16, but they are convergent factors prior to age 16. This research must be replicated, however, since it is possible that the vocabulary and reading level required to complete the questionnaires could be in part related to our results.

On several occasions we have had psychiatric ratings of impulsiveness and anxiety; the average correlation between the ratings of anxiety and the TMAS was +.68; the average correlation between the impulsiveness ratings and the BIS was +.74 ($N = 50$ for these ratings). In making these ratings, the psychiatrists were only instructed to label each person as high, medium, or low on anxiety and impulsiveness.

We have administered the BIS-5 and the TMAS to subjects at least twice a year over a three year period. Over the three year period, the test–retest reliability for the TMAS was +.74 and for the BIS-5 it was +.78 ($N = 85$).

In summary, our psychometric data indicate that anxiety and impulsiveness are orthogonal behavioral predispositions (traits) among males in the age range 16–50 years; further, these two traits are fairly stable over at least a three year period.

Parenthetically, we obviously do not consider these two traits to be all encompassing behavioral predispositions. After we obtain fairly stable relationships across all four classes of data for these two traits, we will then include other personality traits in this research.

Laboratory Behavioral Research (Human)

In our process research we operationally define anxiety and impulsiveness by the scores made on psychometric questionnaires, usually the BIS and the TMAS or IPAT Anxiety Scale. Using these questionnaires, we select four groups of subjects: high impulsiveness, low anxiety (HILA); high impulsiveness, high anxiety (HIHA); low impulsiveness, low anxiety (LILA); low impulsiveness, high anxiety (LIHA). Subjects divided into these four groups have been run on a wide spectrum of laboratory performance tasks including a battery of perceptual-motor tasks, classical eye-blink conditioning, time estimation, and verbal learning tasks.

Subjects among these four groups differ significantly in their performance on perceptual-motor tasks. In general, the HILA subjects are less efficient than the other three groups in their performance on most of these tests (Barratt, 1967a). For example, on a pursuit rotor task (Figure 5.2), these subjects were significantly less efficient than the other three groups. In a complex jump reaction time task, they were also significantly slower in removing their finger from the home key (Figure 5.3; latency R.T.) and in the time between release of the home key and closing the appropriate response key (Figure 5.4; transport R.T.); the transport measures involved more of a motor response and the HILA subjects' poorer performance was more obvious here.

The overall results from the exploratory perceptual-motor research suggested that impulsiveness did not relate as much to sensory input or signal processing

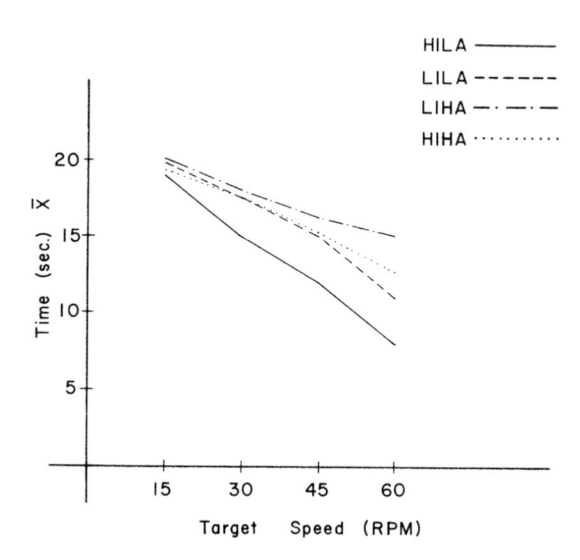

Figure 5.2. *Mean time (seconds) on target on pursuit rotor per 1 minute trial.*

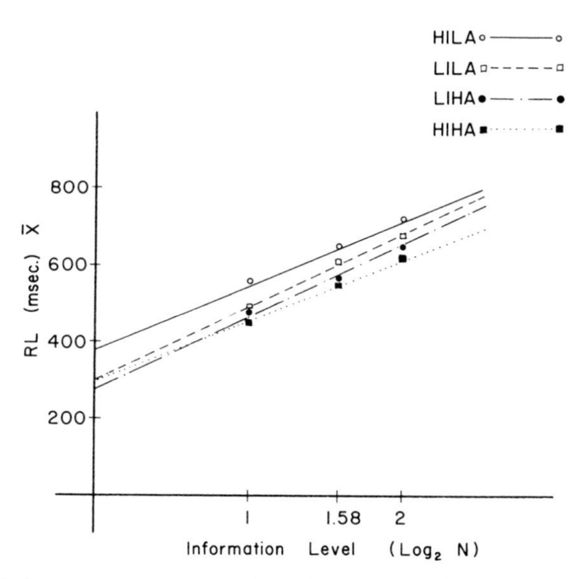

Figure 5.3. *Mean response latencies (msec.) on complex jump reaction time task.*

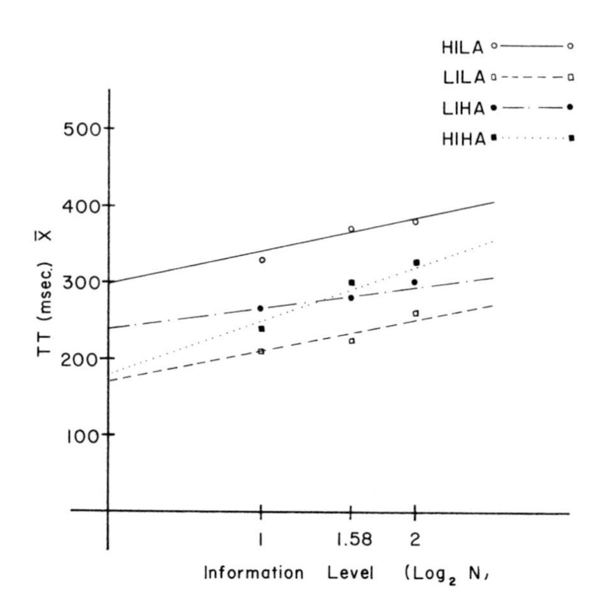

Figure 5.4. *Mean transport time responses (msec.) on complex jump reaction time task.*

per se but, rather, was more related to motor output, especially when anxiety was low. It appeared that these subjects had difficulty in being flexible or in changing a "set" (Barratt, 1967a). In performing tasks where a "set" was established, the HILA subjects had more difficulty in changing their response set than did the other subjects. For example, in a complex choice reaction time experiment in which seven or eight trials of similar stimuli were followed by test trials involving a new pattern, the HILA subjects were much slower on the test trials than were the other subjects (Table 5.4); it is obvious that impulsiveness was more related to performance on these test trials than was anxiety.

TABLE 5.4[1]

Sum of Transport Times (msec.) for Ss *in Each of Four Groups on Three Different Series of Response Sets*[a]

Group	Response set series			
	A	B	C	Total
HILA	598	393	379	1370
HIHA	628	264	283	1175
LIHA	409	238	205	852
LILA	211	201	249	661

[a] Each cell is the sum of *TT*s (msec.) for three response-set tests for all *S*s in each group.
[1] Barratt (1967a, p. 490).

In comparing the results of several visual reaction time experiments, the HILA subjects appeared to be slower in reaction time performance when there was an auditory warning signal preceding the visual stimulus. When there was no warning signal, the HILA subjects did not appear to differ significantly from the other groups in their performance. Again, these data suggest that the HILA subjects had established a set to the warning signal which interfered with their responses on the test trials. This experiment is currently being replicated.

On the basis of the process research, we have compiled a battery of perceptual-motor tests that we are administering to a large population of medical students ($N = 600$), high school students ($N = 600$), and patients. These tests represent varying amounts of "sensory" input discrimination versus motor "output" involvement. Stimuli are all presented automatically and responses are automatically recorded. The perceptual-motor tests include: (1) critical flicker frequency (cff) where both ascending and descending thresholds are obtained; (2) perceptual speed where subjects indicate whether two meters have the same or different settings; (3) reponse orientation where a lever moved as quickly as possible in one of four directions, depending on which one of four lights flashes;

(4) control precision where subjects track a dot on an oscilloscope in two dimensions by moving one control stick; (5) arm–hand steadiness where a subject repeatedly inserts a stylus into a hole without touching the rim; (6) simple tapping where a subject taps key as fast as possible; (7) two hand coordination where a dot is kept centered on oscilloscope using two control sticks simultaneously; (8) visual reaction time where there are four levels of information with and without an auditory warning signal; (9) mirror tracing involving reversed tracing over a complex maze. We have run about seventy medical students to date on the above tests and the results indicate that impulsiveness and anxiety do interact to effect performance in much the same way as in our past research. Two previous findings were not replicated: (1) the differences in reaction time with and without an auditory warning signal were not found; on all reaction time tasks, the HI subjects (especially the HILA subjects) were slower than the LI subjects; (2) the pursuit rotor performance scores were in the same direction as the past experiments, but the results were not significantly different among the four groups.

In a study of classical differential eye-lid conditioning, impulsiveness and anxiety interacted to influence eye-blink acquisition (Barratt, 1970). These data were analyzed for "V" and "C" type conditioned responses (CRs) as well as for the combined data. The V type CRs involve a slower rate and a longer duration of closure, while the C type CRs have a faster rate and shorter duration of closure. The V type CRs have been suggested to be more "voluntary" type closures. The CS+ (reinforced conditioned stimuli) were either correct or incorrect arithmetic problems. The anxiety–impulsiveness interaction effects were exactly reversed for the V and C type CRs. When the CS+ was a correct arithmetic problem, the HILA subjects and HIHA subjects made more V type CRs while the LIHA subjects made fewer V type CRs; the LILA subjects made slightly fewer (but not significantly less) V type CRs under these same conditions (Figure 5.5). The overall results of this experiment indicated that impulsiveness and anxiety do interact with the truth value (correct–incorrect) of the CS+ to effect acquisition of the CRs. Considering the analyses of the combined CRs (both V and C type CRs), impulsiveness had a more clear effect on the acquisition of CRs (Figure 5.6) than did anxiety (Figure 5.7). Again, the results suggest that impulsiveness is related to a "set" to respond a specific way.

In a risk taking experiment in which subjects bet on their performance on a pursuit rotor task, impulsiveness was significantly positively related to a risk taking quotient ($r = +.52; N = 28$), but anxiety was not. The risk taking quotient was a weighted combination of the amount of money bet over a series of three trials plus, the speed at which the subjects requested the pursuit rotor to run. They could make more money by either betting more money or requesting faster speeds, or both. The results of this experiment primarily relate to the risk-taking subset of items among the impulsiveness items. The HILA subjects

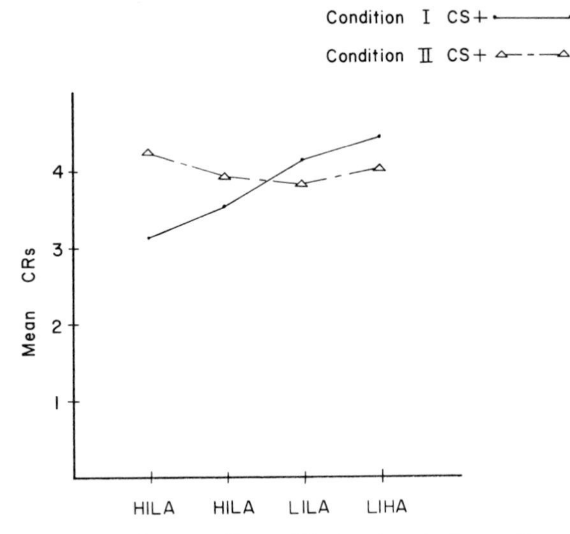

Figure 5.5. *Acquisition of C type CRs to CS related to the interaction of the four groups under Condition I (CS+ = incorrect arithmetic problems) and Condition II (CS+ = correct arithmetic problems).*

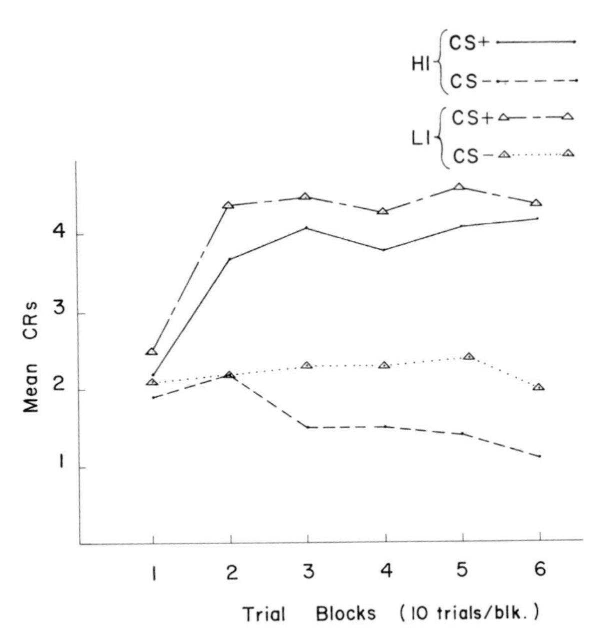

Figure 5.6. *Acquisition of CRs for high impulsive (HI) versus low impulsive (LI) subjects. (Combined CRs.)*

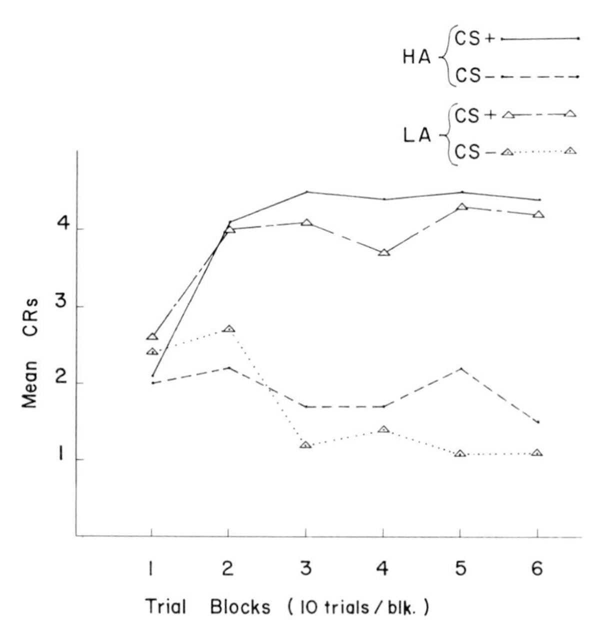

Figure 5.7. *Acquisition of CRs for high anxiety (HA) versus low anxiety (LA) subjects. (Combined CRs.)*

had the highest level of risk taking among the four groups. Anxiety and impulsiveness did not significantly relate to cognitive risk-taking tests developed by Kogan and Wallach (1964).

In a "time estimation" experiment, anxiety was significantly related to performance (Figure 5.8), but impulsiveness was not (Figure 5.9). Again, however, there were differences among the four groups with the HILA subjects making the longest time estimates and the HIHA subjects making the shortest time estimates. In the first half of the experiment, the subjects were instructed to press a key after they estimated two seconds had elapsed; the time period for the second estimate was four seconds. All of the subjects had previously participated in a reaction time experiment and each subject's time estimation scores were corrected on the basis of their reaction time scores.

In summary, then, impulsiveness and anxiety do interact to influence behavior on a wide spectrum of laboratory tasks. On the basis of our results, we hypothesize that impulsiveness tends to make subjects less efficient in perceptual-motor performance because of their being less flexible in changing a "motor set".

Parenthetically, related to our "motor-set" hypothesis, the perceptual motor performance scores for the HI subjects are often significantly more variable than

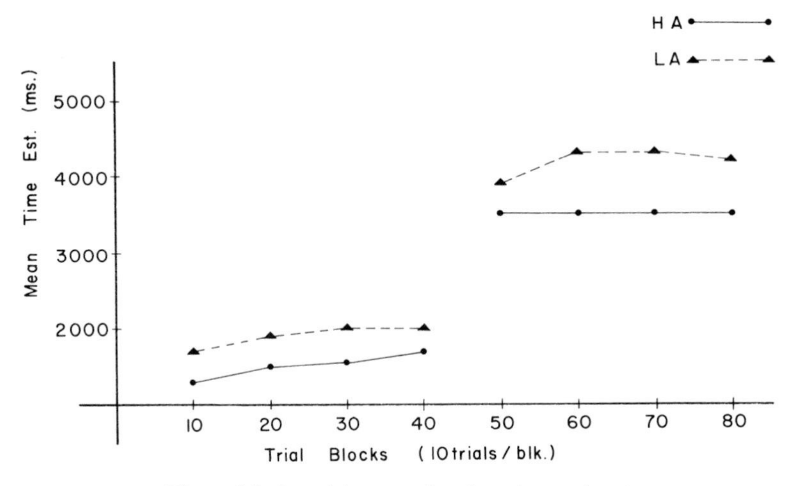

Figure 5.8. *Impulsiveness related to time estimation.*

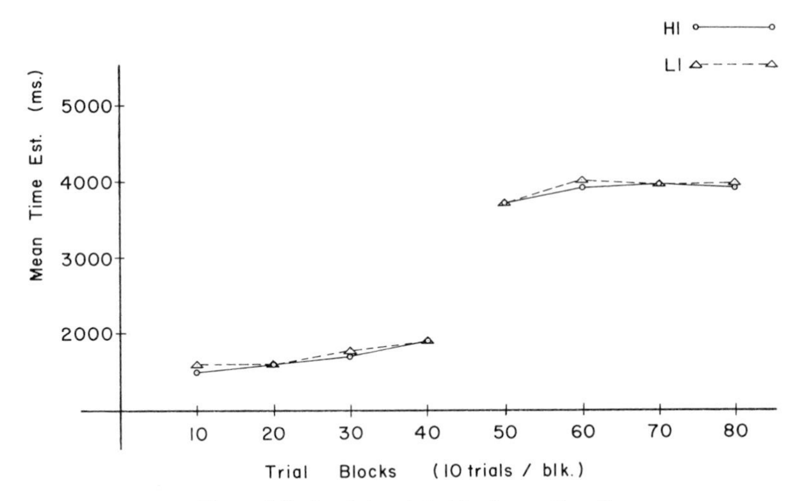

Figure 5.9. *Anxiety related to time estimation.*

those for the LI subjects; anxiety does not appear to relate to variability of performance. For example, for the discrimination reaction time experiment currently in progress, the HI subjects were significantly more variable than the LI subjects (Figure 5.10) while there was not a significant difference in the variability of performance related to anxiety (Figure 5.11) among the subjects run to date. In an earlier experiment (Barratt, 1963a), impulsiveness was also related to variability of reversed mirror tracing. This variability of performance

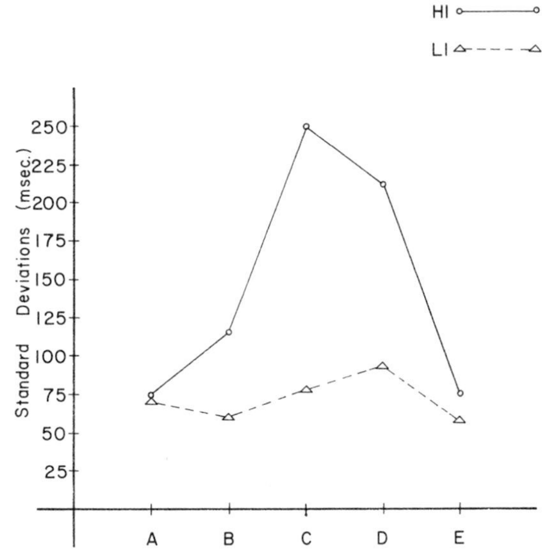

Figure 5.10. *Impulsiveness related to the variability of reaction time latencies for different levels of visual information. (A = one light, one response key; B = two lights, two keys; C = three lights, three keys; D = four lights, four keys; A through D involve auditory warning signal; E = one light, one key and no warning signal.)*

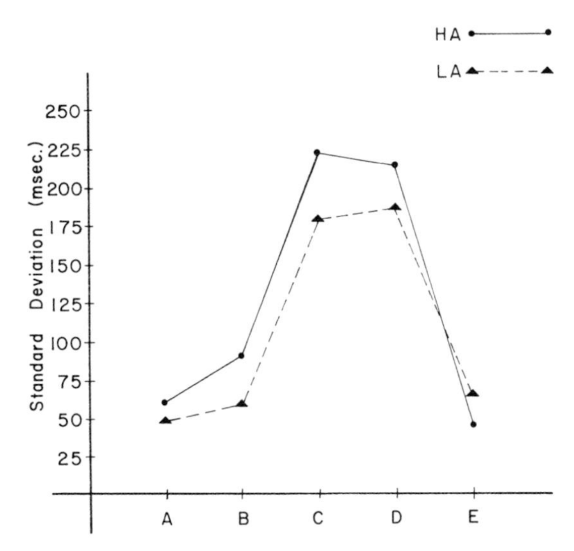

Figure 5.11. *Anxiety related to variability of reaction time latencies for different levels of visual information. (A = one light, one response key; B = two lights, two keys; C = three lights, three keys; D = four lights, four keys; A through D involve auditory warning signal; E = one light, one key and no warning signal.)*

among HI subjects compared to LI subjects may relate to a "motor set" involving the interaction of the limbic system and basal ganglia nuclei as discussed later.

Psychophysiological Research (Human)

Psychophysiological data have been recorded while the subjects performed many of the laboratory behavioral tasks. Some experiments have also been designed to exclusively obtain psychophysiological data related to impulsiveness and anxiety. Our psychophysiological results have been more difficult to replicate than have the data from the other three classes of measurements. There are probably several reasons for this: (1) slight variations in biological state such as hunger (blood sugar level) or sleep deprivation probably have a more marked influence on the psychophysiological measures than on performance or psychometric measures; we try to control for these influences, but it is impossible to do so completely; for example, we request subjects not to smoke for at least one hour before coming for an experiment; frequently, the HILA subjects walk into the laboratory smoking; (2) our first psychophysiological data analyses involve separate parameter analyses; our feeling is now that patterns of the interrelationships of psychophysiological responses over longer time periods are more meaningful in differentiating among the four groups than are specific psychophysiological responses to specific stimuli. One of the problems related to obtaining replicable psychophysiological data is the operation of the "second signal system" (Luria, 1961) as the subjects participate in the experiments.

In an orienting response experiment (Barratt, 1968), subjects listened to 45 presentations of a 1000 cps tone of either 30 minutes, 60 minutes, or 90 minutes duration. The tones were 45 dB above hearing threshold and were presented binaurally through earphones. GSR, BSR, EEG (frontal and parietal-occipital leads), heart rate, and respiration were measured. Data were analyzed for both "on" and "off" responses to the tones. The first analyses involved analyzing psychophysiological response to each stimulus separately for each system; these analyses did not indicate any significant relationship between habituation of the orienting response in the various systems and impulsiveness and anxiety. However, we did find that if we looked at the relative habituation time for the EEG's versus the Autonomic N.S. measures, there were significant and opposite differences between two groups: the HILA subjects consistently habituated the EEG after the ANS measures; for the LIHA, the ANS measures were habituated after the EEG was habituated. This finding was consistent for all of the subjects in both groups. For the LILA subjects and the HIHA subjects, these relationships were equivocal. Although there were inter-individual differences in the number of tones presented before habituation, the intraindividual differences for the HILA and LIHA subjects were consistent as stated above. This experiment has been replicated with a larger sample and the results were consistent.

During the classical eye-blink experiment discussed above, we recorded the same psychophysiological variables that were recorded in the orienting response experiment. There were differences between HI and LI subjects in the analyses of the EEG records. The HI subjects had a higher percentage of alpha in their EEGs than did the LI subjects. The percentage of alpha in the EEGs and the impulsiveness scores were related to the conditioning data in exactly opposite directions: the HI subjects had a higher percentage of alpha and fewer CRs than did the LI subjects. The HILA subjects had the highest percentage of alpha of all subjects with the LIHA subjects having the lowest percentage of alpha. Although there were some isolated instances of the other physiological measures being related to the conditioning data, these measures were not consistently related to both the conditioning data and personality measures. Computer analyses of the EEG data for the four seconds immediately preceding the presentation of the CS+ were consistent with the EEG differences reported above between HI and LI subjects.

We have also recorded psychophysiological data during several of our reaction time experiments. The results indicate that the HI subjects generally have a higher percentage of alpha than do the LI subjects while frequency of GSRs relates to anxiety level; the HA subjects have a higher frequency of GSRs than do the LA subjects. Parenthetically, our overall results are in line with Lacey's suggestion (Lacey, 1967) that all psychophysiological variables are not equally and concurrently responsive to changes in activation level.

At this point, then, our most consistent psychophysiological finding appears to be the relationship of percentage of alpha in the EEG to impulsiveness and the relative differences between the HILA subjects and the LIHA subjects in habituating their EEG and ANS responses.

We are currently recording visual and auditory evoked potentials as part of the data which we are gathering along with our perceptual-motor experiments. We are also replicating the OR data using a different series of stimuli as part of this research. In an earlier experiment, we found a significant relationship between impulsiveness and intraindividual variability of ANS measures; anxiety level was related to the mean level of ANS functioning in the same experiment. We will analyze the data from our current experiment to check on this earlier finding.

Everyday Life Experiences (Human)

In a three year in-depth study of sixteen medical students, we interviewed them repeatedly about their everyday life experiences. Each student was interviewed over 40 times in the three year period. We also interviewed their professors and their peers to obtain data about their interpersonal relationships. These sixteen medical ştudents represented the four most extreme cases in their class of the four combinations of impulsiveness and anxiety. The rank correlations between the first testing and a retest three years later for these sixteen students was +.84 for the BIS and +.88 for the IPAT Anxiety Scale. The results of this study (Barratt–White, 1969) indicated: (1) differences in achievement among the four groups; even though there were no significant differences among the four groups in the Medical College Aptitude Tests, the LILA subjects and the HIHA subjects had significantly lower grade point averages over the three year period than did the other two groups; (2) differences among the four groups between concepts of self and ideal self and between concepts of self and a typical medical student; for example, the HILA subjects saw a typical medical student as being less friendly and more unhappy than they were; the HIHA subjects saw a typical medical student as less friendly, less happy, and clearer thinkers than they were; (3) the students were aware of being anxious and/or impulsive; all but two students answered in accord with their personality questionnaire scores when asked if they were impulsive or anxious; (4) all of the HIHA subjects sought psychiatric help during their first three years in medical school; only one other subject (a LIHA subject) sought psychiatric help; (5) the HI subjects (especially the HILA subjects) were unreliable in keeping appointments and in general had sociopathic tendencies; it is interesting that their peers expressed negative attitudes toward the HILA subjects while their professors, in general, expressed positive attitudes; the professors often described these subjects as hard working and highly motivated while their peers described them, in general, as trouble makers; (6) the HIHA subjects had the greatest discrepancies between self and ideal self.

We have kept records on all of our subjects in terms of punctuality in arriving for an experimental session, attitudes about participating in the experiment, general impressions of their social behavior in the laboratory, family relationships, and their attitudes toward their peers. The HI subjects (especially the HILA subjects) are very lax about keeping appointments and their presence in the laboratory is very obvious. The HIHA subjects have the most negative attitudes about participating in the research and often have to be verbally reinforced to get them to return. The HIHA subjects also have the most difficulties in home adjustments, both with their own parents and also with their spouses if they are married. The LILA subjects are less highly motivated toward academic or professional status goals; for example, among the medical students, very few aspire to be well known in whatever speciality they choose, and they don't aspire to large financial incomes. The LIHA subjects are very highly motivated in academic pursuits and often worry about not doing well in school even when they are doing well. These results on over 300 subjects (high school and medical students) are consistent with the results of the intensive three year study.

In a study (Barratt, 1967b) relating impulsiveness and anxiety to social adjustment among high school male students ($N = 320$), the students were divided into three groups on the basis of infractions reported to the central office: (a) serious offenders; students who had been reported at least three times for fighting or truancy or both (10% of the students); (b) moderate offenders; students reported for disrupting class or smoking in the halls (28%); (c) non-offenders (62%). Using a median split test for the scores on the BIS-5 for the entire group, there was about a 50–50 split for both moderate offenders and nonoffenders; however, the chances were 9 out of 11 of being above the median on impulsiveness for the serious offenders. Anxiety scores were not significantly different among the three groups. In this study, neither impulsiveness nor anxiety was significantly related to teachers' conduct scores nor to standardized achievement scores in mathematics, English, or science.

In a peer rating study in progress involving two medical fraternities ($N = 110$) and group of Catholic priests who live together ($N = 19$), impulsiveness scores were inversely related to positive peer ratings for both fraternities but not for the priests. Anxiety was not related to peer ratings. These peer ratings will be repeated two more times this year.

In a study (Levy, 1967) of 269 sophomore male high school students, those students who had good study habits as measured by the Brown–Holtzman Survey of Study Habits and Attitudes (Brown–Holtzman, 1965) were low scorers on the BIS. The most discriminating impulsiveness items in this study were: I like to take a chance just for the excitement; I usually act before I think; I don't like detailed work; I am not always careful; I always have a ready answer; I don't like work requiring patience and carefulness (items reworded here to indicate impulsive tendencies).

In general, then, impulsiveness and anxiety are related to everyday life experiences. The most conspicuous relationship is the suggestion that high impulsiveness is related to sociopathic tendencies, especially when anxiety is low.

Infrahuman Research

As noted earlier, the purpose of the research with infrahuman subjects is to extend the human research in two ways: (1) to duplicate a human task requirement as nearly as possible to obtain data that cannot meaningfully be obtained with humans; (2) to study neural systems that may relate to impulsiveness and anxiety.

Because of the consistent differences in reaction time performance among the four groups of human subjects, we have concentrated much of our infrahuman behavioral research on reaction time experiments. One of our main interests in the reaction time experiments has been in neural centers that might relate exclusively to either the control of intraindividual variability of reaction times or the mean level of reaction time performance. In a reaction time experiment (Barratt, 1963b) with cats, stimulating the basolateral amygdala increased intraindividual variability of reaction times but did not change the mean level. Stimulating the reticular activating system changed the mean level of the reaction time responses, but did not significantly change the variability.

Following this research, we studied the effects of subcortical electrical stimulation and selected drugs on the release of a suppressed response (Barratt, 1967c). Squirrel monkeys were trained to perform on a chained operant schedule that included a "conflict" sequence of "crf with 50% random shock." A light panel signaled when the monkeys would receive either a food reward or a shock during the conflict portion of the schedule. Suppressing the functioning of the basolateral amygdalae by drugs (Thiazesim) or bilateral lesions (checked by histology) resulted in the release of the suppressed responses. Stimulating the ascending midbrain reticular formation or the use of amphetamines increased the overall activity level of the animals, but did not result in a release of the suppressed bar-pulling response. Unilateral stimulation of the basolateral amygdala also did not result in the release of the response.

In this experiment, the effects of Thiazesim on the release of the suppressed response were reversible; after the acute phase of the drug activity passed, the monkeys again appropriately suppressed their bar-pulling responses. At the time Thiazesim was becoming effective in releasing the suppressed response, there were concurrent EEG changes that suggested an amygdala-frontal lobe interaction in the release of the suppressed response. We speculated that

> From a neuroanatomical viewpoint, it is possible that the amygdala is acting as a "control center" that has both downstream and upstream effects. Upstream it is involved in the activity of the frontal lobes . . . this *interaction* could produce a change in behavioral inhibition if one accepts the popular conception that certain frontal areas are related to impulse control. . . . The downstream influence could be manifest at various basal-ganglia nuclei as Gloor suggests. This downstream influence could result in a general change in motor output [Barratt, 1967c, pp. 238–239].

Following this experiment, Dr. Colin McDiarmid developed a complex operant task that has a reaction time requirement as part of the sequence (McDiarmid and Barratt, 1969). This operant task involves a time out period signaled by a blinking light, a fixed ratio period (FR4, FR8, and FR12 counterbalanced) signaled by a white light, and a reaction time task. On the last FR response, a green light comes on and the animal has to hold the lever down for a specified period of time; at the end of this time period, a red light comes on and the monkey has to release the lever within a specified time period (the reaction time response). If he pulls the lever down during the time-out period, this period is lengthened. The FR sequences are counterbalanced against varying time periods during which he has to hold the lever down.

Once an animal has reached a stable level of performance on this task, the performance is very resistant to the effects of many psychoactive drugs. Thiazesim increases the variability of the reaction times in line with our earlier finding, but the effect is not as marked. Dilantin has a very marked effect on performance on this task. Under the influence of Dilantin (10 mg/k), the latencies of the reaction time responses increase slightly and variability increases significantly; also, the number of incorrect responses increases. We are also currently studying the effects of other psychoactive drugs on the performance of monkeys on this task (drugs include marijuana and alcohol).

On a series of acute experiments with cats, we have been exploring the functional interrelationships among the orbital frontal cortex, the amygdala, hypothalamus, hippocampus, septum, several basal ganglia nuclei, and the cerebellum. In this research we are interested in the relative latencies for evoked potentials among a system of nuclei which we feel relate to impulse control and anxiety. We are also interested in the effects of certain drugs on these relationships. Our current drug research has involved primarily dilantin, lithium carbonate, and selective psychoactive drugs which obviously have an effect on impulse control (e.g., LSD, alcohol, and marijuana). We are interested in lithium because of its positive therapeutic effects on manic patients who usually have impulse control problems. A brief summary of selected results of our acute experiments will indicate the scope of this reasearch: (1) we have demonstrated a functional interrelationship between the basolateral amygdala and globus pallidus and putamen which suggest to us the possibility "that the basolateral amygdala has a facilitory influence upon striatal elements which, in turn, have an initial inhibitory effect upon pallidal elements.... In any event, the establishment of an amygdalofugal connection to the basal ganglia provides a pathway whereby limbic system activity may exert an influence upon somatic motor mechanisms" (Russell, Barratt, Deaton, & Taylor, 1968); (2) we have evidence that the primary locus of activity of lithium is in the orbitofrontal cortex (Creson, Barratt, Russell, & Schlagenauf, 1967; Barratt, Creson, & Russell, 1968); (3) in research recently completed, we obtained evoked potential evidence for olivonuclear collateral afferents to the deep cerebellar nuclei of the cat; (4) we have also obtained suggestive evidence of a topographical representation of several limbic system nuclei (hippocampus, septum, basolateral amygdalae) on the inferior olive; considering the suggested inhibitory role of the cerebellum (Eccles, Ito, & Szentagothai, 1967) it is possible that the inhibitory functions of the cerebellum may be selectively influenced by these limbic system nuclei; (5) we have observed that Dilantin inhibits the activity of the cerebellar cortex before and to a greater degree than it does the olive; the effects of Dilantin are dose related, the maximum reversible inhibitory effect occurring at about 10 mg/k (IV via the sublingual branch of the carotid artery in encephale isolé preparations); 5 mg/k appears to have little or no effect; 7.5 mg/k has a reversible effect but it takes longer to achieve an effect at this dosage level; 20 mg/k produces an irreversible isoelectric effect throughout the cerebellum and brainstem where we have recorded and eventually throughout the entire cerebral cortex; at this dosage, the cortex will stay isoelectric for at least 30 hours; the heart continues to function well even though the cortical activity is isoelectric. Parenthetically, related to impulsiveness and brain function, Dilantin has been used clinically for behavioral disorders that involve impulse control symptoms (Turner, 1967; Resnick, 1967).

We have recently developed some psychometric scales for measuring activity and mood changes in the squirrel monkeys following the administration of drugs (Francois, Barratt, & Harris, 1970). We felt that we were observing drug related changes in the spontaneous behavior of monkeys that were present even though the monkeys were performing well on the operant tasks. Many items in psychiatric rating scales for human subjects do not involve verbal communication between rater and rated. The rating scales which we have developed for monkeys are comparable to the nonverbal scales for human subjects. Thus, in addition to the everyday life measures that we ordinarily observe (e.g., eating habits or percentage of sleep time), we can now objectively measure some of the more subtle drug related changes in the spontaneous behavior of monkeys (Francois, *et al.*, in preparation).

Toward a Neuropsychological Model of Impulsiveness and Anxiety

I will briefly outline some of our thoughts about neural systems that might relate to impulsiveness and anxiety. Although our main interest is in a neuropsychological model, we do not propose that impulsiveness and anxiety can be meaningfully understood without considering acculturation processes, especially the early developmental histories of individuals. James (1890) insightfully contrasted the volatile Latin-American temperament and the more stable Anglo-American temperament more than a half century ago. In our research, we have observed that the impulsiveness scores of high school students from first generation Latin-American families are significantly higher than scores for students from Anglo-American families; anxiety is slightly higher for the Latin-American students. Among freshmen medical students approaching exams at the end of the first year, their mean level of anxiety is significantly higher than when they are registering at the beginning of the year; impulsiveness does not change significantly in this instance. Obviously, environmental influences relate to the acquisition and expression of impulsiveness and anxiety.

With regard to the acquisition of these behavioral predispositions, we suggest that during early childhood, individuals become conditioned to respond to a wide variety of stimuli with patterns of responses or behavioral predispositions which have survival value for the individual (or group). The more frequently used response patterns become readily available behavioral predispositions or "personality traits." The conditioning that results in the formation of these patterns is probably a very subtle (nonconscious) type of conditioning, similar to that which Miller (1969) and his colleagues have demonstrated for many visceral and glandular processes. These behavioral predispositions are related to changes in neuronal structures and functioning; different behavioral predispositions involve different neural circuits or systems which interact with each other. More inclusive behavioral predispositions such as impulsiveness and anxiety probably involve fairly elaborate neural-endocrine systems. We propose that impulsiveness (impulse control) involves a neural system which includes, primarily, interrelationships among the orbitofrontal cortex, selected limbic system nuclei (especially the basolateral amygdala), basal ganglia nuclei, and the cerebellum. Anxiety involves essentially the hypothalamic-hypophyseal axis, the ascending reticular activating system, and the orbitofrontal cortex; the effects of the reticular system on cortical functioning are especially important here.

Our rationale for proposing these two systems relates to the characteristics which we have observed to date in individuals with varying levels of anxiety and impulsiveness. Let us briefly summarize these characteristics. The impulsive person typically: acts without thinking, acts on the spur of the moment, is restless when required to sit still, likes to take chances, is happy-go-lucky, has difficulty in concentrating, and is a doer and not a thinker. The anxious person typically: is aware of bodily functions in stressful situations (blushing, hands sweating, nausea, heart beating), worries, feels tense, feels more sensitive than other people, has difficulty sleeping because of fears, is not calm, angers easily. Essentially, impulsiveness involves the control of the expression of thoughts and actions while anxiety involves feelings about external or internal stimuli. We suggest that anxiety is a feeling. Without going into detail, only a few observations will be made to tie together, then, our "neuropsychologizing" with the behavioral and feeling characteristics of impulsiveness and anxiety.

The forebrain, especially the orbitofrontal cortex, has been related in many studies to inhibitory control (neurophysiological) of other cortical and subcortical nuclei and to changes in motor (behavioral) control (Schlag & Scheibel, 1967). Both limbic system nuclei (e.g., the basolateral amygdala) and the reticular activating system have been functionally related to orbital frontal activity. Thus, our two separate systems could have a combined effect in the orbital frontal cortex, although this is obviously not the only point at which a combined effect could occur.

The amygdala has been suggested to be related to approach-avoidance behavior (Goddard, 1964). Our findings of the functional connections between the basolateral amygdala and the putamen and globus pallidus suggest a possible route by which the amygdala could be involved in "monitoring" of motor performance. Further, the functional relationships which we found between the amygdala and hippocampus and the olive and cerebellum could also be related to the inhibitory role of the cerebellum relative to the neocortex. Dilantin, which suppresses the activity of cerebellar cortex, has been reported to be effective in controlling impulsiveness in patients (Turner, 1967). The uncal area is known to be a locus for generating seizure activity (Gloor, 1960) which certainly represents an involuntary change in level of motor control. Last, our findings that lithium appears to be related to the functioning of the orbital frontal cortex coupled with the therapeutic effects of lithium in manic patients suggests the possible involvement of this area in impulsive behavior. The inefficiency of high impulsive subjects (especially the HILA subjects) in motor tasks could relate to this system.

The feelings which characterize anxiety could be related to: (1) the hypothalamic-hypophyseal control of endocrine functions which result in the ANS changes and other somatic changes (nausea) felt by the anxious person; many recent research findings suggest this possibility (e.g., Levi, 1969); (2) the cognitive awareness of tenseness resulting from nonspecific reticular control of cortical activity; the orbitofrontal cortex could be a key area for the effects of the reticular activating system relative to feelings of tenseness.

I labeled this section "toward a neuropsychological model" because there are many alternative ways of speculating about the bases of these two traits (e.g., Eysenck, 1967). We feel that our conjectures are in line with several other recently proposed themes (e.g., Pribram, 1969). The facts are not yet clear enough to propose "the" model of anxiety or impulsiveness. If we are going to improve validity coefficients for predicting behavior significantly beyond the .50 level (Rundquist, 1969), we feel that it will be through an in-depth study of the interaction of separate personality traits, gradually including more traits in the research design.

References

Barratt, E. S. Anxiety and impulsiveness related to psychomotor efficiency. *Perceptual Motor Skills,* 1959, **9**, 191–198.

Barratt, E. S. Intraindividual variability of performance: ANS and psychometric correlates. *Texas Reports on Biology & Medicine,* 1963, **21**, 496–504. (a)

Barratt, E. S. Behavioral variability related to stimulation of the cat's amygdala. *Journal of the American Medical Association,* 1963, **186,** 773–775. (b)

Barratt, E. S. Factor analysis of some psychometric measures of impulsiveness and anxiety. *Psychological Reports,* 1965, **16,** 547–554.

Barratt, E. S. Perceptual-motor performance related to impulsiveness and anxiety. *Perceptual & Motor Skills,* 1967, **25,** 485–492. (a)

Barratt, E. S. Impulse control and anxiety related to social adjustment and academic achievement among high school males. In *La contribucion de las ciencias psicologicas y del comportamiento al desarrollo social y economico de los pueblos.* University of Mexico, Mexico City, 1967. (b)

Barratt, E. S. The effects of Thiazesim, LSD-25, and bilateral lesions of the amygdalae in the release of a suppressed response. *Recent Advances in Biological Psychiatry,* 1967, **9,** 229–240. (c)

Barratt, E. S. Orienting reflex related to impulsiveness and anxiety, *Psychophysiology,* 1968, **4,** 501–502.

Barratt, E. S. Psychophysiological correlates of classical differential eyelid conditioning among subjects selected on the basis of impulsiveness and anxiety. Paper presented at the Annual Meeting, Society of Biology Psychiatry, San Francisco, California, May, 1970.

Barratt, E. S., Creson, D. L., & Russell, G. The effects of lithium salts on brain activity in the cat. *American Journal of Psychiatry,* 1968, **125,** 530–536.

Barratt, E. S., & Fruchter, B. The relationship of anxiety and impulsiveness factors among high school males. Paper presented at the Annual Meeting, Society for Multivariate Experimental Psychology, Berkeley, California, November 1967. (Mimeo.)

Barratt, E. S., & White, R. Impulsiveness and anxiety related to medical students' performance and attitudes. *Journal of Medical Education,* 1969, **44,** 604–607.

Brown, W. F., & Holtzman, W. H. *Survey of study habits and attitudes* (Manual). New York: The Psychological Corporation, 1965.

Cattell, R. *Handbook for the IPAT anxiety scale,* Champaign, Illinois: Institute for Personality and Ability Testing, 1957.

Creson, D. L., Barratt, E. S., Russell, G. V., & Schlagenauf, G. K. The effect of lithium chloride on amygdala frontal cortex evoked potentials. *Texas Reports on Biology & Medicine,* 1967, **25,** 374–379.

Eccles, J. C., Ito, M., & Szentagothai, J. *The cerebellum as a neuronal machine.* New York: Springer, 1967.

Eysenck, H. J. *The biological basis of personality.* Springfield, Illinois: Thomas, 1967.

Eysenck, H. J., & Eysenck, S. B. G. *Manual of the Eysenck personality inventory,* London: University of London Press, 1964.

Francois, G. R., Barratt, E. S., & Harris, C. Assessing the spontaneous cage behavior of the squirrel monkey. *Journal of Primatology,* 1970, **11,** 89–92

Francois, G. R., Barratt, E. S., & White, R. A rating scale to assess the effects of psychotomimetic drugs on behavioral and "mood" patterns in the squirrel monkey (Saimiri Sciureus). Unpublished paper.

Gloor, P. Amygdala in *Handbook of neurophysiology.* Vol. II. Washington, D.C.: American Physiological Society, 1960. Pp. 1395–1420.

Goddard, G. V. Functions of the amygdalae. *Psychological Bulletin,* 1964, **62,** 89–109.

Gough, H. G., & Heilbrun, A. B. *The adjective check list manual.* Palo Alto, California: Consulting Psychologists Press, 1965.

Guilford, J. P., & Zimmerman, W. S. *The Guilford–Zimmerman temperament survey* (Manual). Beverly Hills, California: Sheridan Supply, 1949.

James, W. *The principles of psychology.* New York: Henry Holt and Company, 1890.

Kogan, N., & Wallach, M. A. *Risk taking.* New York: Holt, Rinehart and Winston, 1964.

Lacey, J. I. Somatic response patterning and stress: some revisions of activation theory. In Appleby & Trumbull (Eds.), *Psychological stress: issues in research.* New York: Appleton-Century-Crofts, 1967. Pp. 14–42.

Levi, L. Neuro-endocrinology of anxiety. *British Journal of Psychiatry,* Special Publication No. 3, 1969.

Levy, E. W. A study of impulsiveness as related to study habits among high school male students. MA Thesis on file, Library, University of Houston, 1967.

Luria, A. R. *The role of speech in the regulation of normal and abnormal behavior.* New York: Liveright, 1961.

McDiarmid, C. G., & Barratt, E. S. Techniques for Psychophysiological research with squirrel monkeys. *Proceedings of the second international congress of primatology,* Atlanta, Ga., 1968, vol. 1. New York: Karger, Basel, 1969. pp. 246–253.

Miller, N. E. Learning of visceral and glandular responses, *Science,* 1969, **163,** 434–445.

Overall, J. E., & Gorham, D. R. The brief psychiatric rating scale. *Psychological Reports,* 1962, **10,** 799–812.

Penney, R. K., & Reinehr, R. C. Development of a stimulus-variation seeking scale for adults. *Psychological Reports,* 1966, **18,** 631–638.

Pribram, K. H. Neural servosystems and the structure of personality. *Journal of Nervous & Mental Disease,* 1969, **149,** 30–38.

Resnick, O. The psychoactive properties of Diphenylhydantoin: experiences with prisoners and juvenile delinquents. *International Journal of Neuropsychiatry,* 1967, 3(suppl. 2), S30–S38.

Royce, J. R. A synthesis of experimental designs in program research. *Journal of General Psychology,* 1950, **43,** 295–303.

Rundquist, E. A. The prediction ceiling. *Mental Health Digest,* 1969, **1,** 13–15.

Russell, G. V., Barratt, E. S., Deaton, J. M., & Taylor, R. R., Jr. Evoked responses in the putamen and globus pallidus following stimulation of the basolateral amygdala. *Brain Research,* 1968, **7,** 459–462.

Schlag, J., & Scheibel, A. Forebrain inhibitory mechanisms. *Brain Research,* Special Issue, 1967, **6.**

Spielberger, C. D., Gorsuch, R. L., and Lushene, R. E. *Manual for the state-trait anxiety inventory.* Palo Alto, California: Consulting Psychologists Press, 1970.

Taylor, J. A. A personality scale of manifest anxiety. *Journal of Abnormal & Social Psychology,* 1953, **48,** 285–290.

Turner, W. J. The usefulness of Diphenylhydantoin in treatment of non-epileptic emotional disorders. *International Journal of Neuropsychiatry,* 1967, **3** (suppl. 2), S8–S20.

Twain, D. C. Factor analysis for particular aspects of behavioral control–impulsivity. *Journal of Clinical Psychology,* 1957, **13,** 133–136.

COMMENTS ON DR. BARRATT'S PAPER

Beeman N. Phillips

There are three types of comments I'd like to make on Dr. Barratt's paper, although I am not really sure how much leeway we have as discussants at this symposium. I'd like first to talk about the things that most impressed me. Then I'd like to say something about the things I'd like more information on. And, third, I want to talk about some things which intrigue me. In passing, I want to add that I am impressed with my own lack of background to make judgments about this paper. As an educational, human-oriented psychologist, I do not have the best background to deal with this area. There are others here who are more competent to react to this paper, and I assume that Dr. Levitt will comment later.

Things I am very much impressed with:

First, I am impressed with the sophistication of the general research design and the collection of comparable classes of data at both the human and infrahuman level. I understand that the collection of such data is very difficult, and that it takes a great deal of time and skill.

I am also impressed with the inclusion of the elaborate array of psychological and physiological measures, and the apparently high quality of the data obtained.

Third, I am impressed with the extensiveness, and the logical coherency and continuity, of this series of studies, and with Dr. Barratt's obvious plans to continue this productive line of research.

Things I would like more information on:

First, I am interested in the possible implications of using only subjects with extreme scores on the anxiety and impulsiveness scales, as the research paradigm requires. The use of high and low groups is very common, as you know, in anxiety research. This is a very efficient way in which to proceed, at least in an exploratory phase. However, the use of extreme groups also contains several potential problems.

There is the problem of a lack of precise knowledge of what "high" and "low" really mean in terms of the variable on which the selection of subjects occurs. What is a "high" anxious subject, for example, depends on the nature of the population sampled and upon the cut-off point used. Even if, for example, one used the top 10 percent of the scorers, the mean of the top 10 percent in one population which is sampled may not be the same as the mean of the top 10 percent in some other population. Therefore, in this approach, one needs a normative frame of reference, and I would like to know more, comparatively speaking, about the anxiety and impulsiveness levels of Barratt's high and low subgroups.

Another problem with the use of extreme subgroups is that one implicitly assumes that the variable on which extreme subgroups are selected is linearly related to the other variables one is interested in. Yet it is frequently found that anxiety is not linearly related to performance, learning, and other measures. When this is the case, one is in danger of obtaining misleading results and making inappropriate generalizations about his findings.

Second, I would like to know more about the possibility of whether or not sex is an important factor in the results obtained in Barratt's studies. I am reminded here of Seymour Sarason's early research at Yale University on anxiety where he somewhat belatedly discovered that sex did make a difference in anxiety research. As he reports, he did not think about this possibility at the outset because at that time there were only male students at Yale.

This might turn out to be an important consideration in Barratt's research and some of his findings might be modified where females are used as subjects. Of course, I realize some of the problems that one runs into in gathering physiological data on females, and I am not being critical of Dr. Barratt's decision to use only males. (Parenthetically, I would like to add, somewhat facetiously, that while he used only males in the portion of his studies dealing with humans, I am not sure whether he applied this same restriction to that part of his research which dealt with infrahumans. However, sex differences perhaps are not as pronounced among infrahumans.)

Also, with regard to the sex factor, the fact that only males were used may have some influence on the character of the impulsiveness scale which was developed. In the discussion of the results one might want to qualify interpretations in terms of the possibility that the Barratt Impulsiveness Scale is really an impulsiveness scale for males. Obviously, females are also impulsive, but they may not manifest impulsiveness in quite the same way, and it may be differently related to other variables.

Things I am intrigued by:

I am intrigued by several things, so let me briefly discuss these. First, I am surprised by the lack of relationships between anxiety tests and standardized achievement tests and teacher conduct ratings among the 12- to 15-year-old boys. Typically, we would expect significant correlations between anxiety and such measures in this age group, and I have to admit that I am really not able to account for this. I have reread parts of Barratt's paper and I still have no explanation except the possibility that sex may be involved. Nevertheless, it is sufficiently intriguing to raise questions about it.

Second, I am intrigued by the lack of relationship between anxiety and peer ratings. Here again, there have been a number of studies of peer ratings, and correlations on the order of .3 to .4 have usually been obtained. I should add that Barratt's peer ratings were obtained in a fraternity, while peer ratings in the studies referred to ordinarily have been obtained in a public school setting. Perhaps peer status acquired in the context of a school setting differs from peer status acquired in the context of a fraternity setting, or any other setting in which people live together, in contrast to working together. In addition, school settings are much more achievement-oriented than fraternity settings, and this may be important. In any case, it would be interesting to look into these possibilities in relation to Barratt's results.

I also would like to comment briefly on the fact that Mexican-American males were not significantly more anxious than Anglo males. We have been doing research on anxiety in elementary school children for a number of years at U. T., and we typically find that Mexican-American children are more anxious than Anglo children. I suspect that a selection factor may have operated in Barratt's high school sample of Mexican-Americans, in contrast to the studies done with younger subjects. The typical Mexican-American adult in Texas has about seven years of schooling, and has probably repeated at least one or two grades. This would mean that, in a high school sample, a significant number of Mexican-American males already has been lost. Also, it is probable that students who repeat grades and leave school early have higher anxiety. Thus selective attrition with respect to anxiety probably occurs, and this would serve to reduce the anxiety level of the high school age Mexican-American males in Barratt's research.

I would like also to comment on Barratt's report that medical school students showed increases in anxiety during their first year in medical school. On this type of measurement, and with self-reports generally, a person typically "looks better" (e.g., less maladjusted or anxious) on the second administration than on the first. Therefore, my guess is that the increase in anxiety is actually larger than it appears to be. Consequently, I think that we might conclude that the medical school setting is very stressful, at least to first year students.

This raises in my mind the possibility of further research, and I am, in this context, thinking particularly about Epstein's research. Briefly, Epstein in his studies of sport parachutists found certain patterns of change in anxiety levels, and in coping responses, as subjects approached the actual jump. Roy Martin, a student of mine, has done a similar study of a group of Ph.D. candidates preparing for qualifying examinations. He studied their level of anxiety, both state and trait I might add, and a number of other aspects of their behavior, in the month prior to qualifying examinations. The patterns of anxiety and coping responses he found are similar to those reported by Epstein. If I could put myself into Dr. Barratt's academic shoes, I would add the investigation of stress and anxiety in medical school, and how students cope with it, to the project.

Also, I am very intrigued with the failure of anxiety and impulsivity to separate into factors for Barratt's 12- to 15-year-old male group. I am reminded of Kagan's research on reflectivity and impulsivity, as well as the work of others with subjects younger than Barratt's, where impulsivity apparently has been differentiated as a separate factor. Unfortunately, I have no ready explanation for why impulsivity does not show up as a separate trait in Barratt's 12- to 15-year-old group. These boys would be in the adolescent period, however, and at this time they are experiencing marked physiological and other changes which usually have profound psychological effects. Perhaps impulsivity (i.e., control of the expression of thoughts and actions), and anxiety (i.e., feelings about external and internal stimuli) coalesce during the adolescent period. Obviously, this is speculative thinking at this time, but research comparable to Barratt's, using younger subjects to see whether impulsivity and anxiety separate, would help to clarify this matter. In any case, it's an intriguing problem which may have important developmental implications.

Finally, I am intrigued with the professors at the medical school in Galveston in that they were apparently deceived by the sociopathic subjects in Barratt's project more than fellow students were. I think he has probably explained what was going on but this does raise questions about the use of faculty, in contrast to using peers, in research like Barratt's.

In conclusion, these are some of my reactions. I think I have probably exhausted my time and should turn the floor over to Dr. Levitt.

Chapter 6

A BRIEF COMMENTARY ON THE "PSYCHIATRIC BREAKTHROUGH" WITH EMPHASIS ON THE HEMATOLOGY OF ANXIETY

Eugene E. Levitt

The paramount vestige of the once-mighty influence of psychoanalysis on American psychiatry and psychology is the prevalent view that the primary etiology of mental illness, psychopathological symptoms, and emotional response in general, is psychosocial. This has not discouraged research into possible physiological causation. The rationale of the physical cause is invitingly appealing. Psychosocial influence, with its multiplicity of nuances and its duration, has a strong flavor of irreversibility. What hope can psychotherapy offer to the patient who has "taken 35 years to get that way"? But if the etiology resides in a hormonal or biochemical imbalance, a defect in metabolism, or a neurophysiological anomaly, the patient could be thoroughly altered in a short time by appropriate chemotherapy, revision of diet, or surgical procedure.

The search for physiological causes was encouraged in past years by the well-demonstrated fact that severe emotional and mental abnormalities can result from avitaminosis, especially thiamine and riboflavin deficiency. More recently, as interest turns more and more to the biochemical, the encouragement has come from work with psychotomimetic drugs. Evidently there are chemicals which can induce anxiety, hallucinations, paranoid reactions, and other emotional aberrations. One of these substances, LSD-25, is structurally similar to an endogenous protein, serotonin, which is normally found in the human brain. If psychosis can be artificially induced by exogenous introduction of a chemical, the possibility of natural causation by an endogenously occurring substance is not unreasonable. One need only postulate a defect in metabolism of that substance.

The Hematology of Anxiety

The favorite place to look for physiological causes is in the veins. A large number of substances are found in human blood, and more are being isolated each year as methods of biochemical assay become increasingly sophisticated. The relationships between mental illness, especially schizophrenia—and therefore by implication, anxiety—and many endogenous blood components have already been investigated. The prevalent, popular technique of injecting other organisms with the blood or serum of individuals suffering from mental illness goes back at least to a 1904 experiment by Berger.[1] Berger injected serum from schizophrenic patients into the brains of 25 dogs, of whom 13 were eventually regarded as unaffected by the surgical procedure itself. In all of these 13, postmortem examinations revealed lesions in corticomotor centers.

Berger warmed up for his dog study by injecting himself subcutaneously with varying amounts of blood and spinal fluid taken from schizophrenic patients. An injection of five milliliters of blood produced in Dr. Berger such symptoms as vertigo, salivation, palpitations, headache, insomnia, and depression. Let us not suppose that the investigations at Tulane, the Lafayette Clinic, and the Worcester Foundation during the last 15 years are pioneer work, either methodologically or with respect to style of results.

Research on possible blood-inspired causes of mental illness was pursued with considerable intensity in European laboratories prior to World War II. Favorite subjects for study were the leucocyte and nitrogen balance. A number of these early European studies appeared to show that either leucocytosis or leucocytolysis is associated with mental illness. Others indicated that psychotics tended to have excessive blood nitrogen (a waste product of protein breakdown), presumably a function of defective nitrogen metabolism. Unfortunately, as seems to be always the case, there are too many negative,

[1] Much of the investigative work prior to 1940 is admirably presented by Malis (1961). Malis' own extensive research has led him to the conclusion that schizophrenia may be caused by a filterable virus.

conflicting or confusing reports in addition to the handful of positive results. Verification by independent laboratories is rare.

During the past two decades, interest in blood-borne etiology has centered on protein substances and immunological mechanisms. So far, the fate of research on proteins has been the same as that of the earlier lines of investigation.

THE 1950's: TARAXEIN AND SCHIZOPHRENIA

The psychiatric breakthrough of the 1950's was taraxein, a protein substance allegedly found only in the serum of schizophrenic patients by Heath and his associates at the Tulane School of Medicine. It was first announced in a paper presented at the American Psychiatric Association Convention in 1956 (Heath, Leach, Martens, & Cohen, 1956). This protein fraction was reported to have produced unmistakable psychotic reactions when it was injected into the bloodstreams of normal people (Heath, Martens, Leach, Cohen, & Angel, 1957). No similar reactions were produced by the injection of five different placebo substances.

The taraxein findings from Tulane were subjected to a thorough review by the Fourth Conference on Neuropharmacology (Heath, 1959) shortly after their first airing at the APA convention in Chicago in 1956. Many sophisticated drug researchers participated, including Harold A. Abramson of the Biological Laboratory at Cold Spring Harbor in New York. Dr. Abramson made a significant comment about the Tulane findings.

> I was very surprised to hear Dr. Heath say that he did not get reactions of a fairly violent type with his controls. In the experiments which I have done with LSD-25, we found that it was more important to give placebos than to give the drug, so to speak. If we were to evaluate what the drug did, we had to have negative subjects, and it was quite a task to find subjects who would consistently give a negative response to taking water by mouth. In fact, from two ounces of tap water I have seen reactions so severe that they bordered on the psychotic . . . the literature abounds with data showing that even after the administration of salt tablets, people get violent skin reactions as well as all sorts of other somatic symptoms . . . the effect of placebo is so well known that if placebo reactions do not occur, the experiment has been manipulated to avoid it.

To which Eli Robins of the Washington University School of Medicine added,

> In the literature, there are numerous studies indicating that in any group of persons a certain proportion are placebo reactors. The real question . . . is whether or not there are studies in which a group of 20 or 30 persons there was not a single placebo reactor? That seems to me to be the crucial question, since Dr. Heath and his group have not had a single positive response to any of the control materials which they gave.

To which Henry K. Beecher, dean of American anesthesiologists, responded,

> There are such findings published, but I don't believe them.

I don't suppose anyone will be terribly surprised to learn that Robins failed to replicate the Tulane results using the original serum prepared by the Tulane group, as well as fresh serum from schizophrenic patients. Heath countered by suggesting that the potency of the schizophrenic serum was strictly time-limited. Serum which produced florid schizophrenic symptoms in an experimental monkey in the morning might turn out to be totally inactive in the afternoon. In fact, Heath was so dedicated to his results that he used any negative finding as a basis for concluding that the particular quantum of serum had become inactive. The circularity is evident.

Doubts about the taraxein findings were summed up a few years later by Seymour Kety, Chief of the Laboratory of Clinical Science of NIMH, and a primary exponent of the theory of biochemical causation of emotional illness. In brief, he dismissed the Tulane findings as, at best, "by no means resolved" (Kety, 1959). Kety pointed out that the only independent attempt to replicate the Tulane findings (the work by Robins) was essentially negative; that reports from the Tulane Laboratory strongly suggested "the operation of unconscious bias;" and it was still not clear that taraxein was qualitatively different from ceruloplasmin, another protein fraction, but one which is associated nonspecifically with illness and stress.

Heath, undaunted, keeps going. He was still publishing on taraxein (now officially labeled as a gamma immunoglobulin) as recently as 1968 (Heath and Krupp, 1968). But psychochemistry seems not to have recovered from its disillusionment of ten years ago. It is doubtful that any finding which might come out of the Tulane laboratory at this point could rekindle a serious interest in taraxein, the psychiatric breakthrough of an earlier decade.

The 1960's: Lactate and Anxiety

The most recent development in the physiology of emotions is blood lactate as the cause of anxiety symptoms. The story opens with a paper read before the 1967 meeting of the American Psychiatric Association by Pitts and McClure (1967a). The presentation found its way that same year into the sedate, *New England Journal of Medicine* (Pitts and McClure, 1967b). There was some mild enthusiasm among psychiatrists, but no great uproar, not even a rush to attempt to replicate findings. Then Pitts published a somewhat simplified version of the original work in the semiprofessional publication, *Scientific American* (Pitts, 1969). From this vantage point of exposure, it was picked up by the popular media and ballooned into the latest psychiatric breakthrough.

The hypothesis pursued experimentally by Pitts and McClure is based on the long-established fact that exercise produces excessive sodium lactate in the blood of patients suffering from anxiety neurosis. Free calcium, which is necessary for nerve conduction and activity, is inactivated by lactate. Pitts and McClure reasoned that the excess of lactate, by interfering with neural activity, produces anxiety.

They experimented with 14 patients diagnosed as anxiety neurotics, and 10 normal controls. On separate occasions, each subject received (1) an infusion of sodium lactate; (2) sodium lactate with calcium chloride added (to test the hypothesis that hypocalcemia rather than the lactate itself produced the symptoms); and (3) a placebo. The design was the traditional double-blind. The dependent variable was "a systematic checklist of 50 symptoms, containing the symptoms of anxiety neurosis dispersed in a random order" (Pitts and McClure 1967b).

The findings are summarized as follows:

> In 13 of 14 subjects with anxiety neurosis, anxiety attacks . . . developed with infusion of lactate. Two of the 10 normal subjects had such attacks with lactate infusion . . . in 1 subject with anxiety neurosis, a probable anxiety attack developed with the infusion of lactate with added calcium; none of the controls did. . . . None of the subjects in either group had anxiety attacks, or even significant symptoms, with the glucose in saline infusion (placebo) [Pitts and McClure, 1967b].

The presentation was an excellent one for *Scientific American,* appealing as it does to biochemists and neurophysiologists, as well as psychiatrists. The article is replete with bar graphs, graphic depictions of the earlier works which demonstrated the excessive lactate in the blood of the exercising neurotic, and schema illustrating the metabolic process.

The inferences from the data are stated more forcefully than in the 1967 publication.

> Our conclusion is that a high concentration of lactate ion can produce some anxiety symptoms in almost anyone, that it regularly produces anxiety attacks in patients but not in controls, and that calcium ion largely prevents the symptoms in both patients and controls. Together with earlier findings on abnormal lactate metabolism in anxiety neurotics, we believe, our experiments demonstrate that the lactate ion may operate in a very specific way to produce naturally occurring anxiety symptoms [Pitts, 1969].

It is hardly any wonder that the science writers were impressed.

The *New England Journal of Medicine* article had been followed closely be several brief notes which pointed out that Pitts and McClure had made a couple of trifling errors. Instead of infusing their subjects with the naturally occurring

L+ lactate, they included also a D– form which does not occur naturally in the human organism (Eldridge, 1968; Henderson, 1968). It was pointed out (Agus, 1968) that the symptoms produced by lactate infusion (which results in a blood alkalosis) are also produced by hyperventilation (which also produces an alkalosis). Patients who are strongly affected by hyperventilation produced twice as many such symptoms as those who seemed to have a higher tolerance for alkalosis. The potential influence of an unknown number of hyperventilators on the findings of Pitts and McClure is, of course, obvious.

These defects alone would probably not have undermined the lactate-anxiety hypothesis. The destruction was completed by a devastating blast of logic and experimentation fired by Grosz and Farmer (1969), that contained the following points:

1. Excessive production of lactic acid is a nonspecific reaction. It occurs following exercise in people afflicted with a number of physical diseases, such as those of the heart, liver, and lungs, in addition to anxiety neurotics.
2. It has not yet been demonstrated that raising the lactate level naturally produces anxiety attacks consistently in patients with anxiety neurosis.
3. The infusion of lactate results in an alkalosis, in contrast to an acidosis which is the consequence of a naturally occurring increase in lactate production.
4. There is a linear correlation between blood lactate concentration and amount of inactivated calcium. At the point in time when anxiety symptoms were allegedly appearing in Pitts and McClure's subjects, the level of blood lactate could not have been high enough to inactivate any significant amount of calcium (no more than about 3%) and thus could not have accounted for the symptoms.
5. The findings of Pitts and McClure depend upon an incorrect calculation without which it would be apparent that the symptoms of hypocalcemia require at least four times as great an infusion of lactate as was used by Pitts and McClure in their study.

And so the lactate-anxiety hypothesis, the psychiatric breakthrough of the '60's, is on its way along the path to oblivion down which blood nitrogen balance has disappeared and taraxein is disappearing.

The 1970's have dawned; who can predict what breakthrough may be lurking ahead?

A Critical Commentary on Breakthrough Research

Breakthrough research appears to have a number of common elements, in addition to its inordinate appeal to the communications media. They help to explain why breakthrough research becomes breakthrough research, and why breakthrough research is rarely a true breakthrough.

1. The crucial experimental ploy is manipulation–infusion or injection. Merely to find a substance in the blood of the anxious or emotionally ill person is not nearly as impressive as inducing anxiety or psychosis in normal people by injecting them with that tainted blood.

2. Biochemical, electrophysiological, and other physical techniques of methodology and measurement are highly sophisticated, and are commonly described in abundant detail.

3. In contrast, psychological and behavioral measurement is usually primitive and often accorded scant attention. For example: "All patients receiving taraxein developed symptoms which have been described for schizophrenia [Heath *et al.*, 1958]," and "Globulin fractions of . . . acute schizophrenic adult patients with full-blown psychotic symptoms caused functional and behavioral aberrations in test monkeys . . . [Heath and Krupp, 1968]."

4. Routine precautions against the encroachment of experimenter bias, such as the use of independent observers and the computation of inter-observer rating reliability, are typically neglected.

5. Control subjects and/or occasions appear in the experimental design of the breakthrough study, and sometimes even those magic amulets against error, the placebo and double-blind. A certain naiveté still pervades the laboratory, witness the doubts about the taraxein findings expressed at the Fourth Conference. In the taraxein research and the lactate experiment of Pitts and McClure, the contrast of experimental and control occasions is absolutely perfect. Every experimental occasion, but not a single control occasion, produced a psychopathological reaction. Placebo effects are ubiquitous (to say nothing of an occasional serum reaction which might have marred the perfection of Heath's results). The experiment which fails to turn up a single placebo reaction must be suspect. The experimenter should have a paranoid reaction of his own.

6. Despite the suspicious cleanliness of the results, no effort is made to replicate the study after having removed from it the most potential source of bias, the original, principal investigator.

To sum up, breakthrough research is low caliber work masquerading as top drawer work. Refined, elaborate physiological measurement creates a specious aura of sophistication which serves to mask primitive behavioral measurement and slipshod methodology. The investigators invariably fail to play devil's advocate to their findings as careful scientists should. As the barrage of critical comments mounts, they become–perhaps understandably–dedicated to their original work and apparently less able than ever to perceive its shortcomings.

The search for an ultimate, physiological cause of emotional reactions and illness goes on but the patiently awaited breakthrough still seems far off in the future. The totality of experimental findings remain confused, conflicting, and ambiguous. Assuming that the ultimate cause is biochemical, many possibilities have already been investigated, but the unexplored area is vast. The current situation (e.g., Levitt, 1967; Stern & McDonald, 1965) has changed little since Kety's (1959) gloomy summary:

> . . . how large is the haystack in which we are searching for the needle; one cannot avoid a feeling of humility when one realizes how slight the chance is that any one of us has already found it, or will find it in a relatively short time.

References

Agus, B. Anxiety and lactate metabolism. *New England Journal of Medicine,* 1968, **278,** 628–629.

Eldridge, F. Anxiety and lactate metabolism. *New England Journal of Medicine,* 1968, **278,** 629.

Grosz, H. J., & Farmer, B. B. Blood lactate in the development of anxiety symptoms: a critical examination of Pitts and McClure's hypothesis and experimental study. *Archives of General Psychiatry,* 1969, **21,** 611–619.

Heath, R. G. Clinical studies with taraxein. *Transactions of the Fourth Conference on Neuropharmacology,* 1959, 37–151.

Heath, R. G., & Krupp, I. M. Schizophrenia as a specific biologic disease. *American Journal of Psychiatry,* 1968, **124,** 1019–1024.

Heath, R. G., Leach, B. E., Martens, S., & Cohen, M. Studies in mind–brain relationships: behavioral changes with administration of taraxein, a substance extracted from schizophrenic serum. Paper read at the American Psychiatic Assoc. convention, 1956.

Heath, R. G., Martens, S., Leach, B. E., Cohen, M., & Angel, C. Effect on behavior in humans with the administration of taraxein. *American Journal of Psychiatry,* 1958, **114,** 14–24.

Henderson, T. R. Anxiety and lactate metabolism. *New England Journal of Medicine,* 1968, **278,** 629.

Kety, S. S. Biochemical theories of schizophrenia. *Science,* 1959, **129,** 1528–1532; 1590–1596.

Levitt, E. E. *The psychology of anxiety.* New York: Bobbs–Merrill, 1967.

Malis, G. Yu. *Research on the etiology of schizophrenia.* New York: Consultants Bureau, 1961.

Pitts, F. N. The biochemistry of anxiety. *Scientific American,* 1969, **220,** 69–75.

Pitts, F. N., & McClure, J. N. Lactate metabolism in anxiety neurosis. Paper read at the American Psychiatric Association convention, 1967. (a)

Pitts, F. N., & McClure, J. N. Lactate metabolism in anxiety neurosis. *New England Journal of Medicine,* 1967, **277,** 1329–1336. (b)

Stern, J. A., & McDonald, D. G. Physiological correlates of mental disease. *Annual Review of Psychology,* 1965, **16,** 225–264.

COMMENTS ON DR. LEVITT'S PAPER

Ernest S. Barratt

I found Dr. Levitt's paper precise, to the point, and very enjoyable. He has pointed out some of the major pitfalls that are involved in the research which attempts to relate bodily functions to psychological (intervening) variables.

I would just like to elaborate on several of the points that Dr. Levitt made because I think they are important. First, the personality and value system of the investigator are important considerations in the public release of research findings. This is especially true in interdisciplinary research where several investigators are responsible for the data. The press is looking for news–hopefully sensational news or "breakthroughs"–and they exert pressure to generalize beyond one's data. I was involved in an example of this recently. We are currently doing research with marijuana–it is an interdisciplinary research project. We had a simple finding that chronic administration of a marijuana extract to cats prolonged EEG changes beyond the immediate toxic effects of a single adminstration of the drug. This information accidentally got out of the lab—I'm not sure how—and we had phone calls from all over the country inquiring about our "proof" that marijuana caused permanent brain damage. We had no such proof and it seemed that the more we denied it, the more people became convinced that we did have. It is a very real problem to try to keep so called "breakthroughs" away from the press, especially when they are not "breakthroughs."

Also, I think another problem related to negative "breakthroughs" is that there may be an element of truth in the findings, but because of an error in experimental design or technique, the results are not only not accepted by the scientific community, but often forgotten. There have been those who have observed the administration of taraxein to monkeys in Heath's Lab and who have reported that the behavior of the monkeys was peculiar. I'm not certain how schizophrenic monkeys are supposed to appear, but these observers report that the behavior of the injected monkeys was schizophrenia-like. I've also heard of some recent replications of Heath's findings in other labs— I don't recall exactly which labs. The point is that "an element of truth" in a finding may be lost for many years unless an investigator really "believes" in his finding and persists in trying to demonstrate it. There are many instances of early statements of investigators not being seriously considered until years later when social pressure or a later investigator's findings made the earlier finding relevant. Moreau, for example, published a book in 1845 outlining many of the psychological effects that are currently being reported with marijuana usage. Until current social pressure made marijuana research important, the ideas in Moreau's book did not receive much attention.

With regard to the lactic acid research, it is possible that the investigators whom Dr. Levitt mentioned should have looked at lactic production in the cerebrospinal fluid instead of in the blood. During hypoxia, changes in lactic acid levels in cerebrospinal fluid have been demonstrated with no significant changes in the blood levels. Possibly controlling for hyperventilators and then examining levels of lactic acid in cerebrospinal fluid during stress may indicate that lactic acid levels here are related to stress, but not in the blood. The point I wish to make is that although I agree wholeheartedly with Dr. Levitt's criticisms of reporting research findings prematurely or in a sensational way, we also have to be cautious not to "throw the baby out with the bathwater."

This brings me to the main observation that I would like to make about research involving physiological, behavioral, and personality measures. If your criterion variables are behavioral or personality measures which are fairly complex (e.g., anxiety), I don't think you will find any one physiological predictor to account for a major portion of the criterion variance. I doubt that the "cause" of mental illness or personality changes relates to a single chemical change, except for a few specific conditions such as PKU. I feel that you must employ a multivariate model and look at patterns or profiles of predictor measures that relate to the more complex criterion measures.

I could go on about this but if I do, someone may not consider my remarks those of an expert on "breakthroughs" in science, so perhaps I had best stop at this point.

AUTHOR INDEX

Numbers in italics refer to the pages on which the complete references are listed.

A

Agus, B., 232, *234*
Allport, F. H., 77, *104*
Altman, I., 38, *49*
Angel, C., 229, 233, *234*
Appley, M. H., 7, *18*
Appley, M. T., 26, *46*
Aquinas, St. T., 67, *104*
Arnold, M. B., 26, 27, *46*
Atkinson, J. W., 31, 39, *46*
Auerbach, S. M., 38, *46*
Averill, J. R., 65, 67, 68, *104*
Ax, A. F., 27, *46*
Axelrad, S., 7, *18*

B

Bandura, A. 162, *178*
Barratt, E. S., 199, 201, 203, 204, 206, 207, 210, 212, 214, 215, 216, 217, 218, *220, 221*
Barrett, J. E., 34, *46*
Bartlett, H. W., 129, 130, 160, 165, 177, *178, 179*
Barton, K., *178*
Barton, V., 177, *182*
Basowitz, H., 29, *46*, *57*, *104*
Beck, A. T., *179*
Berkowitz, L., 26, 28, 40, *46*
Biase, D. V., 35, *49*
Birney, R. C., 7, *18*
Borgatta, E. F., 33, *46*
Branch, C. H., 7, *18*
Brodgen, H. E., *179*
Brody, S., 7, *18*
Brown, W. F., 199, 215, *221*

Burdick, H., 7, *18*
Buss, A. H., 26, *46*

C

Campbell, D. T., 31, *46*
Cannon, W. B., 177, *179*
Carlson, W. A., 162, *183*
Castaneda, A., 6, *18*
Cattell, A. K. S., 120, 129, *180*
Cattell, R., 196, 199, *221*
Cattell, R. B., 6, *18,* 23, 26, 29, 34, *46, 48,*57, 58, *104,*117, 118, 120, 121, 123, 124, 128, 129, 130, 131, 132, 135, 137, 138, 141, 142, 146, 150, 154, 155, 156, 157, 158, 159, 160, 161, 162, 163, 164, 165, 169, 171, 173, 175, 176, 177, 178, *178, 179, 180, 181, 182*
Chambers, W. W., 55, 72, *106*
Chappell, J. E., 80, *105*
Clausen, J. A., 33, *49*
Cleghorn, R. A., 42, *48*
Clyde, D. J., 33, 34, *46, 180*
Cohen, J., 3, *18*
Cohen, M., 229, 233, *234*
Conner, D. V., *178*
Coombs, C. H., 158, *180*
Creson, D. L., 217, *221*
Cross, K., 129, *180*
Curran, J., 129, *180*

D

Damarin, F., 135, *180*
Darrow, C. W., 163, *180*
Darwin, C., 5, *18,* 61, 92, *104*
Daston, P., 33, *47*
Davidson, K. S., 6, *19,* 26, *48,* 56, *105*
Davis, J. F., 42, *48*
Deaton, J. M., 217, *222*
Deese, J., 27, *47*
Denny, J. P., 40, *46*
De Young, G. E., *180*
Dimascio, A., 34, *46, 47*
Dollard, J., 6, *18*
Duffy, E., 25, *47,* 162, *181*

E

Eccles, J. C., 217, *221*
Edwards, A. L., *181*
Edwards, C. D., 6, *19*
Edwards, K. R., Jr., 38, *47*
Ekman, P., 77, 86, *104*
Eldridge, F., 232, *234*
Endler, N., *181*
Endler, N. S., 6, *18,* 139, *181*
Epstein, S., 72, *104*, 162, *181,* 188, 191, *192*
Erbaugh, J., *179*
Eysenck, H. J., 26, *47,* 199, 220, *221*
Eysenck, S. B., 199, *221*

F

Farmer, B. B., 232, *234*
Felling, J. P., 38, *47*
Fenz, W. D., 191, *192*
Fischer, W. F., 7, *18*
Fleishman, E. A., 154, *181*
Francois, G. R., 218, *221,*
Freeman, G. L., 163, *181*
Freeman, M. J., 6, *18*
Freud, S., 5, *18,* 23, 29, *47,* 56, *104*
Friesen, W. V., 77, 86, *104*
Fruchter, B., 203, *221*
Funkenstein, D. H., 27, *47*

G

Gaudry, E., 7, *18*
Gelhorn, E., 55, 72, *104*
Gleser, G. C., 58, *104*
Gloor, P., 220, *221*
Goddard, G. V., 220, *221*
Goodman, A. J., 42, *48*
Gorham, D. R., 196, *222*
Gorsuch, R. L., 6, *19,* 35, 36, 38. 41, *49,* 57, 82, 90, *106,* 173, *181, 222*
Gottschalk, L. A., 58, *104*
Gough, H. G., 199, *221*
Graham, B. F., 42, *48*
Green, R. F., 33, 34, *47, 48*
Grinker, R. R., 28, 29, 40, *46,* 130, *181*
Grinker, R. R., Sr., 56, 57, *104*
Grosz, H. J., 232, *234*
Gruen, W., 135, *180*
Guilford, J. P., 196, *221*
Guttman, L., 33, *49*

H

Hall, B., 38, *47*
Hamburg, D. A., 66, *104*
Hansen, D. N., 37, 38, *48, 49*

Harris, C., 218, *221*
Haverland, E. M., 129, *181*
Hay, G., 177, *182*
Haywood, H. Carl, 162, *181*
Heath, L. H., 163, *180*
Heath, R. G., 229, 230, 233, *234*
Heilbrun, A. B., 199, *221*
Henderson, T. R., 232, *234*
Herrington, L. P., 163, *181*
Hildreth, H. M., 33, *47*
Hoch, P. H., 6, *18*
Hodges, W. F., 38, 41, *47*
Holtzman, W. H., 215, *221*
Horn, J. L., 135, 173, *181*
Horn, J. R., 124, 160, *180*
Howarth, E., 135, *180*
Hull, C. L., 165, *181*
Hundal, P. S., 155, 156, *181*
Hundleby, J. D., 132, 155, 164, *181*
Hunt, J. M., 6, *18*
Hunt, J., McV., 139, 162, *181*
Hurley, J., 129, *182*

I

Ito, M., 217, *221*
Izard, C. E., 51, 52, 53, 55, 60, 61, 62, 66, 67, 68, 71, 72, 73, 75, 77, 80, 86, *105*, 121, *181*

J

James, W., 24, *47*, 218, *222*
Janis, I. L., 26, *47*, 65, 75, 92, *105*
Jennings, J. R., 77, *105*
Jolly, A., 66, *105*

K

Kao, R. C., 158, *180*
Karvonen, M. J., 129, *181*
Katahn, M., 77, *106*
Katkin, E. S., 41, *47*
Katz, P. K., 58, *105*
Katzoff, E. T., 163, *181*
Kawash, G. F., 129, *180*
Kety, S. S., 230, 234, *234*
Kierkegaard, S., 72, *105*
Kogan, N., 209, *222*
Komlos, E., 165, 169, 176, *180*
Korchin, S. J., 28, 29, 40, *46*, 57, *104*
Krause, M. S., 28, *47*
Kritzeck, J., 4, *18*
Krug, S., 129, *181*
Krupp, I. M., 230, 233, *234*
Kunnas, M., 129, *181*
Kurzweil, Z. E., 7, *18*

L

Lacey, B. C., 122, *182*
Lacey, J. I., 122, *181*, *182*, 213, *222*
Lamb, D. H., 38, *47*
Langer, T. S., 26, *47*
Lazarsfeld, P. F., 33, *49*
Lazarus, R. S., 7, *18*, 26, 27, *47*, 65, 67, 68, 75, *105*
Leach, B. E., 229, 233, *234*
Levi, L., 220, *222*
Levitt, E. E., 7, *18*, 26, *47*, 57, *105*, 234, *234*
Levy, E. W., 215, *222*
Lighthall, F. F., 6, *19*, 26, *48*, 56, *105*
Lindsley, D. B., 25, *47*
Livsey, W., 77, *105*
Lorr, M., 33, *47*, *48*
Lubin, B., 6, *19*, 33, 35, *49*
Luborsky, L. B., 129, 160, 163, *180*
Luria, A. R., 212, *222*
Lushene, R. E., 6, *19*, 23, 35, 36, 38, 41, *47*, *49*, *222*
Lushene, R. L., 57, 82, 90, *106*

M

McAdoo, W. G., 23, 38, *48*
McCandless, B. R., 6, *18*
McClure, J. N., 230, 231, 232, *234*
McDiarmid, C. G., 216, *222*
McDonald, D. G., 234, *234*
McDougall, W., 121, *182*
McNair, D. M., 33, *48*
McReynolds, P., 6, *18*
Maher, B. A., 58, *105*
Malis, G. Yu., 228, *234*
Mallama, A. D., 54, *105*
Malmo, R. B., 42, *48*, 59, *105*
Mandler, G., 6, *18*, *19*, 40, *48*
Marks, I. M., 7, *18*
Martens, S., 229, 233, *234*
Martin, B., 7, *18*, 28, *48*
Mason, F., 5, *18*
May, R., 4, 5, *18*, 57, 72, 100, *105*

Mefferd, R. B., 129, *182*
Mefferd, R. B., Jr., *182*
Mendelson, M., *179*
Meyer, R. E., 34, *47*
Michael, S. T., 26, *47*
Miller, N. E., 6, *18,* 219, *222*
Mock, J., *179*
Montouri, J., 6, *19*
Moran, L. J., 129, *182*
Mosher, D. L., 57, 58, *105*
Mowrer, O. H., 6, *18*

N

Nesselroade, J. R., 117, 129, 135, 157, 164, *182*
Nowlis, V., 33, 34, *47, 48,* 55, *105*

O

O'Neil, H. F., 37, 38, *48, 49*
Opton, E. M., Jr., 27, *47,* 67, *104*
Osler, Sonia F., 27, *47*
Overall, I. E., 196, *222*

P

Palermo, D. S., 6, *18*
Parrino, J. J., 38, *48*
Pavlov, I. P., 5, *19*
Pawlik, K., 132, 155, 162, 164, *181, 182*
Penney, R. K., 202, *222*
Persky, H., 28, 29, 40, *46,* 57, *104*
Peterson, D. R., 135, *180*
Pierson, G. R., 177, *182*
Pitts, F. N., 11, *19,* 230, 231, 232, *234*
Plutchik, R., 24, *48,* 61, *105*
Pribram, K. H., 55, *105,* 220, *222*

R

Radcliffe, J., 160, *180*
Reinehr, R. C., 202, *222*
Resnick, O., 218, *222*
Rhymer, R. M., 120, 129, *180*
Ricks, D. F., 33, 34, *49*
Rosenblueth, A., 177, *179*
Rosenstein, A. J., 6, *18,* 139, *181*
Rosenthal, I., 135, *182*
Rosenthal, L., 162, *178*
Rourke, B. P., 7, *19*
Royce, J. R., 198, *222*
Ruebush, B. K., 6, *19,* 26, *48,* 56, *105*
Rundquist, E. A., 220, *222*
Russell, G. V., 217, *221, 222*
Rycroft, C., 7, *19*

S

Sarason, I. G., 7, 8, *19,* 39, *48,* 54, *105*
Sarason, S. B., 6, *18, 19,* 26, 40, *48,* 56, 58, *105,* 132, 177, *182*
Schachter, J., 27, 29, *48*
Schachter, S., 28, *48,* 177, *182*
Schacter, S. S., 75, *106*
Schagenauf, 217, *221*
Scheibel, A., 219, *222*
Scheier, I. H., 26, 34, *46, 48,* 58, *104,* 117, 123, 129, 130, 131, 132, 135, 155, 161, 165, 173, 176, 177, 178, *180, 182*
Schlag, J., 219, *222*
Schoonmaker, A. N., 7, *19*
Shagass, C., 42, *48*
Shotwell, A., 129, *182*
Sidhu, K., 155, 156, *181*
Skinner, B. F., 165, *182*
Smith, I. R., 33, *47*
Smith, L. H., 40, *49*
Snyder, C. R., 77, *106*
Sorenson, E. R., 77, 86, *104*
Spearman, C., 154, *182*
Spence, J. T., 40, *48,* 54, *106, 182*
Spence, K. W., 40, *48,* 54, *106,* 176, *182*
Spiegel, J. P., 56, *104, 181*
Spielberger, C. D., 6, 7, *18, 19,* 23, 26, 35, 36, 37, 38, 40, 41, 43, *47, 48, 49,* 53, 57, 58, 82, 90, *106* 138, 154, 168, 170, 176, *182, 222*
Sprague, J. M., 55, 72, *106*
Star, S. A., 33, *49*
Stellar, E., 55, 72, *106*
Stern, J. A., 234, *234*
Stifler, L., 34, *47*
Stouffer, S. A., 33, *49*
Suchman, F. A., 33, *49*
Sudhakar, Y. P., 155, 156, *181*
Sullivan, H. S., 56, *106*
Sweney, A. B., 160, *180*
Szentagothai, J., 217, *221*

T

Tatro, D., 165, 169, 176, *180*
Taylor, D. A., 38, *49*
Taylor, J. A., 6, *19,* 36, 41, *49,* 199, *222*
Taylor, R. R., Jr., 217, *222*
Taylor, S., 188, *192*
Teevan, R. C., 7, *18*
Thome, F. C., 31, 32, *49*
Titchener, E. B., 25, *49*
Tomkins, S. S., 51, 52, 53, 55, 57, 60, 61, 66, 68, 72, 73, 75, 77, 92, *105, 106, 181*
Trumbull, R., 7, *18,* 26, *46*
Tucker, L. R., 154, *182*
Turner, W. J., 218, 220, *222*
Twain, D. C., 199, *222*
Tyl, M. M., 33, *49*

U

Unger, S. M., 58, *106*

V

Valerius, E., 33, *49*
Van Egeren, L. F., 129, 130, *182*
Venables, P. H., 162, *182*
Vogel, L., 33, *49*

W

Waite, R. R., 6, *19,* 26, *48,* 56, *105*
Wallach, M. A., 209, *222*
Warburton, F. W., *180*
Ward, C. H., *179*
Ward, W. D., 162, *183*
Warwick-Evans, L. A., 162, *182*
Weaver, F., 80, *105*
Wehmer, G. M., 77, *105*
Wells, H. P., *183*
Wenger, M. A., 163, *183*
Wessman, A. E., 33, 34, *49*
Wheeler, L., 38, *49*
White, R., 214, 218, *221*
Wilde, G. J. S., 32, *49*
Williams, H. V., 129, 130, *183*
Williams, J. R., 129, *183*
Wolff, S., 7, *19*
Wolpe, J., 54, *106*
Wundt, W., 25, *49*

Y

Young, P. T., 24, *49*

Z

Zigler, P. K., 58, *105*
Zimmerman, W. S., 196, *221*
Zubin, J., 6, *18*
Zuckerman, M., 6, *19,* 33, 35, *49,* 55, *106*

SUBJECT INDEX

A

Achievement,
  anxiety and, 214, 225
  impulsiveness and, 214
Acquired behavioral dispositions, 31
Adjustment Process Analysis, 165–168, 173–176
Affect Adjective Check List, state anxiety measurement using, 35
Affective state(s), *see* Emotional state(s)
Amphetamines, suppressed response release and, 216
Amplification reduction, as component of depression, 109
Amygdala,
  in impulsiveness, 219–220
Amygdala–*cont.*
  interrelationship with globus pallidus and putamen, 217
  reaction time and, 216
  suppressed response release and, 216
Anger,
  in Adjustment Process Analysis, 166–167
  as component of anxiety, 76
Anguish, as component of anxiety, 76
Anorexia, 111
Anxiety, *see also* State anxiety; Trait anxiety
  as anticipatory reaction or arousal, 72–74
  artificial physiological induction of, 177
  "as if" behavior and, 110

Anxiety—*cont.*
- cognitive factors in, 11–14
- components of, 56–59, 74–77, 94–95, 102–104
  - correlations among, 113–114
  - definitions of, 76
  - measurement of, 77–81, 87–91, 93
- concept of, 45, 52–55
- conditioning and, 176–177, 207, 208–209
- conditions evoking, 12
- cultural influence on expression of, 218–219
- defenses against, 28, 43–44
- definition of, 5, 28, 54, 56–58
- differentiated from fear, 12, 74, 111, 164–165, 168
- everyday experiences and, 213–215
- hematology of, 11, 228–229
- historical perspective, 3–6
- lactate and, 230–232
- measurement of, 6, 10, 198–203
  - analysis of scales for, 155–158
- methodology for study of, 195–198
  - factor analytic, 117–119
  - limitations of, 185–192, 224–226
- nature of, 10–11, 12, 23–24
- neural system involved in, 215–219, 220
- neuropsychological model for, 11
- perceptual-motor tasks and, 204–207
- phenomenological aspects of, 56
  - analysis of, 83–86
- physiological aspects of, 26
- proneness to, 139
- psychophysiological data related to, 212–213
- relationship to guilt, 187
- relationship to motivation, 176–177, 214
- risk taking and, 207, 209
  - as second order factor, 95–96, 97
  - as source state, 10–11, 41, 122
- therapy for, 64–65, 214
- time estimation and, 209, 210
- typical, 219

Apprehension, dependence of emotion on, 67–68

Arousal, 158
- anxiety as, 72–74
- measurement of, 117

Arousal—*cont.*
- as state, 164
  - nature of, 161, 162
  - source, 122

Ataxia, reduction of, 132

Autonomic nervous system, habituation of, 212, 213

Avitaminosis, 227

Avoidance, fear as, 74

B

Barratt Impulsiveness Scale, 199, 225

Basal ganglia nuclei, in impulsiveness, 219

Behavior, role of cognition in, 69

Bivariate methodology, compared to multivariate, 116–119, 175

Brainstem, effect of Dilantin on, 218

Bulemia, 111

C

Cat, reaction time in, neural centers related to, 216

Cerebellar nuclei, 217

Cerebellum, in impulsiveness, 219–220
- inhibitory role of, 217, 220

Ceruloplasmin, 230

Cognition, role in emotion, 65–69

Conditioning,
- anxiety level and, 176–177
- eye-lid, 207, 208–209
- of personality traits, 219

Contempt,
- as component of anxiety, 76
- as component of depression, 109

Cortertia, 164

Cortical activity, reticular control of, 11

Culture,
- influence on activation of emotions, 62
- influence on impulsiveness, 218–219
- state and, 121

D

Defense, against anxiety, 28, 43–44

Depression, 158
- components of, 109
- nature of, 161
- as source state, 122

Differential Emotion Scale, 10, 77–78, 80–81
combination with State-Trait Anxiety Inventory, 81–82, 84
development of, 78–80
Dilantin,
in controlling impulsiveness, 218, 220
effect on reaction time, 217
inhibitory effects of, 217–218
Discouragement, 111
Disease, analogy with emotion, 69
Disgust,
as component of anxiety, 76
as component of depression, 109
Distress,
as component of anxiety, 56, 57, 74, 75, 101
definition of, 76
measurement of, 87–91, 92, 93
as component of depression, 109
role of cognition in, 65–66
Drive, in Adjustment Process Analysis, 165–166
Drugs, *see also specific names*
induction of psychopathological symptoms by, 228–233
reaction time and, 217
Dynamic process theory, anxiety and other states in, 165–178

E

Ego-involving instructions, 45
effects on performance, 40
Electroencephalogram,
habituation of, 212–213
percentage of alpha in, 213
suppressed response release and, 216
Emotion(s),
activation of, 66
analogy with disease, 69
components of, 63–64
interaction of, 64–65
as components of anxiety, 56–59, 102–104
concept of, 53–54
historical perspective, 24–27
definition of, 59–60
in expectancy, 73
external stimuli in, 70, 71
Emotion(s)–*cont.*
facial expression in, 63–64, 78, 111–112, 121
fundamental, 59, 76–77
activation of, 60–63
definitions of, 76
interrelationships among, 110–112
measurement of, 77–81, 87–91, 93
patterns of, 96–102
interaction of, 73
neuromuscular component of, 59–60, 69–70, 71–72
as personality subsystem, 60–61
interaction with other systems, 61
phenomenological aspects of, 25–26, 27, 59, 60
measurement of, 27–28
physiological aspects of, 25–27, 59
pure, 91–94
reflective, 75–76
as response syndrome, 68–70
versus intraperson emotion system, 71–72
role of cognition in, 65–69
semantic difficulties in study of, 113–114
Emotional states, 23, 45
anxiety as, 28–30
personality traits and, 31–32
physiological components of, 28–29
self-report scales in measurement of, 32–35
State-Trait Anxiety Inventory, 35–38
Endocrine functions, hypothalamic-hypophyseal control of, 11
Enjoyment, as component of anxiety, 76
Evoked potentials, in impulse control, 217
Evolution, emotional *versus* cognitive primacy in, 66–67, 70
Excitement,
as component of anxiety, 73, 75
definition of, 76
reduction in, 111
Expectancy, 12–13, 72–74
Experience,
emotional response and, 27
in etiology of trait anxiety, 44–45
influence on activation of emotions, 62
Extraversion, 158
impulsiveness and, 199

Extraversion—*cont.*
trait and state dimensions of, 124

F

Facial expression, 63–64, 111–112, 121
in fundamental emotions, 78
Factor analytic technique, 117–119
dR-technique in 120, 123, 128
G-technique in, 150
limitations of, 185–192
P-technique in, 120, 123, 128
R-technique in, 123
in separation and identification of trait, trait change, and state structures, 127–137
trait change and, 122–127
Fear,
as component of anxiety, 56, 57, 58, 75, 101
definition of, 76
measurement of, 87–91, 92, 93
as component of depression, 109
differentiated from anxiety, 12, 74, 111, 164–165, 168
equated with anxiety, 53, 57
of failure, 39
effects on performance, 40–41
of loss of control, 110
objectless, 70, 109
object of, 108
sequence in, 108–109
Feedback, in integration of emotion components, 63

G

Gamma immunoglobulin, *see* Taraxein
Globus pallidus, 217, 220
Guilt,
as component of anxiety, 74–77, 101, 129
measurement of, 87–91, 92, 93
as a fundamental emotion, 110–111
relationship to anxiety, 57–58, 187

H

Habituation, impulsiveness and anxiety and, 212–213
Harm anxiety, 40–41, 57
Heart rate, stimulus onset and, 189
Helplessness, 14
Hematology, 11, 228–229
Hildreth Feeling and Attitude Battery, 33
Hippocampus, 217, 220
Humiliation, as component of anxiety, 57, 77
definition of, 76
Hyperventilation, psychopathological symptoms and, 232
Hypocalcemia, psychopathological symptoms and, 231, 232
Hypothalamic-hypophyseal axis, 219

I

Impulsiveness,
cultural influence on, 218–219
everyday experiences and, 213–215
eye-lid conditioning and, 207, 208–209
measurement of, 198–203
methodology for study of, 195–198
limitations of, 224–226
neural system involved in, 215–220
perceptual-motor tasks and, 204–207
psychophysiological data related to, 212–213
risk taking and, 207, 209
time estimation and, 209, 210
typical, 219
Individual differences,
personality traits and, 31–32
R-technique in study of, 123
in trait anxiety, origin of, 44–45
Infants, separation distress in, 65–66
Inferior olive, 217
Inhibition,
of cerebellar cortex, 217–218
orbitofrontal cortex in, 219
role of cerebellum in, 217, 220
Interest,
as component of anxiety, 66, 70, 73, 75, 76, 101
definition of, 76
measurement of, 90–91, 92, 93
Introversion, 158
trait and state dimensions of, 124
IPAT Anxiety Scale, 34, 155, 156, 158, 199

J

Joy, as component of anxiety, 76

L

Labels, for physiological arousal, 29
Lactate, anxiety and, 230–232
Learning,
anxiety level and, 176–177
role of in emotion, 67
Leucocyte balance, psychopathology and, 228
Liability modulation, states and, 142–145
Limbic system nuclei, 217
in impulsiveness, 219
Lithium,
impulsiveness and, 220
locus of activity of, 217
LSD-25, psychopathological symptoms and, 228, 229

M

Maladjustment,
impulsiveness and anxiety and, 214, 215
motor component of emotion in, 59–60
Manifest Anxiety Scale, 6, 41, 42, 155–157, 199
in definition of anxiety, 54
Memory, of facial expressions, 63–64
Midbrain reticular formation, suppressed response release and, 216
Monkey,
activity and mood measurement in, 218
release of suppressed response in, 216
Mood, *see also* State
measurement of, 32–35
Motivation,
in emotion, 69
impulsiveness and anxiety and, 214
relationship to anxiety, 176–177
Motives, definition of, 31
Multiple Affect Adjective Check List, 33, 35
Multivariate methodology, compared to bivariate, 116–119, 175
Muscle tension, emotion and, 59–60

N

Neural programs, activation of emotions and, 62
Neuromuscular patterning, 63
in emotion, 69–70, 71–72
Neurosis, 5,54
lactate and, 231
measurement of, 155
Nitrogen balance, psychopathology and, 228–229

O

Objective-Analytic Anxiety Battery, 34–35
Olive, 220
Olivonuclear collateral afferents, 217
Orbitofrontal cortex, 217
in anxiety, 219–220
in impulsiveness, 219–220
Orienting response, impulsiveness and anxiety and, 212–213

P

Peer ratings,
anxiety and, 215, 225
impulsiveness and, 215
Perception,
emotional response and, 27
of threat, 30, 39–45
Perceptual-motor tasks, impulsiveness and anxiety and, 204–207
Performance, stressors affecting, 39–40
Personality,
emotion in, 27, 64
as a subsystem, 60–61
state and trait anxiety as factors in, 29
Personality learning, anxiety level and, 176–177
Personality states, 31, 32
measurement of, 32–34
Personality traits, 31–32
behavioral expression of, 32
conditioning of, 219
measurement of, 34
Placebo, in studies of etiology of psychopathology, 229–230, 233
Population research, 197
Process research, 197–198
Proprioception, in emotion, 63–64
Proteins, psychopathology and, 229–230
Psychopathology, etiology of, 227–229

Punishment, development of anxiety and, 58
Putamen, 217, 220

R

Race prejudice, emotions characterizing, 80–81, 100–102
Rage, as component of anxiety, 76
Reaction time, neural centers in, 216–217
Reflectivity, relationship to impulsiveness, 226
Reliability, impulsiveness and anxiety and, 214
Response set, in perceptual-motor tasks, 206, 207, 209–212
Response syndrome, emotion as, 68–70
  versus intraperson emotion system, 71–72
Reticular activating system,
  in anxiety, 219
  reaction time and, 216
Revulsion, as component of anxiety, 76
Risk taking, impulsiveness and anxiety and, 207, 209

S

Schizophrenia,
  blood components and, 228
  taraxein in, 229–230
School children, anxiety in, 14–16
  intervention to reduce, 15
Scorn, as component of anxiety, 76
Self-awareness, impulsiveness and anxiety and, 214
Self-concept, relationship to ideal self, impulsiveness and anxiety and, 214
Self-deprecation, 58
  in anxiety, 132
    evocation of, 39, 41, 44, 45
    test anxiety development, 56
Self-report scales, as measures of personality states, 32–35
  limitations of, 32–33, 38
  State-Trait Anxiety Inventory, 35–38
Sensitivity, selective, in activation of emotions, 62
Septum, 217
Serotonin, 228
Sex, in study of anxiety and impulsiveness, 224–225
Shame,
  as component of anxiety, 57, 74, 75, 77
    definition of, 76
  as component of depression, 109
  as fundamental emotion, 110–111
Shame anxiety, 40–41, 57
Shyness, 111
  as component of anxiety, 76, 77
    measurement of, 87–91, 92, 93
Skin conductance, 213
  stimulus onset and, 189
Sociopathic tendencies, impulsiveness and anxiety and, 214
Startle, as component of anxiety, 76
State(s),
  changes in, 123–124
  combinations of, 122
  correlations among, 173–175
  correlation with trait, 140
  definition of, 121, 153
    models for, 154
  development of, 165–173
  distinguished from traits, 147–153
  estimation of variance for, 146–153
  liability modulation and, 142–145
  models for, 120–122
  nature of, 127
  oscillation of, 139
  relation between traits and, 123, 140
  relations among dimensions of, 141
  as response pattern, 120–122
  rise and fall of, 140–141
    measurement and, 157–158
  trait variance in measurement of, 123–124
  unitariness of, 120, 121–122
    source state model and, 121
  variability in, 139–140
State anxiety, 10–11
  conditions evoking, 30–31
  definition of, 39, 129
  development of, 166–173
  as general autonomic activity factor, 162–164
  inference of, 28
  measurement of, 29, 34–35, 158
    self-report in, 30

State anxiety–*cont.*
State-Trait Anxiety Inventory for, 35–38
nature of, 29–30, 64, 159–160, 161
stressors evoking, 39, 43, 44
State-Trait Anxiety Inventory, 10, 46
combination with Differential Emotion Scale, 81–82, 84
construction of, 35–36
limitations of, 38
uses of, 37–38
validity of, 38
Stimulus, external, in emotion, 70, 71
Stress, 26, 158
definition of, 30
nature of, 160–161
as source state, 122
state anxiety evocation by, 39–42
Study habits, impulsiveness and, 215
Suppressed response release, neural centers in, 216
Surprise as component of anxiety, 101
definition of, 76
Sympathetic nervous system, arousal of, 28–29

T

Taraxein, in schizophrenia, 229–230
Terror, as component of anxiety, 76
Test anxiety, 14
development of, 56
Test Anxiety Questionnaire, 6
Therapy,
analysis of anxiety and, 64–65
for impulsiveness and anxiety, 214
Thiazesim,
reaction time and, 217
suppressed response release and, 216
Threat,
effects of, 188
expectancy and, 73
perception of, 30, 39–45
real-life, patterns of emotion in, 100–102
Time estimation, impulsiveness and anxiety and, 209, 210
Trait(s),
distinguished from states, 147–153
identification of, 123–124
relation between states and, 123, 140
unitariness of, 120
Trait anxiety, 10
component emotions in, 64
definition of, 39
factor pattern of, 132
measurement of, 29, 35
State-Trait Anxiety Inventory for, 35–38
physiological changes in, 129–132
threat perception and, 39–45
Trait change, 122–127
model for, 126–127
Trait-State Anxiety Theory, 42–45

W

Wessman-Ricks Personal Feeling Scales, 33
measurement of state anxiety using, 34